Cherokee Women in Crisis

CONTEMPORARY AMERICAN INDIAN STUDIES

J. Anthony Paredes, *Series Editor*

Cherokee Women in Crisis

Trail of Tears, Civil War, and Allotment, 1838–1907

CAROLYN ROSS JOHNSTON

THE UNIVERSITY OF ALABAMA PRESS
Tuscaloosa and London

29.95

Typeface: Minion and Triplex

An earlier version of chapter 2 was published as "Burning Beds, Spinning Wheels, and Calico Dresses," *Journal of Cherokee Studies* 19 (edited by William L. Anderson) (1998): 3–17, and is reprinted here with the permission of the Museum of the Cherokee Indian.

An earlier version of chapter 4 was published as "The 'Panther's Scream Is Often Heard': Cherokee Women in Indian Territory during the Civil War," *Chronicles of Oklahoma* 78, no. 1 (edited by Mary Ann Blochowiak) (2000): 84–107, and is reprinted here with the permission of the *Chronicles of Oklahoma* (Oklahoma City: Oklahoma Historical Society, © 2000).

∞

The paper on which this book is printed meets the minimum requirements of American National Standard for Information Science–Permanence of Paper for Printed Library Materials, ANSI Z39.48-1984.

Library of Congress Cataloging-in-Publication Data

Johnston, Carolyn, 1948–
Cherokee women in crisis : Trail of Tears, Civil War, and allotment,1838–1907 / Carolyn Ross Johnston.
       p.   cm. — (Contemporary American Indian studies)
Includes bibliographical references and index.
ISBN 0-8173-1332-X (cloth : alk. paper)
ISBN 0-8173-5056-X (pbk. : alk. paper)
1. Cherokee women—History. 2. Cherokee women—Social conditions. 3. Cherokee women—Government relations. 4. Trail of Tears, 1838. 5. Indians of North America—History—Civil War, 1861–1865. 6. Indian allotments—United States—History. I. Title. II. Series.
E99.C5 J615 2003
305.48′89755′009034—dc21

2003002593

British Library Cataloguing-in-Publication Data available

For Caldonia, Salina, Margaret, and Alta

Contents

Illustrations

Preface and Acknowledgments

In Search of Caldonia

Growing up in Cleveland, Tennessee, we were surrounded by Red Clay, the council ground where the Cherokees met when they had to leave Georgia, the sacred city of Chota just to the north near Loudon, and Rattlesnake Springs where they left from on the Trail of Tears. Nothing was ever taught in the schools about the Cherokees who once lived in the area. They were erased from the historical memory of the descendants of those white settlers who took their land and drove them out of their ancestral homeland.

James F. Corn, who helped ensure that Red Clay became an historical site maintained by the state, once gave me a copy of his book *Red Clay and Rattlesnake Springs* for my winning a speech contest in 1963. Then my Uncle Ernest Ross, who was an educator, worked relentlessly on our family's genealogy. He discovered his great-great-grandmother's grave, marked only by a mountain stone, and he commissioned a marble marker for it. When he told me about Caldonia, I was astonished that I had never heard about her. She remains a mystery since little is known of her life before and after removal. She was a Cherokee woman born c. 1772, in Cocke County, Tennessee, who moved southward to Bradley County, Tennessee and married Richard Hyden, a white man, and had children, including Anderson Hyden, my grandmother's grandfather. Caldonia died in 1843.

Years went by before I sought to find her grave myself in 1993. Powerfully, I was drawn to understand her life, culture, and her experience of living in two worlds. Since my grandmother, Margaret Ross, was a healer, midwife, and divinator, I wondered what her connection might be to Cherokee religion and healing. She spoke of an owl that perched by the house as a harbinger of death. Cherokees believed an owl was a booger, an embodied witch. Such an owl alerted her to my grandfather's murder in the field by robbers during the Great Depression in 1939. She delivered babies, could stop bleeding, heal wounds, take the burn out of burns, and cure other ailments. Had her mother, Salina, passed on this knowledge to her? She would have heard stories from her mother of her great grandmother, Caldonia, but I never thought to ask about her. Why the silence? Perhaps her Indian ancestry was considered best hidden, especially when hiding it in 1838 meant survival itself.

I have also sought to learn about another Cherokee relative, John Ross, the principal chief of the Nation. My relationship to him stems from Scotland, rather than Tennessee. Nathaniel Green Ross (my great-great-grandfather), his contemporary and relative, fought with Jackson in 1812, as did John Ross, and later helped in the painful removal process; Lewis Ross's child (John Ross's brother's child) is buried next to Margaret Anderson, Nathaniel Green Ross's wife. Caldonia was in the same clan as John Ross, the Bird clan, adding another layer of mystery.

The search for Caldonia has led me to write this book about Cherokee women. The journey has led me through Tennessee, North Carolina, Georgia, over the route of the Trail of Tears to Tahlequah, then to Oklahoma City, Tulsa, and Norman, Oklahoma, the Library of Congress, and Harvard University. Thus, the research for this book has been intensely personal as well as scholarly, capturing my imagination as well as my passions. The story of Caldonia runs like an invisible thread throughout the text with glimpses of her experiences.

Acknowledgments

In the course of researching and writing this book over the past ten years I have been extremely fortunate to enjoy the help of some extraordinary people. I wish to especially thank Theda Perdue, Steven Mintz, Sarah H. Hill, Nancy Hewitt, Alice Taylor-Colbert, Terri Baker, Wayne Flynt, Nancy Shoemaker, Mike and Sue Abram, Kathryn Holland Braund, Constantina Bailly, and Tony Paredes, who generously read the manuscript and gave me the precious gift of their brilliant criticism. I only hope I was able to follow half of their wonderful suggestions. I also want to thank Michael Green, David LaVere, Brian Hosmer, Richard Persico, Virginia Paulk Kriebel, and all the members of the National

Endowment for the Humanities Seminar on Southeastern Indians. The National Endowment for the Humanities and the Ford Foundation supported research for this book.

I want to thank the staff of the Oklahoma Historical Society, especially Bill Welge, Sharron Ashton, and Chester Cowen. Bill took me back into the vault and let me hold one of the Cherokee Nation volumes. Anyone who has worked there in the Indian Archives knows the amazing experience. When the new facility opens and scholars are reading in an elegant room, it will simply not be the same as sitting at the long table reading manuscripts while dozens of people try to prove their Indian ancestry. What dramas unfold there daily. I wish to thank the staff of the Houghton Library at Harvard University, where I spent long hours poring over the papers of the ABCFM (American Board of Commissioners for Foreign Missions), and the Wider Church Ministries of the United Church of Christ for permission to quote from these historic documents. I am one of those historians who feel that mystical connection when holding the actual letters and diaries: an experience scholars in the future may miss with the electronic versions. Our widened access will be traded for the person to person connection. I wish to thank the staffs of the Western History Collections at the University of Oklahoma in Norman (especially John R. Lovett), William Eigelsbach, and others at Special Collections, University of Tennessee at Knoxville, the McClung Museum, the Newberry Library, the National Archives, the Library of Congress, Jeannie Sklar and Daisy Njoku at the Smithsonian Institution, the Thomas Gilcrease Museum and Institute in Tulsa, Barbara Fagan and the staff of the History Branch and Archives, Cleveland Public Library, and the Bradley County Historical Society in Cleveland, Tennessee, Special Collections, Northeastern State University in Tahlequah, Oklahoma, the Eckerd College library, and the Museum of the Cherokee Indian in Cherokee, North Carolina (especially Bo Taylor and Ken Blankenship). I am also grateful for the wisdom and stories of members of the Eastern Band of Cherokees and of the Cherokee Nation in Oklahoma.

For their enduring friendship and relentless encouragement I wish to thank Elie and Marion Wiesel, whose writing and work for all oppressed people challenge and inspire me. I also wish to thank Jewel Spears Brooker, Nancy Wood, Jim Goetsch, Patricia Perez-Arce, Jim Moore, Lia Glovsky, Dick Lee, Catherine Griggs, Christine Payne, Paul Newman, Judith and Devorah Ritter, Mike Magee, Linda Lucas, Mary Jane Warde, Bill Dickman, Jesus Subero, Santiago Nunez, Claire Bell, Jeffrey Kennedy, Susan Pomerantz, Xavier Landon, Susan Hyde, John McNeilly, J. D. Wilson, Theresa Turner, Hollis Lynch, Dudley De-

Groot, Margaret Rigg, Barbara Haber, April Bradley Sinclair, Meredith Jordan, Moby Johnston, Mary Ann Marshall, Jane Lackey Lehn, Gary Meltzer, N. Scott Momaday, Vine Deloria, Rayna Green, Katherine Osburn, Abrasha and Peg Brainin, Judy and Bill Chandler, Janice Norton, Mark Fishman, Alex Baehr, Margo and Rodney Fitzgerald, Joe Hamilton, Dick Hallin, William Anderson, Jimmy Moore, Jo Leslie Collier, Judith Green, David Woods, Mary Meyer, Suzan Harrison, Greg Padgett, Barney Hartston, Bill Parsons, Jamie Gill, Bill McKee, Bill Wilbur, David Gelber, Andrew Chittick, Martha Nichols-Pecceu, Jim Reed, Jim Robideau, James E. Billie, Beverly Singer, Michael Solari, Mara Soudakoff, Vais Salikhov, Lina Patridis, Grover Wrenn, David Kerr, Roy Weatherford, Jennifer Ginsberg, Kuuipo Salisbury-Hammon, Lynn Carol Henderson, Shirley Davis Ruggles, and John Galloway.

A special thanks goes to Lloyd Chapin who has always believed in my work and generously supported it as the dean of the faculty at Eckerd College. I wish to thank Don Eastman, Eckerd's president and outstanding leader. My eternal gratitude goes to my mentors Wayne Flynt, Leon Litwack, Natalie Davis, Lawrence Levine, Henry Nash Smith, and John Hope Franklin. I am also extremely grateful to Tony Paredes, the series editor, for his wisdom and generous help.

Finally, I wish to extend my warmest thanks and express my profound gratitude and admiration for my mother Alta Ross Johnston. Sadly, she did not live to see this book completed, but she would have smiled broadly to learn of her relations (she made it into the new millennium). To my courageous father, Eugene E. Johnston, my amazing sister Nancy Smith, and remarkable nieces Jennifer and Patricia Smith go my deepest thanks.

Cherokee Women in Crisis

Introduction

In February 1757, the great Cherokee leader Attakullakulla arrived in South Carolina to negotiate trade agreements with the governor and was shocked to find that no white women were present. Because Cherokee women regularly advised his nation's council on matters of war and peace, he asked: "Since the white man as well as the red was born of woman, did not the white man admit women to their councils?" The governor was so taken aback by the question that he took two or three days to come up with a response. He evaded the question: "The white men do place confidence in their women and share their councils with them when they know their hearts are good." The Cherokees remained incredulous.[1]

Just as European women were absent from the trade negotiations, so have Native American women been absent from traditional histories of the United States and even from histories of Native Americans. This book addresses two important questions: Where are the women? What does Cherokee history look like viewed through the eyes of women? Cherokee women faced different dilemmas and stresses than men did and they responded in different ways. American Indian history has tended to take the form of either tragedy or cultural survival. As Richard White writes, "The history of Indian-white relations has not usually produced complex stories. Indians are the rock, European peoples are the sea, and history seems a constant storm. There have been two outcomes: the sea wears down and dissolves the rock; or the sea erodes the rock but cannot finally absorb its battered remnant, which endures. The first outcome produces stories of conquest and assimilation; the second produces stories of cultural persistence. The tellers of such stories do not lie."[2] This study departs from telling stories of either unmitigated tragedy or of heroic cultural survival; rather, it emphasizes American Indian agency, adaptation, and "negotiated response."[3]

The following chapters analyze three pivotal developments: removal, the Civil War, and allotment of land in Indian Territory, all of which produced crises of gender both in the ways in which Cherokee women defined appropriate behavior and in the ways they related to men. These crises profoundly destabilized Cherokee gender relations and left the Cherokees dispossessed of land. Still, the Cherokees were able to negotiate these changes in such a way as to retain many of their cultural assumptions, ceremonies, and beliefs. Yet, upon the resolution of these events, the role of women had changed. A gendered approach to Cherokee history fundamentally alters our understanding of the process of change in Native American societies and radically revises the way we interpret removal, tribal factionalism, identity, sovereignty, and allotment. In many ways, removal and the Civil War reinforced traditional Cherokee values, but allotment dealt a devastating blow to Cherokee sovereignty. All these developments deprived Cherokee women of some of their rights and changed their roles. They brought new burdens and, at the same time, created some new transient opportunities. Traditional values persisted, but increasingly, assimilation or acculturation became strategies for survival.

Cherokee men were forced to assert their masculinity in new ways. Because of the successive crises, a traditional system of gender reciprocity and equivalence gave way to something quite different, a consensus on what was fundamentally important. Cherokees had contested meanings of gender before these crises, but the upheavals forced the debate into the open, allowing us to see women's differing responses. Some Cherokees resisted actively or passively, whereas others selectively adopted dimensions of a new gender system. Class and ancestry shaped the directions of adaptations, as well as the ways in which new attitudes and behaviors fit with traditional values and practices.

Many of the first studies of Native women by anthropologists focused on a universal sexual asymmetry. In the 1970s a number of scholars contended that separate spheres for men and women led to nearly universal male dominance. From a Marxist perspective, others opposed the view of the universality of women's subordination to men and argued that colonialism and contact between Europeans and Native peoples created inequality between the sexes where autonomy had once existed. In the scholarship on Indian women the major interpretive framework has been the "declension" of women's power.[4]

Anthropologists have been writing ethnographies of American Indian women for many years; however, only recently have historians begun to write extensively about the lives of Native women. This study of Cherokee women has broad significance for the field of women's history. By analyzing three major crises—removal, the Civil War, and allotment—one is able to better understand how and why gender systems change in a culture in which women and men have different work, ritual space, and ceremonies. Native cultures were divided because they found that none of their strategies of resistance to domination succeeded for long. Thus their cultures were arenas of struggle, and meanings of gender were contested.[5]

Exploring the three crises sheds light on how war and economic transformations led to internal struggles and changes in meanings of gender. This study enables us to observe the Cherokee culture—a very different culture from patriarchal European cultures—one in which women had autonomy and sexual freedom, could obtain divorce easily, rarely experienced rape or domestic violence, worked as producers/farmers, owned their own homes and fields, possessed a cosmology that contains female supernatural figures, and had significant political and economic power.[6]

Matrilineal, matrilocal Indian societies such as the Cherokee offer a radically different model of how men and women can create relationships of gender equivalence and harmony. The Cherokee case confirms and challenges standard feminist theoretical explanations. In the traditional Cherokee culture the permeability of public and private spheres reinforced egalitarian values. Similarly, among the Iroquois there was no distinction between the household management and the management of the public economy. In small-scale communities, making distinctions between public and private spheres simply was not meaningful.[7]

Within the context of recent feminist theory, the Cherokee case leads us to a new understanding of the notion of contested gender meanings and suggests that a holographic approach works best in analyzing their culture change. Such a three-dimensional holographic approach assumes that economic transformations seem to be the driving causative forces of change, but because Cherokees adopted conflicting gender strategies, one needs to identify "positionality" of Cherokee women, taking into account class, religious beliefs, kin, age, and other variables in order to explain why particular women or groups of women responded as they did to the crises.[8]

Cherokee women's close association with nature, as mothers and producers, served as a basis of their power within the tribe, not as a basis of oppression. Their position as "the other" led to gender equivalence, not hierarchy. Thus the history of Native women causes us to revise our assumptions about the consequences of sexual difference and our beliefs about whether feminism should be committed to women's fundamental differences from men or similarities to them. Differences among women based on race, class, ethnicity, sexual preference, and culture continue to present challenges to universalizing "women's" condition.[9] In the field of American history, with the exception of Angie Debo's scholarship, few works before the 1970s focused on how Indians were active participants in the making of their own history, and Native women received little attention.

Currently, survival, resistance, accommodation, and adaptation are the primary themes of scholarship in the field. The major questions in American Indian women's history still revolve around whether Indian women lost status and power due to European contact and conquest.[10] What kinds of power did American Indian women have before and after European contact? What were the sources of their authority? What was the impact of U.S. governmental policy on gender roles within tribes? How did American Indian women resist, accept, and transform the relentless attempts to eradicate "Indianness"? What was the nature of gender changes as a result of economic and political transformations? How does the experience of the Cherokees shed light on the broader fields of women's history and feminist theory?

When trying to understand the Cherokees, historians tend to examine culture over time, whereas many anthropologists characterize culture as static.[11] In this study, ethnohistory combines the insights of both fields in order to unravel some cultural paradoxes. Certain cultural markers will help reveal the ways in which the Cherokees defined gender and their identities. The following questions will emerge throughout the story: Is the Cherokee language spoken widely? Which ceremonies do the Cherokees practice and how frequently? Have the ball plays continued? Are there men and women practicing the good medicine or the bad medicine? What is the percentage of converts to Christianity? Do they practice the system of *gadugi* (cooperative labor)? Do they practice menstrual and pregnancy taboos? Do women remain the primary farmers? How is the division of labor gendered?

Recent works by Theda Perdue and Sarah H. Hill challenge the declension theory regarding Native women. In her groundbreaking, highly imaginative book *Cherokee Women: Gender and Culture Change, 1700–1835*, Perdue argues that "the story of Cherokee women, therefore, is not one of declining status and lost culture, but one of persistence and change, conservatism and adaptation, tragedy and survival."[12] She contends that the stories of most Cherokee women were stories of remarkable cultural persistence, and that eighteenth-century Cherokee women may have actually become more secure in their roles as farmers and socializers of children. Perdue goes on to argue that in the early nineteenth century Cherokees were able to adopt aspects of Anglo-American culture without fundamentally altering their values or restructuring gender. She acknowledges that women, as well as Native people in a broader sense, "may well have had less 'power' or 'status' if we define those words in political and economic terms." Moreover, she does not deny that some Cherokee women experienced profound cultural change. These women, who were primarily members of the Cherokee elite, attended mission schools, adopted gender roles of Euro-Americans, and converted to Christianity.[13] Overall, however, she challenges the declension approach.

Focusing on a later period, 1838–1907, this book acknowledges dramatic cultural transformation and loss. Much less change is evident during the earlier period analyzed by Perdue than during the crises of the Civil War and period of allotment. This work differs, however, not only in the choice of time period but also in the fact that it stresses the serious and dramatic destabilization of gender roles in the Cherokee Nation and its consequences. By exploring different aspects of Cherokee women's power—their authority in the community and family, their economic independence, political power, personal autonomy, and spirituality—it is possible to discern that Cherokee women lost and gained power simultaneously.

This approach resembles that of Sarah H. Hill in that it emphasizes adaptation for survival. In her splendid study of Cherokee women and basketry, *Weaving New Worlds: Southeastern Cherokee Women and Their Basketry,* Hill focuses on the preservation of Cherokee culture. She writes, "Baskets have both meaning and reason. The meaning of Cherokee basketry, evident in legend, custom, and history, relates to the role and work of women as the source of food and life, as providers and sustainers for their families. The reason for basketry in the twentieth century is primarily economic."[14] Hill examines the changes in ecology, technology, economy, and cultural politics of the Cherokees' basketry and the persistence of traditions in materials, designs, and processes. Her emphasis is on survival through adaptation. She writes: "Baskets provide a way to examine Cherokee history because of their antiquity, persistence, and importance among Cherokees. Baskets and changes in traditions of basketry serve as metaphors for historical transformation in subsistence practices, rituals and beliefs, exchange networks, social conditions, and ecological systems." Hill points out that "the ceremonial use of baskets disappeared in the nineteenth century, and domestic functions waned in the twentieth."[15]

The books by Perdue and Hill both stress cultural continuity. In addition to these elements and in no way minimizing the horrors and loss that occurred, this study also stresses agency. The Cherokees exercised their agency within an environment that they had not chosen, but, remarkably, they resisted a radical alteration of gender roles.

Even today women occupy a different status in Cherokee society than they do in "white" society. In 1983 Wilma Mankiller was the first woman elected as deputy principal chief for the Cherokee Nation.[16] When Ross Swimmer accepted an appointment as head of the Bureau of Indian Affairs in 1985, Mankiller assumed the office of principal chief. She was the first woman to serve as chief of a major tribe. In 1987 she was elected principal chief of the Cherokee Nation. In 1991 she won her third term in office with 82 percent of the vote. Of the fifteen members in the Cherokee tribal council, six were women at that time.[17] As Chief Wilma Mankiller said in 1993 in an address at Sweet Briar College:

> One of the things I saw, just as if you look at what happened after the Trail of Tears, you can look at some of the positive things that happened among our people . . . [T]hey had unbelievable tenacity. Our tribe is one of the most acculturated tribes in the country, and yet there are thousands of people who still speak Cherokee. Ceremonies that we've had since the beginning of time are still going on in a tribe as acculturated as ours is. Our people are very tenacious, and it was that tenacity that I saw as a strength we could build on.
>
> If you look at history from a native perspective, and I know that's very difficult for you to do, the most powerful, or one of the most powerful countries in the world as a policy first tried to wipe us off the face of the earth. And then, failing that, instituted a number of policies to make sure that we didn't exist in 1993 as a culturally distinct group of people, and yet here we are. Not only do we exist, but we're thriving and we're growing, and we're learning now to trust our own thinking again and dig our way out. So it was that tenacity that I felt we could build on.[18]

Joyce Dugan was elected chief of the Eastern Band of Cherokee Indians in 1995. It is an empowering development to see two Cherokee women being elected chiefs of their respective nations by the end of the twentieth century. Mankiller and Dugan, who bring together diverse gender roles, represent the contemporary resolution of competing and contested conceptions of gender. They combined the traditional roles as wives and mothers with the roles of leaders and producers in the public sphere.

I make no claims in this book about the existence of a static, "essential"

Cherokee identity and culture. When the Cherokees encountered the Europeans, their culture had already changed dramatically. A key to understanding the persistence of traditions, assimilation, and acculturation to white beliefs and values is to begin with the stories, myths, and ceremonies that existed before the Europeans came to the New World.

Chapter 1 describes cultural continuities, Cherokee myths, traditional gender meanings, and their basis in cosmology. Chapter 2 discusses the early catalysts for gender change: the U.S. government and the missionaries who tried to "civilize" and convert the Cherokees. Chapter 3 analyzes how removal created a crisis of gender for Cherokees, and the contested gender identities that emerged from the crisis. In chapter 4 the central focus is the effect the Civil War had in forcing the debate over gender expectations into the open and the differing responses to the crisis. Chapter 5 describes disputes over acculturation and education, increasing domestic conflict, increasing rates of out-marriage, and the impact of economic development on Cherokee women during Reconstruction. Chapter 6 traces the powerful impact that the allotment policy and its implementation had on how Cherokee women defined appropriate behavior and work, as well as their relationships with men.

By studying the culture change within the Cherokee Nation during crises, one can learn a great deal about what American Indians and white Americans fought over in the battle over gender meanings and the ways in which they influenced each other. One sees a poignant irony in the fact that the Europeans encountered these Native societies in which women had significant power and attempted to radically transform them into patriarchal ones. American women struggled for hundreds of years to achieve the kind of equality that Cherokee women had enjoyed for a millennium.

I
Crisis of Gender

I
Cultural Continuity

Their darling passion is liberty. To it they sacrifice everything, and in the most unbounded liberty they indulge themselves through life.

Haywood, *The Natural and Aboriginal History of Tennessee*

When the Europeans encountered the Cherokees in the sixteenth and seventeenth centuries, they were shocked to find that women had so much sexual freedom and held considerable political, economic, and domestic power. To them, Cherokee women represented sexual danger. The Europeans viewed this reversal of patriarchal values as deviant, uncivilized, pagan, sinful, and deeply threatening. They were shocked also by the Cherokees' view of their bodies. The Cherokees did not see nudity as a cause for shame, and women and men were lavishly tattooed. The Cherokee language did not have words for heaven or hell, damnation or salvation, or for grace, repentance, or forgiveness, and the Cherokees did not have laws against fornication or adultery.[1] Understanding traditional Cherokee gender roles and the myths and cosmology in which they were embedded is key to discerning subsequent fights between Cherokees and Europeans over meanings of gender. Men and women had gender-specific tasks, but they occupied interdependent spheres. They had complementary responsibilities in productive and reproductive spheres: men hunted, and women cultivated the earth and gathered food. Survival depended on the balance of male and female contributions. Cherokee women had access to roles, behavior, and power that their European counterparts did not.

Ancient Cherokees had seven clans. The names of the Wolf clan, Deer clan, Bird clan, and Paint clan have been translated with certainty. The other three have been translated variously as Long Hair, Blind Savannah, Holly, Blue, Wild Potato, and Twisters.[2] Today the clans are generally recognized as Deer, Wolf, Bird, Long Hair, Wild Potato, Blue, and Paint. Social identity and rules of con-

Fig. 1. Lizzie Tooni sitting with her daughter, Mary Wolfe (using wooden mortar and pestle), and Mary's children, Bill and Frances. Big Cove, early 1940s. Negative no. 55,445. (Courtesy National Anthropological Archives, Smithsonian Institution)

duct were tied to clan, and the tribe was matrilineal and matrilocal. Fathers did not discipline their own children. Instead, brothers disciplined their sisters' children, and thus women had special relationships with their brothers. Cherokee women owned their dwelling and domestic hearth, and husbands came to live in their houses. Women had control over their property, and, although the land was held communally, domestic improvements belonged to the women.[3] Women also owned the agricultural fields they cultivated. Clans had a strong sense of revenge. A clan member's death would be avenged by the killing of

Fig. 2. Unidentified Cherokee women, n.d. (Courtesy Museum
of the Cherokee Indian, Cherokee, North Carolina)

either the murderer or a member of the killer's clan. This law of blood was a
fundamental dimension of tribal life.[4]

Cherokee women were also influential in political affairs, advising on war
and peace. The women of each clan selected an elder woman to serve on the
women's council, a highly influential body. One of these women, the beloved
woman, who also represented her clan, presided over the council.[5] Frequently
beloved women who had distinguished themselves in battle could decide the
fate of prisoners. Traditional Cherokee women inhabited a separate, complementary sphere defined by their roles as clan members, farmers, wives, and
mothers. They knew the appropriate behavior for women regarding taboos,
dietary and sexual restrictions, and marriage. They were neither subordinate
nor superior to men; the Cherokee division of labor based on one's sex did not
imply hierarchy, but equality.

Traders, travelers, and missionaries described striking changes in Cherokee women's roles between the eighteenth and nineteenth centuries. Although their accounts must be read critically with an awareness of their biases and limited access to the women's world of ritual, the accounts do reveal how Cherokee women defined femaleness, how they related to men, and what they considered appropriate behavior. The accounts generally presented Cherokee women's sexual freedom as licentious and dangerous and their crucial economic role as that of their oppression by Cherokee men.

Private Life: Marriage, Sexuality, Pregnancy, and Socialization of Children

MARRIAGE AND SEXUALITY

In the eighteenth century, James Adair described the marriage ceremony practiced generally by the southeastern tribes during which a man and woman exchanged symbols of their roles. The bridegroom presented the bride with venison, and the bride presented her partner with an ear of corn.[6] The ceremony demonstrated his ability to provide meat for his bride, and her gift symbolized her ability to provide vegetable food for her husband.[7]

Alexander Longe described the marital tie as often temporary: "Sometimes they will live together till they have 5 or 6 children and then part as unconcernedly as if they had never known one another, the men taking the male children and the women the female and so each marry with contrary parties. I have this to say that the women rules the roost and wears the breeches and sometimes will beat their husbands within an inch of their lives."[8] Longe's assertion of a complete reversal of gender roles is suspect; however, he accurately noted that the Cherokees did not conceptualize marriage as a lifelong tie. Divorce within the tribe was easy, as both Cherokee husbands and wives could choose to separate at any time.[9] Lieutenant Henry Timberlake confirmed Longe's observations when he conducted two diplomatic missions with Cherokee leaders in England before his death in 1765. He wrote that though many marriages lasted a lifetime, it was common for a person to change marital partners three or four times a year. He added, in contrast to Longe, that when separations occurred, the children went with the mother. Longe also suggested that the mother-child bond was stronger than the tie between wife and husband.[10]

In contrast to other observers, William Bartram, who visited the Cherokees shortly before the Revolutionary War, saw complementarity and equality rather than female dominance. He wrote that he "never saw nor heard of an instance of an Indian beating his wife or other female, or reproving them in anger or in harsh language. And the women make a suitable and grateful return; for they are discreet, modest, loving, faithful, and affectionate to their husbands." Still, Cherokee women's sexual and economic autonomy shocked most observers. The Cherokees accepted sexuality as natural, and their dances were sometimes overtly sexual in nature. For example, in the friendship dance, as observed in the first half of the twentieth century, men and women enacted the stages of courtship and became openly intimate. During the first song, men formed a line, and women formed another line opposite the men so that they stood face-to-face. They began to dance in a counterclockwise direction, forming a circle. During the second song when the leader began to use words referring to intimacy, the sexual gestures began. During the part of this song when they danced facing each other, the partners held hands. Then they began to dance side-by-side, holding hands crossed in front of their bodies. Dancing face-to-face again, they put their palms upon their partners' palms. Then they placed their hands on their partner's shoulders. Then, dancing side-by-side, they placed their arms over their partners' shoulders. Dancing face-to-face again, they placed hats on the women's heads, and the dancers stroked their partners under their chins. Finally, the male dancers put their hands on their female partners' breasts while they danced side-by-side, and then they began touching the clothing over their partners' genitals. Crowding together during these last two phases concealed the more explicit gestures.[11] The friendship dance was thus an occasion for single people to meet and get together socially.

Louis Philippe's moralistic commentary on the Cherokees in 1797 emphasized the sexual freedom of Cherokee women. Sexual activity before marriage was accepted, and although fidelity was expected after marriage, the Cherokees had no punishment for adultery. In 1807, Major John Norton remarked that in contrast to the Creeks, "the Cherokees have no such punishment for adultery; the husband is even disgraced in the opinion of his friends, if he seeks to take satisfaction in any other way, than that of getting another wife."[12]

Although he recognized Cherokee women's sexual autonomy, Phillipe portrayed Indian women more generally as drudges. He wrote: "The Indians have all the work done by women. They are assigned not only household tasks; even the corn, peas, beans, and potatoes are planted and preserved by the women. The man smokes peacefully, while the woman grinds corn in a mortar."[13] Rayna Green stresses that this image of Indian women as degraded, overworked drudges persisted into the nineteenth century. Euro-Americans did not realize that Indian women's strenuous work brought them power and control over the products of their labor. Green reminds us that the other distinct image of Indian women was the princess, such as Pocahontas, a beautiful daughter of a chief.[14] Thus when Europeans encountered Cherokees, who possessed a radically different gender system from theirs, they saw the women's power and sexual autonomy as deeply threatening. These misconceptions about gender were used to justify campaigns to civilize American Indians and eventually remove them from the Southeast.

Because their women had such considerable power, it is understandable that the Cherokees developed an elaborate system of taboos and rituals to separate purity and defilement.[15] Daniel Sabin Butrick, a missionary sent by the ABCFM in 1818, recorded that the Cherokee women observed all the traditional rules of the Hebrews regarding female "uncleanness," as stated in the twelfth and fifteenth chapters of Leviticus, with the exception that among the Cherokees, the restrictions did not last any longer after the birth of a daughter than that of a son. After childbirth, Cherokee women observed restrictions for twelve to twenty-four days. During their menstrual periods they remained alone for seven days, touching only their own food, clothes, and furniture. They would bathe before reentering their communities.[16]

Warriors remained separate from women for three days before and after going on a raid. Before warriors could be reintegrated into domestic life, they were purified by "going to water" and sweat baths to "wash away the blood." Adair said that wounded warriors were secluded in small huts outside the settlement for an extended period.[17]

In her book *Purity and Danger: An Analysis of Pollution and Taboo*, Mary Douglas explains, "We cannot possibly interpret rituals concerning excreta, breast milk, saliva and the rest unless we are prepared to see in the body a symbol of society, and to see the powers and dangers credited to social structure reproduced in small on the human body." She suggested that when male dominance is accepted in a social organization, beliefs about sex pollution are not likely to be highly developed.[18] Conversely, the Cherokees' beliefs regarding pollution stemmed from the absence of either male or female dominance.[19]

In a society in which rituals were designed to avoid pollution and maintain harmony and balance, the Booger Dance may have been a way for the Cherokees to ritualize and contain the perceived threat of sexual danger. The boogers, representing licentious Euro-American men or Indians from other tribes, were comic figures in the ritual, rather than plundering invaders. They broke rules of sexual restraint and appeared awkward and rejected. The Cherokee term is *tsu`niɢādu'lĩ* (many persons faces covered over); *aɢā`dulā'* is mask. The Booger Dance, then, refers to masked dancing. During a social dance, an announcement would be made that some strangers were expected. The women and children would express their anxiety and excitement. Then the Booger Gang would

Fig. 3. Booger mask. (Courtesy Museum of the
Cherokee Indian, Cherokee, North Carolina)

appear, consisting of four to ten men, and occasionally a couple of women, wearing sheets or blankets and masks representing other cultures such as Chinese, Germans, French, Spaniards, Africans, and other Indian tribes. Their masks were shaped with gourd phalluses and were explicitly sexual. A few masks portrayed Indian women. The Booger Gang also hid gourd phalluses under their blankets, which they would expose to the shrieks of the women.[20] Someone would then ask, "Where are they from? Where are they going?" They generally would say that they had come from "a far distant land."[21] They carried names such as Black Buttocks, Sooty Anus, and Big Phallus, and they would dance around awkwardly with the women. The boogers symbolized aliens, ghosts, the other, and they were rule-breakers. They would make obscene gestures, imitate motions of sexual intercourse, and dance "like white men trying to do an Indian dance." After each of the boogers danced individually, the host would ask them if they would all like to dance. They would reply by dancing either the Bear or the Eagle Dance: after an interlude, a group of women dancers would enter in a line, and they would partner off with the boogers in a dance. As they danced with Cherokee women, they enacted the blending of outsiders with their community in a symbol of intermarriage. The women's participation may have symbolized their submission to the boogers' sexual desires, or they may have been conveying resistance, as they remained poised during the dance. The boogers made explicit sexual movements during the dance. This erotic exhibitionism was more overt during a Bear Dance than an Eagle Dance. After dancing with the women, the boogers would leave as awkwardly and suddenly as they had come. After taking off their disguises, they returned to the dance.[22]

The order of Cherokee society was restored after the boogers left. In addition, the Booger Dance was a way to openly express emotion and sexuality in a stylized manner within accepted rules of restraint. According to Cherokee beliefs, the mythical figure Stone Coat revealed a vision to a medicine man of the coming of white men accompanied by strange Indians from the East and Africans. He offered the Booger Dance as a means of counteracting the social and physical contamination that they brought. The Cherokees probably performed the dance before the Europeans arrived. Therefore, the dance seems to have been both a prophetic and a protective ceremony.[23] In broad terms, the Booger Dance was a medicine dance intended to guard the community from harm and prevent disease.[24] The meanings that the Cherokee people attributed to the Booger Dance probably changed over time, but clearly, the celebration of unbridled sexuality, the fears of contamination and intrusion by foreigners, and the containment of boundaries seem central to the dance. Although the Cherokees feigned fear in the Booger Dance, deeper anxieties remained. The boogers were rebuffed in the dance, but because they left as suddenly as they came, there remained a chance that they might return. And return they did.

PREGNANCY

The Americans misinterpreted the Booger Dance, Cherokee institutions of marriage and sexuality, their gendered division of labor, and their taboos regarding pregnancy and childbirth. Women were defined as quintessentially female when menstruating and pregnant. Cherokee women inhabited female ritual space as mothers. The rituals surrounding pregnancy reinforced the interdependence of men and women. Cherokees believed that men and women both contributed matter that becomes mixed to produce a child. The female contributed blood and flesh to the fetus, and the father provided the skeleton through the congealed sperm. Presumably, the length of time it took to have a child depended on how long the matter took to be mixed. The contributions

 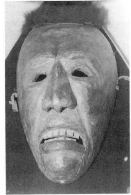 

Fig. 4. Cherokee dance masks. (Courtesy Museum of the Cherokee Indian, Cherokee, North Carolina)

that the mother and father made to the formation of the child have implications that transcend physiology. As Will West Long related, the Cherokees believed in a multiple-soul concept. One soul is located in the head, under the anterior fontanelle (the baby's soft spot). This soul has memory and consciousness and exists forever; it is from the Creator. It creates or secretes the fluids of the body such as saliva, lymph, phlegm, spinal fluid, and sexual fluids. The second soul is located in the liver, and its secretions are yellow and black bile as well as gastric juices. The third soul, the one of circulation, resides in the heart, and its secretion is blood. Finally, the fourth soul is located in the bones. Thus the belief in male and female complementarity in the spiritual and physical contributions to the child is inherent to the concept of the multiple soul.[25]

Cherokee men and women enlisted the services of medicine men and women during pregnancy. A pregnant woman was "taken to the water" every new moon, beginning in the fourth, fifth, or seventh month of pregnancy. This ritual of going to the river to pray, to be prayed for, and be purified was disappearing by the 1930s, but the conservative elder people still practiced it with their young relatives. In the ritual, a pregnant woman went down to the river with a medicine man. The attendant—the mother, husband, or relative of the woman—assisted him and placed a yard of white calico on the ground, and then placed two white beads, symbolizing life, or sometimes two red beads, representing success, and a white thread (50–60 cm long) on the material. As the party stood on the bank of the river facing the water, the medicine man said a prayer while holding a red (or white) bead between the thumb of his right hand and his index finger, and a black bead between the thumb of his left hand and his index finger. At the end of the ceremony the attendant strung the beads and wrapped them up and gave them to the medicine man.[26]

The pregnant woman could request that the medicine man discover through the divination whether the child would live or be stillborn or ascertain the sex of the child. The medicine man brought the beads and cloth home with him. At the next ceremony, the woman brought two more beads that were strung with the others. The medicine man received another yard of white calico as his payment.

The pregnant woman would drink a combination of the following before she went to the river: bark of *dawadzila: Ulmus fulva;* Red or Slippery Elm; stems of *walelu unidzilegisti: Impatiens biflora;* Spotted Touch-me-not; roots of *ganeguwaliski nigohilon itsehi: Veronica officinalis,* L.; Common Speedwell; cones of *notsi: Pinus pungens,* Lamb., and Table Mountain, Pine. The first plant was intended to make the inside of the woman slippery to ensure an easy delivery. The second was intended to "frighten the child" and cause it to "jump down" (the Cherokee expression for delivery). The last two plants were evergreens, which were chosen to give the infant longevity and health. The woman induced vomiting when standing near the water. Thus the practice served as a purification ritual, ridding her of any disease or "spoiled saliva" (which had resulted from malicious conjuring).[27]

Many taboos surrounded pregnancy and menstruation. A pregnant or menstruating woman was believed to be extremely powerful and dangerous to others. Cherokees believed that it was dangerous to eat food that a menstruating or pregnant woman had prepared or to touch an object she had used. Even walking on a trail that she had been on could cause illness. Two or three generations ago (1931 and earlier) a menstruating woman went to an *osi,* a hut set apart from her residence. Women in labor also went there. However, by the early 1930s there were no *osi* on the reservation. Moreover, although menstruating and pregnant women did not leave their homes, they did refrain from cooking meals and from other household duties. Either other female members of the household or the men cooked the meals. The menstruating or pregnant woman was not only dangerous to members of the community but also to her husband. Pregnant women were considered a little less dangerous than menstruating women.[28]

Food taboos for pregnant women were numerous. Cherokees believed that eating certain foods harmed the child or mother. They believed that the child would acquire the characteristics of the particular animal being eaten. The Cherokees were keen observers of the habits of animals, and they developed their dietary taboos based on their observations. For example, the Cherokees believed that pregnant women should not eat squirrel because it might cause difficulty in delivery. The rationale was that a squirrel runs down the tree but may run right back up. Eating ruffled grouse could kill the child because it hatches a lot of eggs, but most do not reach maturity. Speckle-trout would give the child birthmarks or black spots on the face or would cause the mother to hemorrhage during delivery. If a pregnant woman ate rabbit, the child would sleep with its eyes open, or it would have too large eyes. Eating crawfish would cause the child to refuse to come down in labor because crawfish swim backward. The pregnant woman was not supposed to eat any animals killed with bloodshed (shot with a gun or arrow). Taboos did not seem to extend to plant food, with the exception that black walnuts were believed to cause the child to have an ugly broad nose.[29] Douglas suggested that dietary restrictions and taboos relating to purity were tied to a need for order.[30]

As a part of good prenatal care, a pregnant woman avoided menstruating women, who were considered dangerous. She should not look at a corpse. She should not loiter around a doorway, because this might cause a slow delivery; comb her hair backward, because this might cause the child's hair to be unruly; or wear neckerchiefs, belts, or aprons, because this might cause the child to be strangled by the umbilical cord wrapped around its neck. Pregnant women should not look at masks, because a witch could cause the child to look like the mask. She and her husband were urged to go to a spring or creek to wash their faces and hands each morning. Similar taboos pertained to the husband. For example, the husband must not dig a grave or assist in any burial because this caused his child to be stillborn. He was cautioned against putting folds or dents in his hat because the child's head would then have dents. Like his wife, he should not wear a neckerchief or loiter in the doorway. He also had to accompany his wife if she had to go out of the house during the night.[31]

These taboos for the woman and her husband reveal the Cherokees' sense of interconnectedness and the necessity for both of them to ensure the child's health, well-being, and safe delivery. Childbirth occurred within the female circle. Sometimes a medicine man and the husband might be present. A few days before the delivery, the husband made arrangements to have four women attend his wife. The woman's mother, sisters, and relatives frequently served as attendants. One was always a midwife who had knowledge of the necessary formulas and simples (medicinal plants or herbs, or the medicines derived from them). When labor began, the attendants assembled and gave her a warm drink of the barks of a variety of wild cherry, *Prunus serotina*. A medicine man or medicine woman was called to see that all necessary precautions had been taken. He or she then walked out and recited a conjuration while standing at the eastern corner of the cabin, addressing the child, "thou little boy," and calling upon him "to jump down." Then he or she walked to the northern corner of the house and repeated the formula, addressing the child as "thou little girl." Walking to the western corner, he or she called upon the boy again, and at the southern corner he or she called the girl again. The medicine man or medicine woman then left if an old woman was present who could recite the appropriate formulas as needed. But he or she might circle the house again to protect the woman against the power of witches.[32]

The woman delivered while standing, held partially reclining in a slanting position with her feet apart and legs open. Another woman was ready to catch the child in front of the mother. In another position, the woman knelt on the ground and held the back of a chair, while attendants supported her back. A third method was for the woman to sit on her husband's lap, who sat on a chair while he held his arms around his wife's waist. The woman almost never delivered while supine. She was fully clothed with her garments tucked up. After delivery, one of the women cut the umbilical cord, and the other two tended to the afterbirth. Simples and formulas might be used to help in the expulsion of the afterbirth. After the child was born, he or she was bathed in warm water and wrapped in cloth. Then the father, or a near relative if the father was absent, wrapped the afterbirth in an old cloth and usually carried it across two mountain ridges. Then he dug a hole and buried the placenta while reciting, "Now then! Two years from now again I will see it my child" (literal translation of the Cherokee expression). This expression meant, "Well! I will want another child two years from now." Crossing only one ridge meant that the father wanted a child in only one year. He had to be careful that no one saw him, because if someone dug up the placenta, buried it, and heaped four to seven stones on top before filling in the hole, the couple would have no other baby. If someone dug it up and threw it in the open, a child might be born to them before they wished.[33] The husband's absence might mean a longer time between children depending on how far he traveled. Just as the husband participated in rituals regarding pregnancy, he also took part in rituals after childbirth. Initially, however, the husband and wife were separated for a time.

The new mother lay down for two or three days and then went to the *osi*, the menstrual hut, for twelve to twenty-four days. She was considered powerful and dangerous during this time: this power was associated with blood. In addition, the new mother did not eat fish for two days so that the blood that was still flowing would not clot. Fish are cold-blooded and eating them might therefore chill the blood that still flowed, causing it to clot. She also avoided salt and any hot food. Babies were wrapped in a bedsheet for a few weeks, then began to wear the clothes of adults at an early age. Although nursing was common, infants were soon given adult food.[34]

SOCIALIZATION OF CHILDREN

Societies devise techniques of child rearing in order to instill certain distinctive characteristics. The Cherokees wanted to produce boys who were expert hunters and warriors who were brave and courageous; they wanted little girls who would become strong mothers and food producers who were wise and patient. Therefore, little boys of four and five years old were taught by their uncles to make bows and arrows, whereas little girls helped their mothers with domestic chores.[35] Cherokees considered children extremely precious and refrained from physical punishment. Discipline stemmed from fear of embarrassment or ostracism. The Cherokees believed that personal autonomy and communal responsibility must be kept in harmony. Generosity characterized the harmony ethic so that no one was turned away from a meal or denied hospitality.

The Cherokees had lived in the southeastern part of the North American continent for hundreds of years before Columbus, de Soto, and Coronado landed. Although they experienced significant change prior to European contact, there were several themes that characterized Cherokee meanings of gender and identity. Their sense of the sacred filled every dimension of their lives. Everything was connected to everything else. The Cherokee language is not gendered and implies no gender hierarchy. Because of their hunting, gathering, and agriculture, the Cherokees came to know animals and plants intimately. They faced the dilemma of having to kill animals in order to live. Therefore, they were careful to show the animals proper reverence and respect. If they failed to do so, the ghost of the animal would seek revenge on the hunter and cause illness. The Cherokees believed that animals had sent diseases to humans out of self-defense. Feeling pity for human beings, the plants offered themselves as instruments of healing. Cherokee medicine men and women used hundreds of species of plants to cure their people. The men were primarily connected to animals through hunting, and women were associated with plants through farming.

The rhythms of Cherokee life unfolded with the seasons. During the latter part of the summer, men assisted women with the harvest and occupied themselves with ceremonies and with councils. Young men hunted and engaged in warfare during the fall and winter. Cherokee women traditionally farmed, gathered food, brought up the next generation, and participated in civil duties and in ceremonial and spiritual life. Their activities were constant with the

Fig. 5. Walini, a Cherokee woman, Qualla Boundary,
Cherokee, North Carolina, 1887. Negative no. 1011.
(Courtesy National Anthropological Archives,
Smithsonian Institution)

changing seasons. Daily household work, tending children, and farming characterized their lifelong routines.[36]

Children learned the nature of womanhood and manhood from stories of Selu, the Corn Mother, the first woman, who was associated in Cherokee cosmology and myth with fertility, nurture, and the earth, and from stories of Kana'tĭ (the Lucky Hunter), the first man. Cherokees sometimes referred to corn as "Old Woman," and stories tell of cornstalks being transformed into beautiful young women. Selu and Kana'tĭ had two sons, one by natural means and one who sprang from the blood of the meat that his mother had washed in the river. Their sons were curious where their father found the game that he returned with each day. So they followed him and discovered that when Kana′tĭ went to a cave and lifted a large rock, a deer leaped out. When the boys returned to the place a few days later, they lifted the rock and a deer ran out. But, foolishly, they allowed all the animals to get out. They tried to shoot them with bows and arrows and missed. They transgressed the proper conduct of taking only what they needed from nature. Kana′tĭ angrily told them that thereafter they would have to hunt all over the forest for game but that they might not be able to find any. The story embodies an Edenic myth of the lost paradise and explains why humans sometimes experience scarcity.[37]

When the boys returned home, they had no meat for dinner. Their mother, Selu, went into the storehouse and returned with a basket full of corn and beans. Having followed her, the boys saw Selu in the middle of the storehouse, rubbing her stomach and thus producing corn. When she rubbed under her arms, she produced beans. Because the boys thought that Selu was a witch, they decided to kill her.[38]

Selu realized her sons' intentions and told them, "So you are going to kill me. . . . Well, when you have killed me, clear a large piece of ground in front of the house and drag my body seven times around the circle. Then drag me seven times over the ground inside the circle, and stay up all night and watch, and in the morning you will have plenty of corn." The boys clubbed her and cut her head off and put it on the roof of the house. Because they cleared only seven little spots, corn now grows in only a few places instead of all over the earth. They dragged Selu's body around the circle, and corn sprang up wherever her blood fell on the ground. But because they dragged it only twice instead of seven times, Indians work their crop only twice a year. The sons stayed up watching the corn all night and found the corn full-grown and ripe the next morning. Thus, through Selu's sacrifice, the Cherokees received corn from her blood. Eventually, after their father left them and they eluded the wolves he had sent, a panther, and the cannibals who tried to kill them, the boys began their journey to find their father. When they came to the end of the world in the East where the sun comes out, they saw Kana′tĭ and Selu sitting together. Their parents were happy to see them and told them they could stay with them for a time, and then they must go to live in the West, "where the sun goes down." After seven days the boys "went on to the Darkening Land, where they are now."[39]

Thus the original matricide results from the fear of female power, specifically of Selu being a witch. Cherokees believed that witches could read a person's thoughts and cause evil to occur to someone by merely thinking it. Witches

Fig. 6. O., Del's mother-midwife, published as
plate 12b in BAE Bulletin 99, Swimmer
Manuscript, James Mooney. Negative no.
996-d-10. (Courtesy National Anthropological
Archives, Smithsonian Institution)

could change shapes from humans to animals or other humans. Because the
Cherokees lived in small, intense social networks, they were extremely sensitive
to disruptive relationships. The Cherokees believed that illness or injury resulted from one's own misconduct or from someone else's malicious conjuring.
The Cherokees practiced conjury as a response to their fear of these disruptions
in their social element. Conjury was designed to influence the lives of people
and modify the outcome of events.[40]

Cherokees placed value and meaning on anomalies that occurred at the mar-
gins and in the interstices of their classification system. The story of these sons,
the Thunder Boys, gave an explanation why Cherokees did not live in a perfect
world. By being rule-breakers, the boys had introduced uncertainty into an ordered world. Yet, they also could serve as intermediaries between the human
and the Upper World.[41] The story taught that if the people showed respect and
gratitude and did not break a taboo, the blessings of the Corn Mother might
return. The story also portrayed a supernatural couple who shared power and
were both essential in providing for the children. Selu sacrificed herself in order
to perpetuate life. Selu and other female supernaturals both reflected and reinforced Cherokee women's beliefs about gender expectations. As opposed to a

patriarchal religious system, in which the deities are male and women are considered subordinate to men, Cherokee women's and men's power derived legitimacy from myth and female and male supernaturals. Ceremonies, rituals, warfare, and sports helped construct gender meanings for the men and women of the Nation.

Public Life: Ceremonies, Rituals, and Sports

Ceremonies and Rituals

The Cherokees held the Green Corn ceremony to honor Selu, the life-sustaining force. The ceremony affirmed their community, renewed them, and restored balance between them and the natural world. The celebration also reinforced the separate, complementary, and interdependent spheres of men and women. The Green Corn ceremony was held in late summer, corresponding to the ripening of the crop of late corn and held generally in August. It expressed gratitude that the corn crop was successful.[42] Charles Hicks, a Cherokee chief, described the Green Corn ceremony in 1818, an account that was similar to James Mooney's recounting in the late nineteenth century: "The green corn dance, so called, has been highly esteemed formerly. This is held when the corn is getting hard and lasts four days, and when the national council sits—a quantity of venison being procured to supply the dance. It is said that a person was formerly chosen to speak to the people on each day in a language that is partly lost—at least there is very little of it known now."[43]

Accounts of the Green Corn ceremony differ because the same preliminary preparations for the New Moon ceremony were made also for the Green Corn ceremony, and the Green Corn ceremony and Ripe Corn ceremony were sometimes conflated in the reports. The account in the John Howard Payne Papers has been the primary source for a description of these ceremonies. In Payne's version of the Green Corn ceremony, as soon as the young corn was discovered, messengers gathered one ear from a field of each of the seven clans and returned them to the seven Counselors. They then made preparations for the feast. They sent all the hunters out on a six-day hunt. The Counselors then fasted for six days, and on the sixth night all the members of the community except infants refrained from sleeping and kept a vigil. The festival began on the seventh day. In preparation for the First New Moon ceremony and the Green Corn ceremony, the altar was repaired and firewood from seven special trees was gathered. When the evening came, seven elder women performed the friendship dance. When dawn arrived, the whole community gathered to observe the divination using the sacred crystal regarding the success or failure of the crops. A new fire was lit for the sacrifice of a deer's tongue and seven kernels of corn, one from each of the seven ears. After offering a prayer of thanksgiving and gratitude for the harvest, the priest put the corn and the deer's tongue into the fire along with wild tobacco. Then the chief's right-hand man ordered the provisions that had been prepared to be brought in, and the people began to eat the new corn. However, the right-hand man and the seven Counselors had to abstain from eating the new corn until after seven more days. The ceremony was intended to restore balance to the social relations of the community. All the lawbreakers were forgiven (except murderers), and they were able to reenter the community as pardoned human beings. In the afternoon during the ceremony, the men and women played the one-pole ball game and participated in dances in the evenings. Men repaired the public buildings while women cleaned their houses and cooking vessels. Men were not permitted to touch females, including infants, during the time of the ceremony. No one could eat any of the corn before the Green Corn ceremony was performed. Moreover, the men observed a strict fast from the afternoon of the first day until the second sunrise. On the second day the priest prepared an emetic for the men. Through the purification by water, and through the men's act of drinking the black drink, the community was made pure again.[44]

The Ripe Corn ceremony occurred generally in late September when the corn had become hard. The seven Counselors called for a religious dance and set the day of the festival. They ordered an arbor of green boughs to be framed in the National Heptagon and a beautiful shade tree to be cut down and placed in the sacred square. The next morning the festival began; Payne's account spoke of the Cherokees' "unmeasured exultation." Only the men performed the dance, each carrying a green bough and dancing around the tree in the square. The festival lasted for four days. The women were excluded from the square during the special dance, but after the boughs were put away in the evening they could join the men in social dances. This festival has outlasted all the others and continues into the present.[45]

During the Green Corn ceremony men and women played their traditional roles dramatically, and this reinforced fundamental categories. The newly lighted fire in the ceremony replaced the old, "polluted" fire. Adversaries reconciled, and the people who had failed to live up to higher social ideals were reminded of what they should do. Men and women danced in three circles around the fire and then separated. After painting themselves, the people then immersed themselves in the water.[46]

The gendering of the dances and the mythological complementarity of men and women mirrored Cherokee cosmological assumptions. Fire, the symbol of purity, was the earthly representative of the sun, and was an old woman who was a grandmother in terms of kin. In the Cherokee story about the origin of fire, the Thunders sent lightning and started a fire in the bottom of a sycamore tree; a female water spider was the one who succeeded in bringing fire to humans (similar to the story of Prometheus in Greek mythology). Several male animals tried and failed in their mission to retrieve the fire. So Water Spider wove a bowl out of a thread from her body and carried it on her back as she crossed over to the island; she put one burning coal in the bowl and brought it back. Thus a female was responsible for the gift of fire to a cold world; however, the male Thunders were also essential in the process. Cherokee children learned that the sun was female and the moon was male. Cherokees referred to the sun's dividing night and day, and perhaps life and death.[47] In addition to the powerful images of Selu and the sun as female, women's strength was evident in the story of Nûñ'yunu'wĭ (Stone Coat), in which the power of menstruating women was seen as deadly, but also revered. A hunter encountered Stone Coat, a cannibalistic monster, in the mountains. If the monster came to the settlement he would eat them all. The medicine man told them that the monster could not live if he saw menstruating women. So the people arranged for seven menstruating women to line the monster's path, and when he encountered them, he fell down on the trail, blood pouring from his mouth. Then the medicine man drove seven sourwood stakes through Stone Coat, and the people covered him with logs and burned them. Nûñ'yunu'wĭ was a great *ada'wehĭ* (translated as wizard, magician, or to the utmost level of power), and while the fire blazed, he told them medicine for all kinds of sickness and sang hunting songs. When they raked off the ashes, they found a large lump of red paint and a magic *u'lûñsû'tĭ* stone.[48]

Cherokee women's power derived from their ability to give and sustain life. Sustaining life through farming was seen as a source of this power. However, blood was believed to be the ultimate symbol of this power. Selu's blood was shed as she sacrificed her life and gave the gift of corn. Menstrual blood was believed to be dangerously powerful as seen in the story of Stone Coat, who was killed by the sight of seven menstruating women. Women bled each month without dying. Clan membership was determined through the mother's bloodline. War women gained power through shedding blood and taking life in times of war. In the female version of the Stone Coat story, Spear-finger, U'tlûñ'tă, had the ability to change herself into any shape (she was also covered with a stone coat). Spear-finger represented a female monster who took life.

In the mythical story of the daughter of the sun, men are the ones who introduce death into the world. The sun's daughter dies when she is bitten by a

Fig. 7. Four women of Big Cove, by William H. Gilbert. Neg. no. 44,368-R. (Courtesy National Anthropological Archives, Smithsonian Institution)

rattlesnake. Seven men go to retrieve the sun's daughter from the Darkening Land. The little men tell them to put her in a box to carry her, but not to open the box under any circumstances until they get home. They disobey and open the box. They are afraid the daughter is smothering, and when they lift the lid a little, they hear a fluttering sound and a redbird flies past them. The redbird, of course, is the daughter of the sun, and when they get home the box is empty. Thereafter, no one can retrieve a soul that has passed into the Darkening Land; so death enters the world.[49]

Certain people who were highly trained knew magical songs, and they served as intermediaries between the people and the other worlds. These medicine men and women had the ability to heal and to prophesy the future. They were crucial in helping explain the unexplainable and in enlisting the help of animal supernaturals to combat disease and witchcraft. The medicine people's activities were woven into virtually every dimension of the Cherokees' lives from courtship, marriage, pregnancy, childbirth, death, and burial to preparation for war and the ball play. Balance, harmony, and clarity regarding gender roles were apparent in the rituals that reinforced femininity and masculinity. Menstruation, childbirth, motherhood, blood, the sun, clan, corn, and agricul-

Fig. 8. Swimmer, or A'yûñ'inĭ, a full-blood medicine man, 1887. Negative no. 1008. (Courtesy National Anthropological Archives, Smithsonian Institution)

ture defined female identity; warfare, hunting, animals, water, fatherhood, the moon, bone, and the ball play defined and reinforced masculinity.

SPORTS: THE BALL PLAY

When the Cherokees no longer engaged in warfare, the ball play gained even more importance as a way of exhibiting masculinity. The Cherokee ball play resembled modern-day lacrosse.[50] The hickory ball sticks were roughly two feet long. Deerskin, squirrel skin, or Indian hemp was laced across a loop at the spoonlike end of the ball stick. Balls made of deerskin or squirrel skin were filled with deer fur, hair, or with spunk (touchwood, a kind of wood decayed by fungi). The Cherokees played on a field marked by a goal of two poles driven into the ground at each end of the field. The players had to either throw the ball through the poles or run through the poles with the ball, which counted as one point. The first team to score twelve points won the game. An old man walked onto the field and threw the ball into the air between two men—one from each team—with rackets, who tried to bat the ball toward their team-mates in order to start the game. Then the players could pick up the ball with the ball sticks or catch it in the air. A player could carry the ball in his hands only after he had picked it up with ball sticks, but he could not pick up the ball with his hands. The game was violent, and injuries were frequently serious, sometimes even fatal. The ball game—"the little brother to war"—was also an occasion for heavy gambling, sometimes involving large amounts. Chiefs bet one thousand dollars on a game played near Jasper, Georgia, between the Cherokee towns of Hickory Log and Coosawattee.[51]

Cherokee men and women observed taboos regarding sexuality and food for the welfare of the entire community. Young men who were ball players observed a demanding training schedule and certain taboos. The ball game was an intensely masculine ritual. For instance, if a woman even touched a ball stick it could not be used in a game. A man whose wife was pregnant was not permitted to play. In addition, because the Cherokees believed that when humans ate animals they acquired the characteristics of that animal, the ball players observed dietary restrictions. For example, a player could not eat rabbit because rabbits were easily frightened and could make a player timid in the game. Likewise, a player could not eat frog or he might risk having brittle bones. Eating a sucker fish might make him sluggish. He ate no hot food or salt. Players had to fast from dinner of the night before the game until after the game was played the next day. They also abstained from touching any woman for seven or more days before the game.[52]

Because opposing teams came from different towns, the games generated intense communal solidarity and great excitement, as well as hostility toward players on opposing teams. Conjurers were always enlisted to ensure the team's victory and sometimes even to cause an opponent illness or even death. Ceremonial preparations for the game resembled the preparations for war. The night before a ball game between Yellow Hill and Raven Town in 1889, a dance was held that lasted all night. The dance symbolized the specific roles that men and women played in the community. The males were the players of one team and the seven females formed a group, one from each Cherokee clan. Men and women remained physically separate and performed their own dances. Yet during the pre–ball play ceremonies, they formed a symbolic whole that represented the harmony of their interdependence. The groups of men and women danced near the post where the ball sticks were hung. While the women were near the post, the men danced in a circle around the fire to the sound of a rattle. The women stood in a line a few feet away singing and dancing, moving toward the men and then turning and dancing away from them to the beat of a drum.

Fig. 9. Ballplayers. Negative no. 1044a. (Courtesy National Anthropological Archives, Smithsonian Institution)

A conjurer had placed black beads representing players of the opposing team on a flat rock to the side of the ball stick hanger. Through their songs and by occasionally stepping on this stone, the women sought to weaken the opponents. This practice demonstrated the perceived power of women and the important part they performed in the ball play. The men invoked various spiritual beings in their songs to give them strength in the upcoming game and to make them fast runners.[53]

The ballplayers left for the field at sunrise, accompanied by the conjurers and their assistants. Until around noon the players participated in rituals of "going to water." War parties had previously observed these customs. When the players arrived at the field, they went to a sheltered place where the conjurer symbolically marked the ground representing the field and assigned positions to the men. They then stripped for the scratching ritual using a *kanuga*, a comb made of seven sharp splinters of turkey leg or wing bones tied to a frame made from a turkey quill. The turkey was known for its swiftness and for its lung power. Each player was extensively scratched in a ritual manner, and blood flowed from hundreds of scratches. The conjurer gave them a root or a mixture of seven herbs to chew and rub into the scratches. The herbs varied from one medicine man to another. These were intended to strengthen the players. Next, they washed the blood off in the cold water. Sometimes they then greased their bodies with bear's oil or slippery elm bark.[54]

After another conjuring ritual with red and black beads, the players went to

Fig. 10. Two Cherokee women sitting in front of log cabin exhibit. (Courtesy Museum of the Cherokee Indian, Cherokee, North Carolina)

the ball ground. After much rough struggle and a point was scored, the ball would be brought back to the center and play would begin again. The game might last a half hour or as long as seven or eight hours. The betting could be so intense that people might wager their clothing. After the game, winners claimed their bets, and the players immersed themselves in the water again and then broke their fast.[55]

Even though warfare was associated with men, women also participated as war women or by choosing captives. Similarly, although the ball game was primarily considered a masculine activity, women played an important part by participating in the dance to weaken the opponents. Moreover, after the main game, women who supported the team that lost would sometimes play a ball game with the women from the team that won. On occasion, women might form one team and men the other team in a stickball game, usually the one pole version of the game.[56]

The ball play, like warfare, was a test of masculinity, bravery, and physical strength. The ball play also reinforced communal solidarity, served to redistribute wealth through gambling, and reinforced the separate, interdependent spheres of men and women. The role of the conjurer indicated the close connection with supernatural forces. The ability of the conjurers to accurately predict the outcome of the games and to directly affect the outcomes either confirmed or challenged one's faith in the medicine men.

Cherokee ideology and culture reflected gender reciprocity and equivalence. Division of labor for men and women in the Cherokee Nation, ceremonies and rituals reinforcing masculinity and femininity, and myths and legends all helped maintain harmony within the community. Their assumptions about sexuality, economic roles, domestic power, and autonomy differed greatly from the patriarchal assumptions among the white Europeans. The Cherokees' cosmology and their radically different views about gender and sexuality led to the Europeans' determination to dramatically alter the society's beliefs and ceremonies. Contact with the Europeans, colonists, and Americans brought disease, warfare, and dispossession.

2
Early Catalysts for Change

There is no people anywhere who love their women more than these [Chero-
kees] do. . . . They are courteous and polite to the women. . . . An Indian
never attempts, nay, he cannot use towards a woman amongst them any in-
delicacy or indecency, either in action or language.

William Bartram, 1853

There is no synonym in their [Cherokee] language for love, and there cannot
be imagined a more contemptuous profanation of its most sacred rites, of
husband and wife, consecrated in our minds by habitual reverence, hallowed
by the most imposing solemnities of religion,—the holy and mysterious tie
. . . which sustains and invigorates our tenderest sympathies and most ex-
alted sentiments—cannot be said to exist at all among the Cherokee.

Thomas J. Harrison

In 1825, a hired girl named Mary had "criminal intercourse" with a young
Cherokee, Robert Sanders, at Carmel mission in Georgia, and Moody Hall, a
missionary of the ABCFM, described the incident that followed: "We burned
their beds and cabin. Cherokee take such 'abominable crimes' lightly."[1] This
incident sheds light on the radically different views regarding sexuality of
religious-minded Euro-Americans and traditional Cherokees and on the battle
being waged over Indians' land, minds, and bodies. The concerted efforts of
missionaries and the U.S. government to inculcate patriarchal gender roles
met with varying degrees of resistance depending on class allegiances. For the
Cherokees, becoming "civilized" increasingly came to mean nothing less than
a radical alteration of gender roles.

Economic Transformations and Challenges
to Cherokee Gender Balance

The U.S. government and missionaries made a concerted effort to transform
Cherokee gender roles and attitudes toward sexuality and the body. They
sought to inculcate Euro-American values of true womanhood and confine
Cherokee women to the domestic sphere. They met with resistance from tradi-

tional Cherokees, but, over the course of contact, wealthier members of that society, often of mixed ancestry, readily accepted both Christianity and the ideals of "true womanhood." Thus gender inequality intersected with class inequality because more affluent women were freed from much domestic labor by hired help or slaves, and they had the means to acquire education and gentility. By the end of the eighteenth century, Cherokee women no longer agreed among themselves on what it meant to be a woman.

Susanna Wickett epitomized a Cherokee woman who became highly acculturated. In the early 1790s she married Major Ridge and left her clan to live in a log cabin that she did not own. Susanna Ridge became a Christian and a plantation mistress as her husband acquired slaves.[2] The Cherokees knew slavery before this period, but it involved primarily war captives. By the 1830s they began to view Africans as more desirable for slavery than other Indians. By 1835, the plantation system became well established within the Cherokee Nation; there were 207 slaveholders, with 83 percent owning fewer than ten slaves.[3] Where slavery existed, it reinforced Euro-American gender roles by assigning agricultural work to slaves rather than Cherokee women. Thus Susanna Ridge worked primarily inside rather than farming outside, departing from Cherokee women's traditional daily productive role. She insisted that her children, including John Ridge, receive an education from white missionaries. Years later her husband and son were assassinated for signing the removal treaty at New Echota.[4]

Although the majority of Cherokee women continued to embrace traditional values, they felt increasing pressure to abandon them. Over the course of the seventeenth and eighteenth centuries, Cherokee gender roles began to change, due in large part to economic transformations. Trade with Europeans, especially the deerskin trade, created indebtedness and inequalities within the tribe. Men hunted and conducted most of the financial transactions, and women prepared the skins. Before horses were introduced, women transported the deerskins as well. Women also sold corn to forts, such as Fort Loudon, in the eighteenth century. Those women who cultivated the land still owned what they raised and had the right to dispose of it as they wished. The connection to wider markets, however, ultimately subverted traditional gender arrangements.[5]

The deerskin trade diminished women's economic independence. The trade gave men, not women, access to the market economy, and sometimes men who became increasingly involved in hunting were unable to help the women as much in farming. Some women, then, may have actually become more empowered as farmers due to the deerskin trade because they were left with more of the work, but the inequities of the system threw traditional patterns out of balance. For instance, if men were addicted to alcohol, which was traded frequently for deerskins, their families might suffer privation. In contrast to Creek women, Cherokee women did not extensively participate in the trade. Therefore, the trade tended to upset gender complementarity, thus destabilizing Cherokee families as men began to become more economically dominant over women.[6]

"Civilization" Program

After the American Revolution, the Cherokee Nation lost large portions of its lands, including vast stretches of hunting grounds. Subsequently, they had to rely more heavily on horticulture for subsistence. At the same time, it became U.S. government and missionary policy to transform Cherokee men into farmers and Cherokee women into submissive housewives. Cherokee men and women accommodated this "civilization" program within their traditional gender roles, and women were more receptive to changes than men.[7]

From Thomas Jefferson to Andrew Jackson, American presidents confronted the dilemma of whether to "civilize" or remove the Indians. In order to civilize them, the U.S. government gave spinning wheels and plows to the Indians. The spinning wheel represented an entire way of life based on farming, domesticity, and agrarian democracy.[8] Laurel Thatcher Ulrich explains how homespun became a crucial embodiment of this agrarian dream: "The age of homespun provided an ideological haven from the artificiality of Europe and the rudeness of the American landscape. Americans situated their yeoman farmer between aristocrats and sages, seldom invoking one without the other. In poems, sermons, diaries, and in counterpanes, blankets, and tablecloths, they celebrated family solidarity and household industry, even as they spun slave-grown cotton and turned up Indian bones with their plows."[9]

Because of the power of the nineteenth-century cultural myth, white Americans regarded the spinning wheel as the symbol of the republic. Even during the American Revolution, wearing homespun was considered patriotic and represented independence from European trade. Naturally, the U.S. government selected plows and spinning wheels as the most important implements to supply the Native people in order to hasten their civilization. Some American Indian women saw the spinning wheels as attractive additions to their households and adopted them readily. Their response stemmed from the fact that the skins normally used for their clothing became scarce with the deerskin trade, and thus they either purchased cloth—especially calico (which made them dependent on trade with the white traders)—or used the spinning wheel to supply clothing to their families.

Thomas Jefferson believed yeoman farmers in an agrarian setting were crucial to the continuance and health of democracy. His environmental approach considered the Indians as capable of civilization, but he believed that they would become extinct unless they adopted the values of Euro-Americans. Indians needed to turn to agriculture, convert to Christianity, and intermarry with whites. In addition, they had to sever their communal connections with the land, adopt the practice of owning private property, and assume Western European gender roles. Jefferson also encouraged the use of deep-cutting plows, horses, oxen, milk cows, beef steers, spinning wheels, and looms. Skeptical about whether Indians would accept the first alternative, Jefferson planned to move the Indians who lived east of the Mississippi River to the northern part of the Louisiana Purchase.[10]

Presidents Monroe, Adams, and Madison all coveted the Indians' land, but they respected their human rights to the extent that they encouraged civilization programs. Monroe signed an appropriation bill in 1819 that provided ten thousand dollars annually for the civilization of the Indians. Andrew Jackson appeared to support this program when he said that Indians must "become merged in the mass of our population."[11] These early presidents also imagined Cherokee lands as part of the nation's resources. As early as 1805, the U.S. president wanted a post road to run through parts of the Cherokee Nation, the Creek Nation, and the Choctaw Nation, from Knoxville to New Orleans. The building of this road marked the beginning of the end for Cherokee sovereignty.[12] From 1824 to 1852, half of the ten major presidential candidates had made their reputations as either generals in Indian wars or secretaries of war.[13]

Not all government officials differentiated between the fates of Cherokee women and men, but Jefferson specifically addressed the role of women in his *Notes on the State of Virginia*. He perceived the status of women in the Indian cultures as inferior to men, writing:

The women are subjected to unjust drudgery. This I believe is the case with every barbarous people. With such, force is law. The stronger sex imposes on the weaker. It is civilization alone which replaces women in the enjoyment of their natural equality. That first teaches us to subdue the selfish passions, and to respect those rights in others which we value in ourselves. Were we in equal barbarism, our females would be equal drudges. The man with them is less strong than with us, but their women stronger than ours; and both for the same obvious reason; because our man and their woman is habituated to labor, and formed by it. With both races the sex which is indulged with ease is the least athletic.[14]

MISSIONIZING AND EFFORTS TO CONTROL
CHEROKEE WOMEN'S SEXUALITY

The U.S. government and missionaries sought to justify "reform" in the name of liberating Cherokee women from drudgery, but the practical effect was to undermine women's sources of power and destabilize gender and class relations. In this effort to transform gender roles within the Cherokee Nation, the federal government subsidized mission schools such as Brainerd in Tennessee, which was established in 1817. A central dimension of this transformation was controlling women's sexual behavior. In 1822 Jeremiah Evarts commented on the fact that "the intercourse between the young of both sexes was shamefully loose. . . . Boys or girls in their teens would strip and go in to bathe or play ball together naked. They would also use the most disgusting indecent language without the least sense of shame. But when better instructed, they became reserved and modest."[15]

Return J. Meigs was the Cherokee agent in Tennessee in the period prior to removal. He commented in his journal on the Cherokee culture and changes in women's lives. Writing in 1817, he articulated the belief that the Americans were "liberating the Cherokee women." He described the positive effects of introducing the civilization program: "Since the introduction of domestic manufactures the females are held in higher estimation by the men. They are emerging from a partial kind of slavery with their proper place in society. They are more esteemed by the males, & as esteem & love are concomitant between the sexes, love is becoming a sentimental passion never known in a perfect savage state."[16]

The missionaries to the Cherokees shared Meigs's attitudes about the elevation of women through submission to patriarchal values. More missionaries and missionary funds came to the Cherokees in the early nineteenth century than to any other tribe. Various associations supported more than twenty mission stations and twenty schools: the Moravians (or United Brethren) beginning in 1800, the Presbyterians in 1804, the Sarepta Baptist Missionary Association in 1815, the ABCFM in 1816, the Baptist Foreign Mission Board in 1817, and the Tennessee Methodist Conference in 1822.[17] The missionaries sought to inculcate patriarchal family organization and Christian morality. They opposed polygamy, fornication, nudity, gambling, drinking, conjuring, dancing, infanticide, witchcraft, ball play, card playing, and participation in

Cherokee ceremonies such as the Green Corn ceremony. Whether sexual behavior radically changed during the eighteenth and early nineteenth centuries
is difficult to determine, but concepts of modesty and shame about the body
were strongly introduced into the culture during this time. The missionaries
wanted to transform the Indian children into the "white man's and white woman's images."

Those missionaries, such as Baptist minister Evan Jones, who encouraged
Cherokees to accept the new religion while retaining many of their old beliefs
and who supported the people politically were the most successful in winning
converts. For both Evan Jones and his son John Jones, Christianity was a vehicle
for revitalizing Cherokee culture. They preached that the best of the traditionalist worldview could be combined with the best of Christianity in order to
form a shield against the intrusion of white culture. They supported both bi-
lingual education for Cherokees and a vibrant Native ministry.[18]

The Baptist Foreign Mission Board set up a station at Valley Town on the
Hiwassee River in North Carolina in 1820, and Evan Jones arrived there in September 1821. A year later, the Baptists established another station at Notley,
sixteen miles southwest of Valley Town, and then at Tinsawatoo, sixty miles
southwest of Valley Town, in Georgia. Kaneeda, a full-blood, became the first
Native Baptist minister and was given the English name of John Wickliffe. Jesse
Bushyhead, the son of a prominent family in the Amohee district, also became
a Baptist minister, and he established a church in his district. Reverend Bear
Currier, a young Cherokee minister, assisted him. In 1835, 227 Cherokees belonged to the Baptist Church in the Cherokee Nation East.[19]

The Methodists were also active in trying to convert the Cherokees to Christian morality, but they relied primarily on circuit riders. The Indian membership numbered 1,028 when the work of the Methodist missionaries among the
Cherokees reached its peak in 1830. John Fletcher Boot was perhaps one of the
most powerful Native preachers; in 1829 he began under the Tennessee Conference on the Wills Valley Circuit.[20]

The ABCFM stations included 159 church members and 174 students in the
schools in 1829. The Baptist Valley Town School served 54 pupils in 1822. The
Methodists did not establish any schools, but 675 Cherokees had become members of the Methodist Church by 1827; there were 702 Cherokee members in
1828 and 736 in 1829. The ABCFM reported 262 members and 68 pupils in
1833. The Baptists claimed 232 Cherokee members in 1836.[21] The missionaries
of all these denominations sought to instill patriarchal values through the example of model farming communities, schools, church discipline (dismissal of
moral offenders), preaching, and articles in the Nation's newspaper.

They also believed that the life of their most famous convert, Catharine Brown, epitomized the virtues of piety, purity, submissiveness, and domesticity. Brown also symbolized the taming of female sexuality. She entered Brainerd Mission on July 9, 1817. Rufus Anderson, the editor of her memoir, published in 1825, extolled her as an exemplary woman who deserved to be emulated: "It is pleasing to observe here, that her moral character was ever irreproachable. This is remarkable, considering the looseness of manner then prevalent among the females of her nation, and the temptations to which she was exposed, when, during the war with the Creek Indians, the army of the United States was stationed near her father's residence. . . . Once she even fled her home into the wild forest to preserve her character unsullied."[22]

Within sixty days of Brown's arrival at Brainerd, she could read the Bible, and after ninety days she was as proficient as "almost any person with an ordinary education."[23] Mr. Porter, one of the missionaries, described her character: "For sweetness of temper, meekness, gentleness, and forbearance, I never saw one who surpassed her. To her parents she was uncommonly dutiful and affectionate." On January 25, 1818, she became the first Indian baptized by the ABCFM.[24] Evarts described Brown as a beautiful woman who "probably attracted more attention than any other female in the nation." When she first arrived at the mission, the missionaries thought that she seemed vain; but as she became more and more serious about conversion, she became modest in her dress and behavior.[25] When her parents wanted her to accompany them to Arkansas, she dutifully went with them. When her father's trip was delayed, he brought her back. Brown wrote to Mr. and Mrs. Hall at Brainerd from Knoxville on May 30, 1819: "But I will now give myself up entirely to Him (Christ). I should be willing to leave everything for God, and to undergo any sufferings, if it would but make me humble, and would be for his glory. My heart bleeds for my people who are on the brink of destruction. O pray for me, my dear brother and sister." Brown went to teach school at Creek Path, a girls' school, in May 1820.[26] Her devotion was not always matched by that of the male missionaries who met her. Daniel Sabin Butrick, a missionary for the ABCFM, was thoroughly captivated by her. She evoked such a powerful sexual response in him that he agonized over it in his diary. His attraction to her caused him to feel extremely guilty. He confided to the pages of his diary: "My wicked passions rage, the storm beats on my foundering bank, and gaping waves and towering surges threaten my immediate ruin."[27]

In 1822, Brown began to show symptoms of tuberculosis. Her deathbed scene resembled that of Little Eva in *Uncle Tom's Cabin;* her death was romanticized in her memoir, and she quickly became a martyr in the eyes of Christians. Dying chaste, young, and beautiful, Brown became a symbol of true womanhood. Mr. Bascom described her on her deathbed: "The natural mildness of her features seemed lighted with a beam of heavenly hope, and her whole aspect was that of a mature Christian, waiting with filial patience the welcome summons to the presence of her Lord."[28] Likewise, Mrs. Potter described Brown in a letter to the corresponding secretary of the ABCFM: "Her countenance was softened with the affectionate remembrance of an endeared brother, her cheek was a little flushed with the exertion of speaking, her eye beamed with spiritual joy, and a heavenly smile animated the whole scene." She described Brown's last night as labored because she had difficulty breathing. The next day Potter wrote: "Then, turning her eyes towards heaven, an indescribable placidness spread over her countenance. . . . She expired so gently, that even those around the bed scarcely knew that the last breath had left her until the physician informed them she was gone."[29]

Brown died on the morning of July 18, 1823. In the years following her death, she assumed almost mythic proportions. The missionaries' admiration of her was so great that they regarded her as a model of what every young woman should be. An entry in the *Brainerd Journal* tells of a Cherokee woman who became interested in Christianity because of Brown and traveled 120 miles to hear the gospel. Anderson wrote in Brown's memoir that in pagan countries, "man is a lordly tyrant, and woman is a slave. True civilization is found only in Christian countries."[30]

And yet, Brown's life was likely more complicated. Although she was a Christian convert, she also continued traditional Cherokee practices such as fasting, and she participated in women's prayer groups, often in the forests and mountains. Brown and her parents continued to enlist the help of traditional healers. Thus, she may have retained more of her Cherokee beliefs and been less acculturated than the missionaries' account claimed.[31]

Still, the missionaries held on to their image of the saintly Catharine Brown and their belief that Christianity would liberate Cherokee women from the heavy labor of cultivating the earth and elevate them as moral guardians of the hearth.[32] The missionaries found an eloquent spokesperson in Elias Boudinot (Buck Watie), the editor of the *Cherokee Phoenix*. Boudinot frequently published articles extolling the values of true womanhood. For example, in the April 1, 1829, issue an article appeared titled "Who Is a Beautiful Woman?" The author wrote: "She is beautiful because the gentleness of her nature and the kindness of her heart throw a household halo around her person adorning her as a honeysuckle adorns an ordinary tree and impressing her mental image on our minds."[33] On May 27, 1829, an article extolled the "Angel of the House":

Fig. 11. Elias Boudinot Sr. (1802–39). OHS Glass Plate
Collection, no. 19615.43. (Courtesy Archives and
Manuscripts Division, Oklahoma Historical Society)

"A wife! What a sacred name, what a responsible office! She must be the unspotted sanctuary to which wearied men flee from the crimes of the world, and feel that no sin dare enter there. A wife! She must be the guardian angel of his footsteps on earth, and guide them to Heaven."[34]

Boudinot and his cousin John Ridge had both married white women from New England. Boudinot married Harriet Gold, and Ridge married Sarah Bird Northrup in Cornwall, Connecticut, where they attended the mission school.[35] Most instances of intermarriage, however, involved Cherokee women and white men. This profoundly affected the balance of gender roles. In 1825, approximately one quarter of the Cherokee population had some white ancestry. White fathers tended to disregard matrilineal and clan customs. Moreover, the Cherokee slave owners, many of whom had already intermarried, tended to adopt

Fig. 12. Harriet Ruggles Gold Boudinot (d. 1836). OHS
Glass Plate Collection, no. 19615.31. (Courtesy Archives
and Manuscripts Division, Oklahoma Historical Society)

more patriarchal values.[36] In these families it was usual for men to speak English and women, Cherokee. Robert Sparks Walker commented, "Oddly enough, females often refused to speak English at all."[37]

Although the frequency of intermarriage was still negligible in the 1830s, the trend toward white men joining the Nation was already clear. White men were expected to become acculturated into Cherokee society. Children of white women and Cherokee men did not have any clan affiliations. There was not a shortage of Cherokee men as marital partners. Some women may have perceived liaisons with white men as beneficial to their own status as well as the community's if the men brought skills that were needed for tribal survival or if the men were successful traders.

It is clear, however, that missionaries saw white husbands as perfect conduits for their civilization programs. They tried to instill patriarchal values through example in the missions' family structure. Samuel A. Worcester, the prominent missionary of the ABCFM in Indian Territory, wrote to David Greene from Park Hill, in 1846 describing what could happen if someone disrupted the patriarchal hierarchy. He complained about Nancy Thompson, a white missionary who had been a devoted "assistant," but who had not known her place. He said, "It was difficult for her to get along well in families where there were a husband and a wife, who claimed the right of control over all domestic affairs." When his first wife, Ann Orr Worcester, died, Thompson was the head of the domestic department in his family for a time. When he married Ermina Nash, Thompson did not want to be subservient to her.

Worcester wrote, "[I] assured her (Miss T) I could never give up the principle, that whatever is done in the domestic labors of the family, must be done in accordance with the wishes of the head of the family." Then he added, "And I think that no woman ought to be sent into *any* missionary family, without understanding that, in relation to all the domestic affairs of the household, the wife is the head [subject, of course to her own husband,] and wants no helper who is not willing that she should direct—no helper who will do things contrary to her own wishes." Thompson had protested, saying, "We are all sisters, and not subject one to another." Overstepping her place landed her in trouble with the ABCFM.[38] This situation is revealing because the women missionaries apparently did not always practice the ideal of meekness and passivity that they taught.[39]

The missionaries not only modeled patriarchal family values but also sought to provide lessons in domesticity for Cherokee girls. In the Cherokee Nation in 1830, at least half of the fifty-six whites supported by mission boards in the seventeen mission stations were women. Because only ordained ministers held the title of missionary, these women were called "assistants." The assistants, along with the male missionaries' wives, taught in the schools, cooked, served, washed clothes, managed women's dormitories, made cheese, and churned butter. In addition, along with students, they raised vegetable gardens and took care of chickens.[40]

Hannah Moore and Sophia Sawyer, like other missionary women who came from New England, were surprised by the Cherokees' lack of inhibitions. Moore described being shocked to see a company of ballplayers riding full speed, "whiskey bottles hanging at their sides. Though a great many females attend their ballplays, my guide knew I did not wish for a moment to look on a scene so disgusting to refinement as Indians running in a state of nudity." She remarked, "I dare not raise my eyes."[41]

The women missionaries had to adjust to these cultural differences, but they ultimately experienced a sense of personal empowerment even as they sought to diminish Cherokee women's autonomy and power. Sometimes they met with resistance. Once at Haweis, Sawyer tried to convince a Cherokee mother to send her child to the mission school, pursuing her into her chimney corner only to be told by the woman that she would as soon see her child in hell as in the mission classroom.[42] Sawyer served at Brainerd, New Echota, Honey Creek, Running Water, and Haweis, toiling incessantly to inculcate the values of true womanhood in her female students. Although Sawyer taught the girls submissiveness, her own behavior was unruly; she was a strong, independent, outspoken woman who constantly alienated her male colleagues. She traveled alone, for instance, to Dwight Mission in December 1837, and the ABCFM transferred her from place to place in the old Cherokee Nation without hesitation.[43]

On December 27, 1838, she wrote to David Greene, an ABCFM officer: "I often inquire why a poor weak sensative female is thus left to the current alone." Yet this poor, sensitive woman defied a Georgia guardsman during the removal crisis when he came into her classroom.[44] She was violating a Georgia law by teaching a black child to read the Bible, but she asked the sergeant to leave the room while she prayed. She told him that she would not obey any Georgia laws until the U.S. Supreme Court decided in favor of the state.[45] Sawyer had been working on a book called *Lights and Shades of Indian Character in Thirteen Years' Residence among the Cherokees.* Her manuscript, which the ABCFM did not think should be published, contained information on "delicate and exciting subjects." Regrettably, the manuscript appears to have been lost.[46]

Sawyer left New Echota for Running Waters, the residence of John Ridge.[47] There she became a teacher and a member of the extended family, and she moved with the Ridge family in December 1837 to Honey Creek, in Indian Territory. After Major Ridge and John Ridge were killed in 1839, she moved with the survivors of the family to Fayetteville, Arkansas, and started a school for girls.[48] The first students in Sawyer's school were fourteen Cherokee girls, daughters of the Drews, Ridges, Rosses, Adairs, and Starrs. By 1840 there were fifty-one students. The entry in *Noted Daughters of Arkansas* by Mrs. Anthony George described Sawyer as a proper New England lady: "Her dress was of Puritanical severity; her hair was combed smoothly over her ears as was then the custom. Her lace caps were dainty, yet dignified and reserved. No one ever thought of approaching her with the slightest familiarity, so great was her reserve."[49] Still, her mobility, education, and independence suggest that she may have had a difficult time returning to a domestic life in Massachusetts. Women missionaries such as Sawyer and Moore became intermediaries in the private world of Cherokee womanhood and home life. Wade Horton persuasively argues that the high status of Cherokee women enabled female missionaries to develop a significant voice within Cherokee culture. They eventually used their access to attempt to transform gender role expectations of Cherokee women and to control their sexuality. They did so in part by offering their converts laborsaving tools such as looms, spinning wheels, and candle molds.[50] Along with providing these tools, they sought to impose their views of sexuality, marriage, dress, etiquette, and religion.

In mission schools, girls assisted their white counterparts in the kitchen and with laundry and ironing. They cooked, made candles, processed meats, and cleaned buildings. They also learned to spin, weave, and sew.[51] On the mission's model farms the boys fed cattle, made fires, and worked in the fields. As part of their civilization policy, the U.S. government subsidized the Cherokee mission schools and provided looms, spinning wheels, and cards.[52] Hannah Moore described her work in trying to "civilize" the Cherokee girls at Dwight Mission in Indian Territory. She taught ornamental needlework, knitting of stockings and ornamental money purses, carding, spinning, fitting, and making dresses—all in an effort "to teach the savages, or semi-barbarians, the rudiments of civilization."[53] The following report from Brainerd appeared in the annual reports of the ABCFM: "The instructress of the girls informed us, that since the 16th of March last, the girls had made eighty garments, such as shirts, pantaloons, &c. without including smaller articles; that they had pieced thirteen bed quilts, and quilted nine. We examined a part of the work and it appeared well done."[54]

The mission stations were intended to be model homes, schools, churches, and farms, thus instilling the values of piety, learning, and industry.[55] Their indoctrination caused some Cherokee girls to reject traditional values and view their own people as somehow "inferior." Letters written by Cherokee girls reflect the impact of their education. These girls were often mediators with their peers and were confronted with both deculturation and acculturation. Susan Taylor, a nine-year-old at Brainerd Mission, wrote, "We ought to strive to learn very fast, so we can teach our brothers and sisters and other heathen children."[56] Nancy Reece, a fifteen-year-old daughter of a Brainerd church elder, wrote many such letters that were sent to white benefactors, fellow Cherokees, and Choctaws. Her letters reflect a tension between viewing her people as somehow uncivilized and yet capable and as good as whites.[57] In a letter from Brainerd on May 16, 1828, she wrote to a northern woman: "Among others the girls of this school have thought more about the Saviour and that they are sinners. Some of them think that their sins are forgiven. I have thought more than I did and some times I think that my heart is changed and at other times I am doubtful. I love to think about the Saviour and love to pray to Him, and pray that there may be a survival of religion here."[58] Another letter was sent by Brainerd student Christiana McPherson to the president of the United States: "We heard that the Cherokees were going to send you a mink skin and a pipe. We thought that it would make you laugh; and the Scholars asked our teacher if they might make you a present and she told us that she did not know as there was anything suitable in the whole establishment. Then she looked among the articles of the girls society and told me that I might make you a pocket-book. Will you please to accept it from a little Cherokee girl aged nine years?"[59] Elizabeth Taylor wrote from Brainerd to a Miss Abigail [Parker] on June 26, 1828, telling her of Cherokee rituals and dances. After describing conjuring, rainmaking, dances, and other aspects of Cherokee culture, she wrote: "But I have learned that the white people were once as degraded as this people; and that encourages me to think that this nation will soon become enlightened. I hope I feel thankful for the good that missionaries are doing in bringing the word of God to this people."[60]

Northern sponsors would often "adopt" a child and give it an English name as a symbol of religious and cultural conversion. Although the officers of the mission societies were male, the rank-and-file contributors were primarily women, many of whom formed "cent societies" to fund missionary efforts among the Indians. Cyrus Kingsbury wrote to benefactors in Wilmington, Delaware, describing the progress of one of the sponsored students: "While we heartily congratulate you in your exertions to aid the cause of Missions, & to raise the Cherokees from their state of Moral Darkness to the Glorious light & liberty of the Gospel, we would give you some information." He proceeded to describe one of their beneficiaries, Thomas Witherspoon, as "somewhat roguish tho not vicious—he makes pretty good proficiency in study."[61]

Even the "roguish" ones probably adopted new forms of dress. By 1830 most Cherokee women wore cotton or calico dresses in public, and men wore trousers.[62] Outward symbols of acculturation did not necessarily signify that the majority of Cherokees had adopted Euro-American values. Many believed that tribal sovereignty depended on being viewed as civilized. The Cherokee women who wore calico dresses certainly looked radically different from those whom a Seneca war chief described in the eighteenth century. The women, who were in charge of his fate, "each had two snakes tattooed on her lips, with their heads opposite each other, in such way that when she opened her mouth the two snakes opened their mouths also."[63]

Cherokee Resistance and Acculturation

The civilization program, the loss of hunting lands, missionary efforts, and slavery all destabilized gender relations within the Cherokee Nation. Men's roles were more disrupted than women's because men lost their ability to be hunters and warriors. Because farming was considered "women's work," the men would have had to radically alter their views of masculinity if they had chosen to become farmers. Therefore, most Cherokee women continued farming; in addition, they adopted new domestic technologies and continued as mothers. Only a small minority of elite Cherokee women who were slaveholders embraced fully the values of "true womanhood." However, even these women were not willing to give up the ownership of their property. In fact, tribal sovereignty continued to rest on communal ownership of land.

Wilma Dunaway persuasively demonstrates that, shortly before removal, the Cherokees had learned new survival strategies in a world economy and that their agricultural production equaled or surpassed that of their white neighbors. They produced corn, hogs, and cattle at levels equivalent to or higher than the 1840 outputs of white settlers in the former Cherokee territory. By 1828 each Cherokee household averaged three horses, one plow, and a spinning wheel, and probably around a third of the households had looms. However, most traditional Cherokee women continued to weave baskets and produce pottery rather than purchase manufactured ones. Through such ecological accommodations as cotton growing, sheep raising, weaving, and spinning, Cherokee women were able to preserve crucial cultural elements of household production and networks.[64]

Dunaway points out that, historically, agrarian capitalism has shifted control of household, land, and means of production to men; has stimulated public policies that disempower women; and has fostered the "cult of domesticity" in order to justify the inequitable treatment of wives. She makes a convincing case for the ways in which Cherokee women effectively resisted the economic, cultural, and political changes that would have undermined their matrilineal powers and rights. Thus, Cherokee cultural transformation was not as pervasive as historians have previously assumed.[65]

By 1835 fewer than 17 percent of Cherokees were of mixed ethnicity; therefore the full-bloods who were culturally conservative constituted a majority of the Cherokee population. Moreover, fewer than 25 percent of Cherokee families were undergoing or had made the transition to agrarian capitalism by this time. Less than 7 percent of the households used slave labor to produce large enough surpluses to export their crops. Wealthy Cherokee women who were slaveholders tended to spend less time with their kin networks because they supervised the work of slaves, and they thus tended to become more acculturated to Euro-American values. Three-quarters of Cherokee women were full-bloods who preserved matrilineal traditions and continued their historical participation in farming, fishing, hunting, livestock raising, and gender-integrated *gadugi*. They continued to live in extended families in which matrilineal clan ties were preserved, and they continued to participate in local decision making. Through opposing the missionaries, many traditional Cherokee women maintained control over the cultural socialization of their children.[66] As a result, public changes and private continuity created tensions within the Cherokee Nation. Cherokee women no longer agreed on what it meant to be a woman. The contested meanings of gender would remain largely unrecognized until periods of personal, economic, and political crisis.

Cherokees made successful adaptations to new circumstances in ways that were compatible with ancient cultural traditions. In many of their deepest emotional crises, such as sickness, death, traumatic personal loss, fear, or anxiety, they often resorted to traditional explanations and relied on medicine men.[67] Those Cherokees who resisted Christianity and "civilization" held traditional religious beliefs, objected to adopting patriarchal gender roles, favored communal land ownership over private property, and wanted to retain women's voice in tribal affairs. Cherokees expressed their resistance to changes in gender roles through their failure to convert to Christianity in significant numbers, backsliding if they did convert, and their persistence in continuing their ball play, conjuring, and ceremonies. In addition, they actively reasserted traditional Cherokee religion three times between 1789 and 1839.[68]

Cherokee women demonstrated resistance to acculturation in two revitalization movements, the Cherokee Ghost Dance movement during the 1811–13 religious revival, and White Path's Rebellion in the 1820s. Six different versions of the Ghost Dance visions all shared the message from the Great Spirit that he was angry with the Cherokees for forsaking their religious practices and traditions. The Ghost Dance movement never achieved unity or coherence and died out or went underground in 1812, but the intensity of the movement symbolized the tremendous struggle that existed between the older Cherokee values of communal sharing and the materialistic, acquisitive values of the white capitalist system.[69] Elite, highly acculturated Cherokees, who were frequently of mixed white and Cherokee ancestry, began to acquire the best farm sites, purchase slaves, and gain political influence, whereas the more traditional Cherokees remained poor. Other tensions stemmed from the fact that by 1800 the Cherokees had lost half of their original tribal lands in addition to their oldest towns and most sacred sites. The fur trade had waned; men were once again more involved in food cultivation, and women had to become spinners and weavers in order to clothe their families. Thus the gender roles were destabilized because women had traditionally been the primary farmers. This tension over gender relations may help explain why the visions concerned returning to a time when women and men were in complementary and equal roles.[70]

Many Cherokee women opposed the missionaries and schools that directly attacked traditions and chose to maintain control over their children's education. Often, mothers resisted the language shift to English and thus thwarted the teachers' instruction of their children. Cherokee women were central in asserting Cherokee nationalism and cultural autonomy.[71] They creatively accepted those aspects of the civilization program that made their domestic tasks easier, such as using spinning wheels, but the majority rejected the injunctions to become subordinate to men and resisted attempts to diminish their power during the early nineteenth century.

Even those who embraced Christianity did not always assimilate. Backsliding from church membership was quite common. James Adair, a trader in the eighteenth century, wrote an account of a Cherokee woman named Dark-Lanthorn who married a white man and temporarily converted to Christianity. Her story might have been typical of many of the so-called backsliders whom the missionaries lamented. Adair chronicled her encounter with conversion: "There was a gentleman who married her according to the manner of the Cheerake; but discovering that marriages were commonly of short duration in that wanton female government, he flattered himself of ingrossing her affections, could he be so happy as to get her sanctified by one of our beloved men with a large quantity of holy water in baptism—and be taught the conjugal duty, by virtue of her new Christian name, when they were married anew." After the ceremony was over, she went to bed with her husband. He entered her name in the church book of converts. Adair continued, "Afterward to his great grief he [her husband] was obliged on account of her adulteries to erase her name from thence, and enter it anew in some crowded page of female delinquents."[72]

Apparently, a large number of people had their names erased from the church rolls. Although the majority of Cherokees did not join churches, of the sixty-five converts who joined the Moravian churches during their first thirty years in the Nation, McLoughlin claimed that two-thirds were from the same small group of families, two-thirds were of mixed ancestry, and two-thirds were women.[73] It is unclear why these groups appeared particularly susceptible to the attraction of the Christian church. Perhaps they found some solace in Christianity, given the high death rate of children and infants, and they may have welcomed the church's support of temperance because drunkenness threatened family stability. Most expulsions resulted from adultery and intemperance.[74] By the 1830s only 10 percent of the Cherokees were attending Christian churches.[75]

Because the Cherokees did not believe in the depravity of human nature, the majority of the Nation continued to resist this new view of themselves.[76] In 1840 Daniel Butrick wrote to David Greene, complaining about the morals of the Cherokee women: "One Mrs. Safford, it is said uses profane language, one Mrs. Glass, it is said attends dances, and the other Mrs. Broken Canoe, I believe has never been at meeting here since she was baptized in May 1836."[77] When Daniel Butrick began preaching against conjuring, practically his whole congregation deserted him for a while before gradually coming back.[78]

Isaac Proctor was shocked to find out that one of his congregation who had received communion the previous Sunday had cursed through conjuring another member of the congregation on Monday.[79] The persistence of conjuring is indicative of the continuity of traditional values; conjuring played a crucial role in virtually every aspect of the community's life, from childbirth, pregnancy, and illness to ball plays. Throughout his journal, Butrick comments on his view of the immorality within the Nation, citing drunkenness, adultery, domestic violence, rape, wife murder, and marriage without parental consent.[80]

On September 27, 1833, Butrick lamented that the actors in the recent ball play were entirely naked. He forbade any student in his school to go to a ball play or an all-night dance. He despaired, however, that "the young women who have been educated at mission school and by great expense and labour taught to read and understand the Bible, are the first victims of these emissaries of darkness." He wrote that they become "ringleaders of wickedness."[81] Butrick recorded the rules for his students:

1. No scholar must use profane language, nor profane the Lord's Day.
2. No scholar must attend Ball plays, nor engage in any kind of gambling, as card playing, horse racing, etc. nor assemble with companions engaged in those vices.
3. The scholars must not attend dances of any kind.
4. No scholar must drink any kind of intoxicating liquor, unless directed as a medicine (wine at Lord's supper excepted).

5. The scholars must not fight, nor wrestle, nor use provoking language; and must, of course be obedient to all the internal regulations of the school.[82]

We have seen the ways missionaries attempted to radically alter gender roles in the Cherokee Nation. Although they met tremendous resistance among the traditional Cherokees, they found a receptive audience among the economic and political elites, many of whom were of mixed ancestry and accepted Christianity. Because the elites believed that tribal sovereignty depended on being recognized as civilized, they also selectively accepted some aspects of patriarchal gender roles. These changes were reflected in the Cherokee laws and constitution. Whereas economic transformations may be the original stimulus to changes in gender systems, religious beliefs and legal systems justify and codify the changes.

Legal Changes in the Cherokee Nation

Many of the legal changes within the Cherokee Nation in the early nineteenth century excluded women from the formal political process, weakened the power of the clans, and diminished women's autonomy. With the passage of the Cherokee Constitution in 1827, Cherokee women became politically disenfranchised and could no longer vote or hold public office. Because clan membership derived from women, any weakening of the practices of clan revenge, marriage restrictions, and taboos related to clan membership meant challenges to women's power. This loss of formal political power was dramatic. The Cherokee Constitution, modeled after the U.S. Constitution, created a three-branch government with a Supreme Court, a legislature, and the principal chief as executive. The Cherokees hoped that this demonstration of Cherokee sovereignty and acculturation would prevent their removal from the Southeast.

From the early 1800s, Cherokee laws sought to shift the locus of control from clan to nation, undermining traditional forms of power and authority.[83] The National Council passed ninety-seven laws between 1810 and 1827 that were designed to undermine old traditions and push Cherokees toward Christianity and agrarian capitalism.[84] The Brooms Town meeting on September 11, 1808, had marked the beginning of the first written law of the Cherokees, establishing a police force to suppress robbery and horse stealing. The laws also extended protection to children as heirs to their father's property and to the widow's share. On April 10, 1810, clan revenge was abolished. These measures undermined matrilineality and clan customs. Nevertheless, women retained the same rights of property ownership as men. Cherokee women had complete control of their property, which meant that their husbands could not manage their property without their consent. Tribal lands continued to be communally owned.[85]

Legal changes also signaled the Cherokee Nation's intervention into sexual and familial practices. The council enacted a law in 1825 that forbade any Cherokee from having more than one wife at any given time.[86] In addition, Cherokee women traditionally had the right to practice abortion and infanticide, but in 1826 the council made infanticide illegal and punishable by fifty lashes. This shift reflected a departure from women's previous autonomy.[87] Reflecting this interventionist trend, the council passed two laws in the 1820s regarding rape, a rare crime in Cherokee history.[88] Any person found guilty of rape was punished with fifty lashes upon the bare back and had his left ear cropped off close to the head. For the second offense, the penalty was one hundred lashes and the other ear cut off. If someone committed a third offense, the penalty was death.[89]

Legal changes affected all classes of Cherokees, and when the elites began to accept more patriarchal gender roles, even traditional Cherokees were judged thereafter by their conformity or rebellion against them. Controlling Indian women's sexuality and "liberating" them to be housewives was central to dispossessing Cherokees of their land and was used as a justification for it. Their sexual, political, and economic power represented a danger, but by the time of removal in 1838, the Cherokee clan system was significantly weakened and women's political power diminished. Left unchanged, however, was the inviolability of women's property. As seen in the dynamic reassertion of traditional religion, the majority of Cherokees did not adopt the Euro-American worldview. If tribal sovereignty was presumed to be dependent on the appearance of being civilized, Cherokees could dress like whites, adopt a similar constitution, and pass laws that conformed to white expectations. Economic and political transformations, intermarriage with whites, the vigorous civilization program of the U.S. government and the missionaries, and attempts to control Cherokee women's sexuality all created factionalism within the Cherokee Nation. Splits occurred chiefly along lines of class and ancestry. Although the traditional values of harmony, balance, and order persisted within the culture, tensions were present, if largely unrecognized. The crises of removal, the Civil War, and allotment would force this debate into the open.[90]

3
The Trail of Tears

When the strong arm of power is raised against the weak and defenseless, the force of argument must fail. Our Nation has been besieged by a powerful Army and you have been captured in peace from your various domestic pursuits. And your wives & children placed in forts under a military guard for the purpose of being immediately transported to the West of the Mississippi.

John Ross, July 21, 1838

Strangers urge our removal [to make room for their settlements], they point to the West and there they say we can live happy. Our National existence is suspended on the faith and honor of the United States alone. We are in the paw of a Lion—convenience may induce him [to] crush and with a faint Struggle we may cease to be!

John Ridge, "John Ridge on Cherokee Civilization in 1836"

Stockades were going up on the Hiwassee River in 1838. Eventually, numerous stockades would imprison the Cherokee Nation in anticipation of removal from their ancestral lands.[1] Cherokee women's power traditionally originated in their roles as mothers (bearers of life) and as cultivators of the earth (sustainers of life). Because removal and the forced cession of lands were direct attacks on Cherokee women's power, they protested the loss by appealing to their people through their authority as mothers.[2] Our view of Cherokee removal radically changes when we take gender into account. How did women's experiences of removal differ from men's? What role did Cherokee women play in the crisis? By focusing on gender as an independent variable, we discover that most Cherokee women opposed removal, even as their lack of acculturation served to justify U.S. governmental action. The loss of their formal power via the 1827 constitution meant that they could not oppose removal as forcefully as they could have previously. Removal legitimized male political power and excluded women from public participation in politics. All the public players in the controversy were men. Moreover, the land that was being ceded was that which was most closely associated with women: the agricultural fields and villages. Women in the Nation did not respond to the removal crisis in a unified manner. The more traditional Cherokee women responded very differently than the more assimilated women. Wealthy, acculturated women of mixed ancestry supported removal in a much larger proportion than did any other group. The crisis forced into the open the debate over what it meant to be a woman.

Removal created bitter factionalism that many Cherokees erroneously thought was rooted in acculturation. Overall, the removal crisis destabilized Cherokee gender roles, but at the same time, it reinforced the values of family and tradition because detachments usually consisted of extended families and people who were from the same locations. Moreover, Cherokee women's traditional skills became even more essential both on the journey and when they arrived in Indian Territory: they needed to fall back on their traditional skills for survival. Much of the burden of removal fell on women, and this underscored their centrality in Cherokee culture. Men's powerlessness may have even reinforced Cherokee women's power. Yet in some respects, removal weakened certain aspects of women's autonomy. On the Trail of Tears women faced more hardships than men, because they were more vulnerable to rape and because many of them were pregnant.[3] However, it was the Cherokee women who formed the bonds that held together the various social groups in the crisis, a role reflected in oral histories of the Nation.

Removal of the Cherokees from their homeland severely disrupted family life through separation, death, and dispossession of land and property. Because Cherokee men were unable to protect their families in the roundup by soldiers, they experienced a crisis of masculinity. In their sorrow, many turned to alcohol. The experiences of removal also challenged the patriarchal values of the elite, acculturated Cherokees, many of whom supported the Treaty of New Echota, which committed them to removal and stipulated that they would trade their lands in the East for five million dollars and land in Indian Territory. Because a number of the members of the Treaty party had white wives, they may have had fewer ties to the land. The men in this group experienced greater ease with removal, which may have enhanced their power. Their actions inspired hostility among traditional Cherokees, most of whom retained older patterns of language, dress, religion, and marriage, and more traditional gender roles. Thus, in addition to the divisions it created within the Cherokee Nation, removal inspired a revival of Cherokee religion and reinforced traditional beliefs about gender roles.

Cherokee men and women suffered both physically and psychologically because of removal. Women's experiences differed from men's: they bore children while in the stockades and on the road; they carried their children, alive and sometimes dead; and, along with the elderly and very young, they were more susceptible to disease and death. Yet, in a sense, their roles were less disrupted than men's because they were able to continue to function as mothers. Neither men nor women were able to provide for their own families on the Trail of Tears, so men were denied their roles as providers. All had to depend on rations given to them.

Long before soldiers began driving Cherokees from their homes into the stockades, Cherokee women had tried to avoid confrontations with the invaders. Appealing to the respect the Cherokee people held for the power of women as mothers, a Cherokee woman delivered a speech in 1787 urging her people to embrace peace with the American nation. She also wrote to Benjamin Franklin and sent him some of the same tobacco she had used to fill the peace pipe for the warriors. She reminded her people that they should heed women's counsel: "I am in hopes that if you Rightly consider that woman is the mother of All— and the Woman does not pull Children out of Trees or Stumps nor out of old Logs, but out of their Bodies, so that they ought to mind what a woman says."[4]

In 1785, Nancy Ward, the beloved woman (war woman) of Chota, addressed the treaty conference at Hopewell, South Carolina, in an attempt to encourage a peaceful resolution of existing land disputes. This conference, which ultimately resulted in the cession of large areas of Cherokee land south of the Cumberland River in Tennessee and Kentucky and west of the Blue Ridge Mountains in North Carolina, was the last occasion in which women played an official role.[5] However, Cherokee women unofficially continued to oppose further cession of lands. On two occasions (in 1817 and again in 1818) Cherokee women sent messages to the National Council. When the United States attempted to acquire more of the Cherokees' land in 1817, a group of thirteen women signed a communication to the council in which they made a petition on the authority of their maternal role. They equated removal with destroying Cherokee mothers:

> The Cherokee ladys now being present at the meeting of the Chiefs and warriors in council have thought it their duties as mothers to address their beloved Chiefs and warriors now assembled. Our beloved children and head men of the Cherokee nation[,] we address you warriors in council[.] [W]e have raised all of you on the land which we now have, which God gave us to inhabit and raise provisions[.] [W]e know that our country has once been extensive but by repeated sales has become circumscribed to a small tract and never have thought it our duty to interfere in the disposition of it till now, if a father or mother was to sell all their lands which they had to depend on[,] which their children had to raise their living on[,] which would be bad indeed and to be removed to

another country[.] [W]e do not wish to go to an unknown country[,] which we have understood some of our children wish to go over the Mississippi[,] but this act of our children would be like destroying your mother. Your mother and sisters ask and beg of you not to part with any more of our lands.[6]

In the following years, Cherokee women collectively opposed the allotment of land to individuals. Common ownership of land promoted harmony within the culture and also made the sale of lands dependent on the consensus of the Nation. In 1818 they urged the council to continue to hold the land in common:

We have called a meeting among ourselves to consult on the different points now before the council, relating to our national affairs. We have heard with painful feelings that the bounds of the land we now possess are to be drawn into very narrow limits. The land was given to us by the Great Spirit above as our common right, to raise our children upon, & to make support for our rising generations. We therefore humbly petition our beloved children, the head men & warriors, to hold out to the last in support of our common rights, as the Cherokee nation have been the first settlers of the land; we therefore claim the right of the soil.

In the same appeal, Cherokee women lamented the influence of whites who had intermarried with Cherokees, although one element of their argument against removal was that the Cherokees had become civilized:

We will remember that our country was formerly very extensive, but by repeated sales it has become circumscribed to the very narrow limits we have at present. Our Father the President advised us to become farmers, to manufacture our own clothes, & to have our children instructed. To this advice we have attended in every thing as far as we were able. Now the thought of being compelled to remove [to] the other side of the Mississippi is dreadful to us, because it appears to us that we, by this removal, shall be brought to a savage state again, for we have, by the endeavor of our Father the President, become too much enlightened to throw aside the privileges of a civilised life. . . .

Some of our children have become Christians. We have missionary schools among us. We have heard the gospel in our nation; we have become civilised and enlightened, & are in hopes that in a few years our nation will be prepared for instruction in other branches of sciences & arts, which are both useful & necessary in civilised society.

Finally, the women made clear their concern about the influence of whites within Cherokee society. Although they had been agents of civilization, they seemed less interested in Americanizing Indians than in gaining economic and political power over the society:

> There are some white men among us, who have been raised in our country from their youth, are connected with us by marriage, & have considerable families, who are very active in encouraging the emigration of our nation. These ought to be our truest friends but prove our worst enemies. They seem to be only concerned [with] how to increase their riches, but do not care what becomes of our Nation, nor even of their own wives & children.[7]

As late as 1825, Cherokee women argued against removal; some women presented a string of shells (of the wampum) to General William Clark, urging him to resist the policy and to "pursue in our undertaking and not give it up."[8] However, women's political power was waning: under the Constitution of the Cherokee Nation in 1827, voting rights were limited to "all free male citizens (excepting Negroes and descendants of white and Indian men by negro women who may have been set free) who shall have attained the age of eighteen years." Although Stone Carrier had taken two women in his delegation to Washington in 1808, official female participation in the Cherokee political system had ended after 1794. Women could and did continue to exercise rights of petition, but they could no longer command obedience—they could only plead for support.[9]

An article appearing in the January 6, 1829, *Cherokee Phoenix* restated the arguments made in the women's petitions of 1817 and 1818. The circular was addressed to "Benevolent Ladies of the United States." Apparently, a white woman wrote the article in an appeal to other white women to exert their influence in averting disaster for the Indian people. She urged immediate action, but in doing so, made clear whites' ignorance of Cherokee women's traditional power and authority:

> Have not then the females of this country some duties devolving upon them in relation to this helpless race? They are protected from the blinding influence of party spirit and the asperities of political violence. They have nothing to do with any struggle for power nor any right to dictate

the decisions of those that rule over them. But they may *feel* for the distressed, they may stretch out the supplicating hand for them, and by their prayers, strive to avert the calamities that are impending over them. It may be, that female petitioners can lawfully be heard, even by the highest rulers of the land. Why may we not approach and supplicate that we and our dearest friends may be saved from the awful curses denounced on all who oppress the poor and needy, by Him, whose anger is to be dreaded more than the wrath of man.

This communication was written and sent abroad solely by the female hand. Let every woman who peruses it, exert that influence in society, which falls within her lawful province, and endeavor by every suitable expedient to interest the feelings of her friends, relatives and acquaintances, on behalf of this people, that are ready to perish. A *few weeks* must decide this interesting and important question, and after that, time, sympathy and regret will all be in vain.[10]

The pleas of Cherokee women and their white supporters failed to stop removal. Few Americans lamented the knowledge that the Cherokees had lost 90 percent of their precolonial territory by 1819 and that seventeen thousand Cherokees were surrounded by approximately one million whites in Georgia, Alabama, the Carolinas, and Tennessee. Removal became imminent when Andrew Jackson became president on March 4, 1829, and even more so when gold was discovered on Cherokee land in Georgia later that year.[11]

Jackson profited both personally and politically from his adamant removal policy. He claimed (either by himself or with associates) nearly one hundred thousand acres of Cherokee land, which he then put up for sale in Philadelphia.[12] Three months after his inauguration, in June 1829, Jackson said that the Cherokees would be able to live in peace in the West: "There your white brothers will not trouble you; they will have no claim to the land, and you can live upon it, you and all your children, as long as the grass grows and water runs, in peace and plenty. It will be yours forever." Few Cherokees found any consolation in what they believed was another empty promise. One Cherokee told a group of missionaries: "The Indians say they don't know how to understand their Father the President. A few years ago he sent them a plough & a hoe—said it was not good for his red children to hunt—they must cultivate the earth. Now he tells them there is good hunting at the Arkansas; if they will go there he will give them rifles."[13]

Jackson was the dynamic force behind Indian removal throughout the years from 1814 to 1824. He was responsible for all but two of the eleven treaties of cession with the southern Indians. Through his treaties the U.S. government acquired three-fourths of Alabama and Florida, one-third of Tennessee, one-fifth of Georgia and Mississippi, and parts of Kentucky and North Carolina. His military victory over the Creek Indians (made possible by his Cherokee allies) had paved the way for his election as president. As historians have now acknowledged, Jackson's success with the treaties is directly related to the fact that he appealed to feelings of avarice and fear in his dealings with the American Indians. At times he bribed key members of the tribes, and at others he insisted that if they did not accept the terms they would be annihilated.[14]

Jackson supported the pact with the state of Georgia in 1802, in which the federal government promised to remove the Indians from the state as soon as it could be done peaceably. In 1828, in a frontal assault on Cherokee tribal sovereignty, the Georgia legislature declared the Cherokee Nation's constitution and laws null and void; in addition, the declaration claimed all Cherokee lands in Georgia, along with any gold buried beneath.[15] Jackson further weakened tribal sovereignty by not paying tribal annuities. Instead, he authorized a per capita payment of forty-four cents to each Cherokee who made the long trip to the agent's headquarters.[16]

As Jackson was maneuvering to have the southeastern Indians (including the Cherokees) removed, the question arose regarding whether the tribe was economically viable. The campaign for removal took place at a time when the Cherokees were making substantial economic progress. Baptist missionary Evan Jones described the Cherokees' attempts to become acculturated, by which they hoped to avoid removal. Jones wrote:

> Agriculture, Female industry, general knowledge, good order and decency of appearance are making very sensible progress, And our holy religion has produced in some of the natives that happy change which no human efforts can possibly effect! Our school has been very well attend[ed] the past year and many of our pupils have made very pleasing improvements. Several who have left the school have become respectable and useful members of society, among their people—Thus under the benign influance of our happy Government and the prudent management of its principal organs—ignorance and confusion and wretchedness are being chased from the abodes of man.[17]

Historians have debated whether Evans's rosy picture captured the reality of Cherokee daily life. Certainly there were many poor Cherokee households in the Southeast before removal, and class stratification had increased over the course of the late eighteenth and nineteenth centuries. Nevertheless, the 1835 census of the Cherokee Nation revealed that at least half of Cherokee households produced substantial surpluses.[18]

The Cherokee Campaign against Removal

Whereas North Carolina Cherokee women tended to be more traditional than their counterparts in Georgia, Tennessee, and Alabama, they also combined traditionalism with acculturation. They selectively accepted the changes that would help in their domestic production, such as using spinning wheels, and some were responsive to the missionaries. However, they maintained their ceremonies and vigorously opposed removal. In Georgia, the central players were all men, but, as we will see, they could not have acted as such without women's crucial, if often unacknowledged, support. The most public battle revolved around the Cherokee cases before the Supreme Court. Samuel A. Worcester, Elizur Butler, and Reverend James Jenkins Trott all served as missionaries to the Cherokees in Georgia. They were imprisoned for refusing to request a permit from the governor of Georgia to live and preach in the Cherokee Nation. Their refusal to follow Georgia policy raised to a higher level the question of Cherokee sovereignty. The Cherokees sought the opinion of the Supreme Court on the issue of Georgia's right to extend its jurisdiction over their Nation, effectively depriving them of their sovereignty. In the majority decision, Chief Justice John Marshall argued that the Cherokees could not be strictly considered foreign nations, as they had claimed, and must instead be considered "domestic dependent nations." Even though it denied their independent sovereignty, the Supreme Court ruled in the Cherokees' favor in this landmark case and declared Georgia's law unconstitutional. John Ross, the principal chief, was thus confident that they might be able to avoid removal. These hopes were dashed when Jackson announced that he had no intention of enforcing the decision.[19]

The historical emphasis on the missionaries who initiated the case is understandable because of the public controversy surrounding the case and because of the moral victory won by the Cherokee Nation before the Supreme Court. Less attention has focused on their wives, who kept their families and the missions going while their husbands were in prison. Ann Orr Worcester lost a child during the crisis, and all the families suffered in various ways to maintain the missionaries' stance. In many ways, the women's stories resemble those of the Cherokee women who were not public actors but were nevertheless critical to the outcomes. However, these burdens did not begin to compare with what Cherokee women faced when removal was finally implemented.

Opposition to removal was so strong within the Cherokee Nation that fewer than five hundred Cherokees out of seventeen thousand met to discuss the treaty, and there was not a single elected Cherokee official who signed the fraudulent Treaty of New Echota on December 29, 1835.[20] John Ross waged a relentless battle to save the ancient homeland. He trudged to Washington with delegation after delegation, presented memorial after memorial to Congress, and enlisted the support of northern religious leaders. Today, Ross may seem overly optimistic about his crusade to stop removal; however, by enlisting northern support, he ensured that Americans would remember that another strongly supported road had been possible. But all the efforts against removal and even a favorable Supreme Court decision were ultimately futile. Greed and land hunger overcame any stirrings of conscience among members of Congress. On May 28, 1830, the Indian Removal Bill was ratified in the Senate by a margin of eight votes. The final blow came when the U.S. Senate passed the Treaty of New Echota by one vote on May 23, 1836.[21]

The date for removal was set for two years after final approval. It was mandated that if the Cherokees had not voluntarily left for Indian Territory by that time, they would be forced out. In December 1836, General Nathaniel Smith of Athens, Tennessee, was appointed superintendent of removal, and Brevet Brigadier General John E. Wool was ordered by President Jackson to organize the removal of the Cherokees. Because Wool carried out his orders with caution, restraint, and respect for the Cherokees, he angered Jackson and was relieved of his command. General Winfield Scott replaced him, and with his seven thousand men, he was entrusted with implementing forced removal of the remaining fifteen thousand Cherokees.[22]

Elizur Butler described his visit to the camp of the Cherokee "captives" a few miles from Brainerd, Tennessee. He wrote to David Greene in Boston on June 15, 1838: "Whilst at this encampment, I saw several hundred Cherokees marched in by a double rank of soldiers in close file of men all well armed. In this body were the aged and the young; women, and children."[23] As parents and children were corralled into the army encampments, removal disrupted Cherokee family life by separating family members and by dispossessing Cherokees of their land and property.

Previously, we saw how the missionaries attempted to convert the Cherokees to Christianity and to patriarchal gender roles. However, we find that the missionaries also experienced changes through their contact with the Cherokees; some of them paid the price of imprisonment for their loyalty and even chose to go on the Trail of Tears with the Cherokee people. Butler, Butrick, and Jones documented the brutalities from the beginning of removal to the end of the

Trail of Tears. Their accounts of the removal process begin with the stories of the cruel roundup of the people. Soldiers forced people from their homes without even giving them an opportunity to collect their few belongings. Often, family members were separated—husbands from wives and parents from children.

Sallie Butler recalled her grandmother's telling her that the "corn was about waist high when they got orders to leave, and that the Georgia officials did not pay them anything for their crops, or anything else they had to leave." They were allowed only one wagon to take what their family could bring. She said that some of the menfolk wanted to slip back the first night they left and pull up the corn, but they were afraid they would be put in the penitentiary, so they did not go back.[24]

In June 1838, Jones wrote: "The Indians are perfectly still peacefully working in their fields and gardens awaiting the arrival of the appointed day but were lately refusing to recognize the unjust and unauthorized instrument of Echota."[25] Then, in July, he described the roundup that had occurred over the previous weeks:

The Cherokees are nearly all prisoners. They have been dragged from their houses and camped at the forts and military posts all over the Nation. In Georgia, especially, the most unfeeling and insulting treatment has been experienced by them, in a general way. Multitudes were not allowed time to take anything with them but the clothes they had on. Well-furnished houses were left a prey to plunderers who like hungry wolves, follow the progress of the captors and in many cases accompany them. These wretches rifle the houses and strip the helpless, unoffending owners of all they have on earth. Females who have been habituated to comforts and comparative affluence are driven on foot before the bayonets of brutal men. Their feelings are mortified by the blasphemous vociferations of these heartless creatures. It is a painful sight. The property of many has been taken and sold before their eyes for almost nothing; the sellers and buyers being in many cases combined to cheat the poor Indian. . . . Cherokees are deprived of their liberty and stripped of their entire property at one blow. Many who a few days ago were in comfortable circumstances are now the victims of abject poverty. . . . I say nothing yet of several cold-blooded murders and other personal cruelties, for I would most conscientiously avoid making the slightest erroneous impression on any persons, being not in possession of precise and authentic information concerning all the facts in these cases of barbarity.[26]

In his journal entry at Brainerd of May 26, 1838, Butrick described similar wrenching experiences. He noted that if family members were away from home when the soldiers came to drag them off, they were separated from their families. Confrontations occurred when the soldiers tried to remove them from their homes. When one man tried to defend his family and struck a soldier with a stone, he suffered a hundred lashes. Butrick said that one woman stopped to have a baby while being driven to a fort, and then she had to move on to overtake her friends. Another woman fainted and was mercilessly "driven on." Once settled in the camps, the Cherokees faced epidemics that swept through the groups—the elderly and children were especially susceptible. As the march to a new territory became imminent, Butrick wrote, "With regard to the west, all is dark as midnight."[27]

In addition to eyewitness accounts by missionaries, Cherokee participants and their relatives provided oral histories in the years following removal. Their testimonies shed light on both shared brutalities and the differing experiences of Cherokee men and women. Thomas Bluford Downing said that his grandfather told him of the soldiers' drive through the country gathering up every Cherokee they encountered. The first thing the soldiers did when they came to a house was to reach up above the door and get the rifle or old musket if there was one. Then they told everyone to get out. "They were driven out without being allowed to take anything, except what they could carry in their arms." His grandfather buried two thousand dollars, and after two days he went back for it and then caught up with the company. His father, Daniel Downing, was born on the Trail of Tears near Calhoun, Tennessee.[28]

Joanna (McGhee) Jones recalled that her mother was about twelve when they were forced to leave Georgia. Her mother told her that before they left their homes, the white people came into their houses and looked things over. When they found something they liked, they would say, "This is mine. I am going to have it, etc." Jones said, "When they were gathering their things to start they were driven from their homes and collected together like so many cattle. Some would try to take along something which they loved, but were forced to leave it, if it was of any size."[29]

Lucinda Fleetwood recalled her trip west:

We lived betwixt Valley River and Little Heiwassa river in Tocall Dist. and went to school at Jones Mission. We enrolled under Major B. F. Curry, of the U.S. enrolling office and he delivered us to Lt. Harris at Calhoun, where we took [to] water in 1834 in flat bottom boats and came to Waterloo where we took steamboats and came 40 miles above Little Rock at a place called Burnt Caddons. From there we traveled to Fort Gibson in government wagons. My father died at Burnt Caddons and John Miller took charge of the family and brought us on and attended to the drawing of rations and supplies as furnished by the government for the use of the family; [I] had 14 children.[30]

Eliza Whitmire, who was about five years old when she was caught up in the chaos of removal, described the ordeal based on her own experiences and on stories she heard while growing up in Indian Territory:

The weeks that followed General Scott's order to remove the Cherokees were filled with horror and suffering for the unfortunate Cherokees and their slaves. The women and children were driven from their homes, sometimes with blows and close on the heels of the retreating Indians came greedy whites to pillage the Indians' homes, drive off their cattle, horses, and hogs, and they even rifled the graves for any jewelry, or other ornaments that might have been buried with the dead. . . . The trip was made in the dead of winter and many died from exposure from sleet and snow, and all who lived to make this trip, or had parents who made it, will long remember it, as a bitter memory.[31]

Rich and poor alike were evicted from their homes. Joseph Vann, one of the richest men in the Nation, and his family were forced to leave their grand home in bitterly cold, snowy weather to find shelter across the Tennessee line. Their new home was a humble log cabin with a dirt floor. Similarly, John Ross lost his fine estate when a lottery winner took it by force.[32]

After the brutal roundup in June 1838, the first detachment of Cherokees was herded onto boats. Another detachment of one thousand went overland under military guard.[33] Butrick wrote in his journal of a sick woman who was unable to sit up. As the rest of the company was leaving, a soldier went up to her, kicked her in the side, and drove her into the boat. She was soon missing and presumed dead. He continued, "It is said that many old women, driven in this company, cried like children, when they started, saying, they never could walk such a journey this scorching season of the year."[34]

In the same entry Butrick described a scene in which the soldiers at the camp caught a married woman, who was a member of the Methodist society, and dragged her about and forced her to drink liquor. They then "seduced her away," and most likely raped her. Butrick commented that she had become an outcast even among her own relatives, and he lamented, "How many of the poor captive women are thus debauched, through terror and seduction, that eye which never sleeps, alone can determine." He described a number of incidents in which women had babies on the road, while in the middle of a company of soldiers. In one incident he wrote that "a woman in the pains of childbirth, walked as long as possible, and then fell on the bank of the river, when a soldier came up, and stabbed her with his bayonet, which together with other pains soon caused her death."[35] Cherokee men were unable to protect their families and yet did not resort to violence. Butler wrote that he did not know of any Cherokee who had shed the blood of a white person, but at least one deaf and dumb man had been shot in Georgia because he did not stop when ordered to do so.[36]

A drought made water scarce, and the heat was suffocating; seventy people died in three weeks.[37] After the first group left, one hundred Cherokees signed a petition to Colonel Lindsay, one of the officers in charge of the removal, pleading with him to delay any more departures:

We your prisoners wish to speak to you—We wish to speak humbly for we cannot help ourselves. We have been made prisoners by your men but we did not fight against you. We have never done you any harm. For we ask you to hear us. We have been told we are to be sent off by boat immediately. Sir will you listen to your prisoners. We are Indians. Our wives and children are Indians and some people do not pity Indians. But if we are Indians we have hearts that feel. We do not want to see our wives and children die. We do not want to die ourselves and leave them widows and orphans. We are in trouble and our hearts are very heavy. The darkness of night is before us. We have no hope unless you will help us. We do not ask you to let us go free from being your prisoners unless it should please yourself. But we ask that you will not send us down the river at this time of the year. If you do we shall die, and our wives will die and our children will die. We want you to keep us in this country till the sickly time is over so that when we get to the West that we may be able to work to make boards to cover our families. If you send us there now the sickly time be commenced, we shall have no thought to work. We should be in the open air in all the deadly time of sickness, or we shall die and our poor wives and children will die too. And if you send the whole nation, the whole nation will die. We ask your pity. Pity our women and children if they are Indians. Do not send us off at this sickly time. Some of our people are Christians. They will pray for you. If you pity us, we hope your Lord will be pleased and that He will pity you and your wife and your children and do you good. We cannot make a good talk, our hearts are too full of sorrow. This is all we say. The humble petitions of the Cherokee prisoners at and near Ross's Landing, June 11, 1838.[38]

Two days later the soldiers forced another detachment to leave for the West.

Some Cherokees eluded the roundup, and more than a thousand, especially in the mountainous region, ran into the hills and escaped. Others remained in the East because they had received special dispensation, had been permitted to stay by virtue of being intermarried, had accepted state citizenship, or had hidden out. Mary Cobb Agnew's parents were permitted to stay six years longer in Georgia before leaving, most likely because her mother was married to a white man. Agnew was born on May 19, 1840, in Georgia. When Agnew was four, she and her parents joined her grandparents in Indian Territory. Although her parents did not go to Indian Territory on the Trail of Tears, her grandparents on her mother's side did. Agnew stated, "Old men and women, sick men and women would ride but most of them walked and the men in charge drove them like cattle and many died en route and many other Cherokees died in Tennessee waiting to cross the Mississippi River. Dysentery broke out in their camp by the river and many died on the journey but my grandparents got through all right."[39]

Other Cherokees rebelled when faced with a forced march west. Jobe Alexander, a Cherokee, recalled that "the last group that was rounded up revolted; the leader gave the signal to revolt and all turned on the guards and took their guns away and murdered the guards and they made for hideaways in the mountains. That is why the Indians are back in North Carolina, Tennessee, and Georgia. They never were found or hunted much."[40] Their descendants form part of the contemporary Eastern Band of the Cherokee Nation.[41] So much hysteria and fear reigned within the group of thirteen thousand Cherokees who remained in the camps that Lewis Ross and acting chief George Lowrey pleaded with General Scott to permit their families to wait until September 1 before leaving. Scott granted the request on June 19. He also granted their request that they be allowed to conduct their own removal.[42]

The Cherokees spent three to four months in the camps without adequate food or water or proper sanitation. Epidemics quickly swept through the settlements. Butler described the large number of deaths from dysentery, cholera, measles, and whooping cough. Evan Jones wrote in his journal on June 16, 1838, of the immensity of the Cherokees' suffering: "I have no language to express the emotions which rend our hearts to witness their season of cruel and unnecessary oppression. For if it be determined to take their land and reduce them to absolute poverty, it would seem to be mere wanton cruelty to take their lives also."[43]

Two miles south of the Hiwassee River near the present town of Charleston, Tennessee, the remaining members of the Cherokee Nation gathered at Rattlesnake Springs. They held a final council and agreed to continue their old constitution and laws in the West. William Shorey Coodey wrote to John Howard Payne, describing the departure of the first of the thirteen detachments:

> At noon all was in readiness for moving; the teams were stretched out in a line along the road through a heavy forest, groups of persons formed about each wagon, others shaking the hand of some sick friend or relative who would be left behind. The temporary camp covered with boards and some of bark that for three summer months had been their only shelter and *home,* were crackling and falling under a blazing flame; the day was bright and beautiful, but a gloomy thoughtfulness was depicted in the lineaments of every face. In all the bustle of preparation there was a silence and stillness of the voice that betrayed the sadness of the heart.
>
> At length the word was given to "move on." I glanced along the line and the form of Going Snake, an aged and respected chief whose head eighty winters had whitened, mounted on his favorite pony passed before me and led the way in advance, followed by a number of young men on horse back.
>
> At this very moment a low sound of distant thunder fell on my ear. In almost an exact western direction a dark spiral cloud was rising above the horizon and sent forth a murmur I almost fancied a voice of divine indignation for the wrongs of my poor and unhappy countrymen, driven by *brutal* power from all they loved and cherished in the land of their fathers, to gratify the cravings of avarice. The sun was unclouded—no rain fell—the thunder rolled away and sounds hushed in the distance. The scene around and before me, and in the elements above, were peculiarly impressive & singular. It was at once spoken of by several persons near me, and looked upon as omens of some future event in the west. John Ross stood on a wagon and led the people in a prayer. After the thunder sounded, a bugle announced the departure of the first detachment.[44]

The removal required 645 wagons, a large number of oxen, and five thousand horses.[45] Yet even as the Cherokees organized their own removal under difficult circumstances, General Scott objected to the expenses they submitted for supplies and necessities. He wrote to John Ross and other leaders, "I am confident that it will be found that among every thousand individuals, taken in families, without selection, there are at least 500 strong men, women, boys, and girls not only capable of marching twelve to fifteen miles a day, but to whom the exercise would be beneficial, and another hundred able to go on foot half that distance daily. This would leave 450 to ride with 250 horses or ponies and only 200 in 50 wagons."[46]

Nine contingents left at intervals in October, and four left during November. The drought broke in November, and the Cherokees then endured torrential rain.[47] The first two detachments, under John Benge (October 1) and Jesse Bushyhead (October 5), crossed the Tennessee River at Blythe's Ferry where the Hiwassee intersected it, then traveled to Pikesville, McMinnville, Murfreesboro, and Nashville.[48] An alternate land route turned south after crossing the Mississippi at Cape Girardeau and traveled to Smithville, Batesville, then Lewisburg, Arkansas, then turned west and entered Indian Territory at Fort Smith, Fort Coffee, and Fort Gibson, moving north to Tahlequah. Those people who made the trip by steamboat went down the Tennessee, Ohio, and Mississippi Rivers, then up the Arkansas as far as possible, and finally overland into Indian Territory.[49]

Removal dramatically disrupted family life. Some individuals were separated from relatives during the removal process and frantically tried to locate them. Men and women were suddenly dependent on the quartermasters of the detachments for their sustenance and rations. Whenever possible, men hunted game along the way and women reverted to traditional domestic practices. Shamans and medicine men doctored the sick, as did the white doctors. Butler wrote that in the three and a half months of the journey there were as many cases of sickness as there were individual members of the detachment.[50] At times, however, the white doctors and the Native healers were at cross-purposes. During this crisis, some turned to alcohol for consolation, some turned to traditional religion, and others turned to Christianity. Often, members of the same church tried to travel together.[51]

Butler wrote, "[From the first of June] I felt as if I had been in the midst of death." Butler is the source of the estimate that four thousand lives were lost because of removal. He wrote, "From the best estimate I am able to make, I may safely say that of those Cherokees who were in the old Nation the 23rd of last May, between three and four thousand now rest in their graves. I fear that if the exact number were known it would exceed four thousand."[52] Over the course of removal, two thousand to twenty-five hundred died in the camps, one thousand to fifteen hundred died on the trip, and a thousand died within a year after their arrival.[53]

The oral histories of the Trail of Tears are filled with images of the trauma of being rounded up, the terrible conditions in the camps before departure, the bad food on the trip, and the deaths of parents, grandparents, and children. Lillian Lee Anderson's grandfather, Washington, was separated from his father, mother, and sister during the journey. He did not know whether they had died. She described the trip as told by her grandfather:

> The Cherokees had to walk; all the old people who were too weak to walk could ride in the Government wagons that hauled the food and blankets that they were allowed to have. The food was most always cornbread or roasted green corn. . . . The food on the Trail of Tears was very bad and very scarce and the Indians would go for two or three days without water, which they would get just when they came to a creek or river as there were no wells to get water from. There were no roads to travel over as the country was just a wilderness. The men and women would go ahead of the wagons and cut the timber out of the way with axes.[54]

Anderson's grandmother's sister, Chin Deenawash, survived the trip. Her husband died shortly after they got out of Georgia, leaving her to battle her way through the rest of the journey with three small children, one who could not walk. Anderson recalled: "Aunt Chin tied the little one on her back with an old shawl, took one child in her arms and led the other one by the hand; the two larger children died before they had gone very far and the little one died and Aunt Chin took a broken case knife and dug a grave and buried the little body by the side of the Trail of Tears. The Indians did not have food of the right kind to eat and Aunt Chin came on alone and lived for years after this."[55]

Bettie (Perdue) Woodall's mother walked every step of the way to Indian Territory on the Trail of Tears. Her mother told her that not a single woman rode in the wagon unless she was sick and not able to walk. She told her daughter of an incident in which a baby was murdered on the trip by a soldier: "On one occasion she told of an officer in charge of one of the wagons, who killed a little baby because it cried all the time. It was only four days old and the mother was forced to walk and carry it, and because it cried all of the time and the young mother could not quiet it, the officer took it away from her and dashed its little head against a tree and killed it. Mother got transferred after this to another wagon; she feared the officer might kill her to keep her from

Fig. 13. "Trail of Tears" by Robert Lindneux. (Courtesy Woolaroc Museum, Bartlesville, Oklahoma)

telling on him."[56] Even when children died, the parents were not given ample time to bury their dead. Comingdeer told his son Nick the story of his journey on the Trail of Tears. He described how he had seen many old Cherokees carrying their dead children all day until the detachment stopped for the night. Then the fathers of the dead children, with the help of other Cherokees in the group, would dig a shallow grave and bury them.[57] Children sometimes got lost from their parents on the trip. Jennie McCoy Chambers recalled that her mother and her grandfather, Elijah Hicks, picked up two children along the trail who were lost.[58]

Rachel Dodge's grandmother, Aggie Silk, told her of the many hardships of the trip to Indian Territory. She said that many people suffered from chills and fever because of their exposure and because they often went hungry. She recalled, "When they got too sick to walk or ride, they were put in the wagons, and taken along until they died. The Indian Doctors couldn't find the herbs they were used to and didn't know the ones they did find, so they couldn't doctor them as they would have at home."[59]

W. W. Harnage's mother went on the Trail of Tears, and his father was an old settler who had come to Indian Territory before the removal of 1838. His mother told him that when her detachment reached the Mississippi, the river was too high and they had to stay there six or seven weeks before they could

Fig. 14a. *What Have We Done.* Painting by Troy Anderson. (From the permanent collection of the Cherokee Heritage Museum and Gallery, Cherokee, North Carolina. Dr. R. Michael Abram and Susan Abram, curators; photograph by Mike Kesselring. Used by permission.)

Fig. 14b. *Soon My Child.* Painting by Troy Anderson. (From the permanent collection of the Cherokee Heritage Museum and Gallery, Cherokee, North Carolina. Dr. R. Michael Abram and Susan Abram, curators; photograph by Mike Kesselring. Used by permission.)

cross the river. Subsequently, hundreds of them died of dysentery. Harnage said, "She weathered the storm, while others even after arriving, soon died of sorrow and grief."[60]

Rich and poor Cherokees, slaves, and intermarried whites went on the Trail of Tears. Experiences differed widely depending on one's class status. Wealthy Cherokees such as the Vanns, Rosses, Ridges, and Coodeys lost their fine houses and possessions, but many of them took their slaves with them to Indian Territory and traveled in more comfort than the rest of the Nation. Ella Coodey Robinson's father, William Shorey Coodey, and her mother, Elizabeth Fields, emigrated in 1834. She described how her mother was accustomed to many slaves: "Mother had as many servants (slaves) as she had use for, a head cook, a helper (who was being trained) for the cook, a house maid, a serving girl, a nurse for the babies and a house man who did the housecleaning. A laundress and a coachman were not included in the house staff. There was quite a class distinction among the negroes, as those in the house looked down on those who worked on the outside."[61]

Members of the Treaty party such as Major Ridge, John Ridge, Boudinot, and Watie were given preferential treatment throughout the treaty process.[62] Many members of the Treaty party had gone by boat on March 1, 1837, from Ross's Landing. The party had 466 people, half of whom were children.[63] Major Ridge and his family received special treatment with cabin passage, and they received three hundred dollars as opposed to the twenty dollars given to ordinary members of the Nation. As late as 1867, William Medill, the commissioner of Indian Affairs, was haggling over the one hundred thousand dollars promised by the U.S. government to members of the Treaty party for damage claims associated with the Treaty of 1835.[64] But even those of wealth and power faced tragic outcomes on the Trail of Tears. Ross, his wife Quatie, and their children went to the West by steamboat part of the way and overland part of the way. Quatie died en route on February 1, 1839, at Little Rock.[65] Despite the common tragedies of the experiences, removal promoted class, racial, and political divisions within the Cherokee Nation. Comingdeer, Nick Comingdeer's father, went on the Trail of Tears; he described the resentment against the Treaty party that grew as the trip progressed: "They hated the name of the Ridges and Boudinot. They would talk at night of how they were going to kill them when they came to the country where they lived."[66]

After removal, approximately six thousand Cherokees continued as a prosperous literate middle class.[67] Most, however, faced continued hardship even after arriving in the West. Many Cherokees died from malnutrition, disease, and overexposure. Cephas Washburn, a missionary for the ABCFM at Dwight

Mission, described the high mortality rate and the great suffering from sickness endured by the immigrants. He attributed a great deal of their suffering to the consumption of whiskey and the lack of medical aid.[68] A period of eighty days had been estimated for the time it would take each detachment to travel the eight hundred to one thousand miles to Indian Territory. In no case did a detachment reach its destination in less than four months. In fact, one group took six months to complete its journey. The last detachment reached Indian Territory in March 1839. By the close of 1840, many thousands of Cherokees were near starvation. As their physical journey neared its end, some continued to find comfort in their traditional religion, whereas others gravitated toward the mission churches.[69]

Following the horrors of removal and resettlement, U.S. government agents insisted that the policy had been proven right. In a revealing letter in 1848, Medill wrote to the secretary of war to describe the beneficent effects of removal. After painting a caricature of indolent men who only wanted to hunt and do battle, he announced that Indian women were beginning to assume their "true position":

> The most marked change, however, when this transition [from savagery to civilization] takes place, is the condition of the females. She who had been the drudge and the slave then begins to assume her true position as an equal; and her labor is transferred from the field to her household—to the care of her family and children. This great change in disposition and condition has taken place, to a greater or less extent, [in] all the tribes that have been removed and permanently settled west of the Mississippi. It is true, that portions of some of them enjoyed a considerable degree of civilization before they were transplanted; but prior to that event they were retrograding in all respects.[70]

Medill's statement reflected the continuing ways in which the U.S. government justified removal in the context of "liberating" Native women. Disruption of traditional Cherokee gender roles proved key in destabilizing their culture and dispossessing them of their land. Even before removal, the Cherokee Nation had experienced changes in what they believed it meant to be a woman, but the removal crisis forced into the open the debate over meanings of gender. Cherokee men, who could no longer protect their families, probably experienced a crisis of masculinity. Domestic violence most likely increased, as did drunkenness.[71]

Those who had previously been members of the elite class and who had begun to accept Euro-American values saw these values questioned and some-times undermined. Therefore, more traditional Cherokees associated assimila-tion with removal, because even the wealthy Cherokees were dispossessed and forced westward. The Cherokees had learned that neither accommodation nor resistance would save them from removal.

II
Crisis of the Civil War
and Reconstruction

4
The Civil War

There is no reason why we should split up and become involved in internal strife and violence on account of the political condition of the States. We should really have nothing to do with them but remain quiet and observe those relations of peace and friendship towards all the people of the States imposed by our treaties. By this means alone can we avoid every cause for hostility from either section of the country and upon this policy we ought all to be able to attend to our ordinary affairs and avoid all cause of strife among ourselves.

John Ross, July 2, 1861

Feather beds dragged outside and ripped open . . . feathers flying in the wind, children hiding behind their mothers crying as their homes were burned, husbands and fathers shot before their eyes . . . livestock killed or taken . . . long trains of ox-wagons, mile upon mile of refugees—some moving slowly north toward Kansas, others moving South toward Texas. . . . The procession resembled the march of the Trail of Tears. In 1863 the combination of the American Civil War and the results of intratribal factionalism severely strained conventional definitions of gender and disrupted Cherokee family life, leaving one-third of the adult women widows and one-fourth of the children orphans. Historians have told the stories of the battles of Pea Ridge, Cabin Creek, Cowskin Prairie, and Boggy Depot, but the experiences of women in the Indian Territory have gone virtually unrecorded.[1]

The crisis of the Civil War empowered women in the Cherokee Nation, because they had to assume new responsibilities and greater burdens as a result of wartime disruptions. They experienced a new crisis of gender. Cherokee women suffered from refugee status and violence in the form of rape, raids, and robberies. The war also led to a crisis of identity for the elite Cherokee women because they were no longer able to live up to the expectations of "true womanhood" as espoused by white America. However, all Cherokee women did not respond to the war in the same way. The Civil War intensified class, political, and racial divisions within the Nation and prevented the emergence of a consensus on gender. At the same time, the Civil War reinforced older Cherokee gender roles for the traditional and nonslaveholding women by emphasizing the role of men as warriors and elevating the role of women as providers and cultivators of the earth. Elizur Butler noted that the tendency to return to "heathenish practices" was particularly strong in times of crisis.[2]

The degree to which Cherokee women became acculturated to patriarchal, Christian values prior to the Civil War is difficult to determine. Gender roles within the Cherokee Nation had changed during the eighteenth and early nineteenth centuries, when the communal land ownership and matrilineal clan systems were being challenged by an aggressive federal policy to convert Cherokee men from hunters to farmers and to convert Cherokee women from farmers to housewives. We have seen how the adoption of the Cherokee Constitution of 1827 diminished women's political power. At the same time, elite Cherokees came to associate patriarchal gender roles with being civilized, and "any challenge to the precepts of the cult of true womanhood could be interpreted as a reversion to savagery."[3]

The Cherokees responded to Christianity and modernization with negotiated adaptation. The *Cherokee Phoenix* and the *Cherokee Advocate*, along with the instructors at the Cherokee Female Seminary, attempted to inculcate the values of Euro-American gender roles. Elite Cherokees were the most responsive to these changes in gender relationships, but by 1839 probably less than 10 percent of the Cherokee population was officially listed as "members" of Christian churches; by 1860, the number had risen to about 12 percent of the population.[4] Many Cherokees selectively adopted aspects of Christianity while retaining many beliefs, rituals, and practices of traditional Cherokee religion.[5]

Similarly, many Cherokee women may have selectively adopted aspects of the cult of true womanhood—especially the idea of women as moral guardians —while retaining their customary rights, such as their right to own property. Slaveholding families relegated domestic duties to slaves, and therefore domesticity did not pose a burden for elite Cherokee women. However, it is doubtful that they fully accepted the value of submissiveness because traditional Cherokee gender roles emphasized individual autonomy. Moreover, only about 8 to 10 percent of the Cherokee population possessed sufficient affluence to emulate the lifestyles of upper-class white women.[6]

Still, affluent females associated becoming civilized with accepting Christian notions regarding women's proper sphere. The Cherokee Female Seminary, established in 1851, was modeled on Mount Holyoke, whose announced purpose was to make female education "a handmaid to the Gospel and an efficient auxiliary in the great task of renovating the world." Many students at the seminary already held the values of white Victorian women before they enrolled, and the curriculum reinforced these values. Consequently, the seminary's influence disrupted a common sense of gender among women and exacerbated class distinctions and factionalism.

It is likely that, after the trauma of removal, many Cherokees became more committed than ever to proving that they were civilized. Certainly, during the period between resettlement in Indian Territory and the Civil War, more affluent Cherokees forged a distinctive stratum within the larger Nation.[7] Their lifestyles often depended on the institution of slavery. Cherokee and black women interacted with one another in complex ways during the years preceding and throughout the Civil War. Before their emancipation, female slaves owned by the Cherokees did the work previously allotted to Cherokee women. They were instrumental in enabling a small class of acculturated women to pursue gentility and leisure. Thus the relationship between black women and Cherokee women played a critical role in determining gender distinctions.

The African American women told of rapes by masters and masters' sons and of brutal whippings; others noted gestures of kindness by masters and mistresses. They also recounted harrowing war experiences, backbreaking domestic and field labor, and a steady reliance on religion to help them endure their struggles. They told of the moments when they learned that they were free and of how they lived after the war. African American women faced the most dramatic changes after the war, experiencing severe issues of poverty and discrimination.[8]

Just as Cherokee society had divided along class lines, their slaves experienced similar distinctions. Lucinda Vann described the differences among black women's experiences, which depended on their status as house or field slaves. Vann lived on the large plantation of old Jim Vann in Webbers' Falls. Her mother was Betsy Vann, who worked in the big house. Vann claimed that "Master Jim and Missus Jennie was good to their slaves." The master insisted that the house slaves dress well. She described the fine clothes they wore: "[Vann] wanted people to know he was able to dress his slaves in fine clothes. We had fine satin dresses, great big combs for our hair, great big gold locket, double earrings, we never wore cotton except when we worked. We had bonnets that had long silk tassels for ties. When we wanted to go anywhere we always got a horse, we never walked. Everything was fine, Lord, have mercy on me, *yes*."[9] In this case, the house slaves dressed as ladies and reflected the gentility of the elite Cherokee and white women and the wealth of the Cherokee men who could afford such luxuries.

In contrast to Lucinda Vann's portrait of benevolent treatment, Katie Rowe, who was eighty-eight when she was interviewed in Tulsa in 1937, told of cruel treatment under the bonds of slavery. Saunders, the overseer, would use a cat-o'-nine-tails to whip a slave on his naked back and then break the blisters with a wide strap of leather fastened to a stick handle. Rowe recalled: "I seen de blood running out'n many a back, all de way from de neck to de waist. Many de time a nigger git blistered and cut up so dat we have to git a sheet and grease it wid lard and wrap 'em up in it, and dey have to wear a greasy cloth wrapped around dey body under de shirt for three-four days after dey git a big whipping!"[10]

Charlotte Johnson White endured cruelty at the hands of her master, who was a white man married to a Cherokee woman. She told of how he beat her mother so severely that she died. White became the victim of his wrath also. She recalled: "Time I was twelve year old I was tendin' the master's children like what dey tell me to do, and den one day somehow I drop one of dem right by where de old master was burning some brush in de yard. 'What you do that for?' he yelled, and while I was stoopin' to pick up de baby he grabbed me and shoved me into de fire! I sent into dat fire head first, but I never know how I got out. See this old drawn, scarred face? Dat's what I got from de fire, and inside my lips is burned off, and my back is scarred wid lashings dat'll be wid me when I meet my Jesus!"[11]

Nancy Rogers Bean spoke of how fiercely some slave women resisted their bondage. When faced with being separated from her family, her aunt refused, even though it had meant self-mutilation. Bean said: "One of my aunts was a mean, fighting woman. She was to be sold and when the bidding started she grabbed a hatchet, laid her hand on a log and chopped it off. Then she throwed the bleeding hand right in her master's face." Astonishingly, Bean's aunt survived.[12]

Victoria Taylor Thompson recalled that her mistress was a good person who had ensured that none of her slaves were beaten or whipped. Thompson did not experience violence personally until the Civil War broke out, when her father left to fight on the side of the South with Master Taylor. During this time, a man by the name of Uncle Mosie, a white mill owner, stole her and forced her to live in a cabin with him. She remembered: "He branded a circle on my cheek, but in two days I got away and run back to the Taylors where I was safe." Although she only briefly mentioned the incident, she implied that a white man had raped her.[13]

When the war broke out, many Cherokees left the territory, taking some of their slaves with them. Vann's master and mistress stayed and buried their valuables and money. They told their slaves that they could go if they wanted to do so. A group of their slaves—including Vann, who was part Indian and part African—put together their bedclothes, some hams, and a lot of coffee and flour and headed for Mexico with seven horses and a small buffalo.[14] Rochelle Allred Ward also had vivid recollections of the Civil War. She was ninety-one when she was interviewed at Fort Gibson during the winter of 1937–38. "I never was where the fighting went on," she said, "but I heard the cannon go 'Bum! Bum' and the little guns go 'Bang!' in all directions. I seen the soldiers come in after the fights; they be all shot up with blood soaking through the clothes, trying to help each other tie on a bandage— . . . the awfulest sights I ever see."[15]

During the war, hostility erupted against elite Cherokee women. Although the precise relationship between the stress over gender roles and the political ascendancy of traditional Cherokees after the war needs more investigation, the divisions within the female community during the war between traditional and acculturated Cherokee women and between Cherokee women and black women reflected widely divergent conceptions of what it meant to be female and what it meant to be Cherokee.

The elite Cherokee women's crisis of identity during the conflict helps to explain the vigorous reassertion of the values of true womanhood after the war, especially as promoted in the educational system. Anne Firor Scott and other historians have stressed the ways in which the Civil War empowered Northern and Confederate women through their work in the Sanitary Commission and through numerous other organizations that provided essential materiel and services for the war effort. Formal organized women's activities did not exist in Indian Territory. Unlike Confederate women, who were urged to support a noble cause and sacrifice themselves to it, Cherokee women saw no transcendent ideal in fighting the war.[16]

Loyalty to either side during the Civil War was problematic for the Cherokee Nation. Would they join with the Southern states, which had dispossessed them of their homeland in the East? Or would they support the federal government, who had enforced their removal, withdrawn their troops from the territory, and suspended annuity payments? Intense factionalism between the Ridge and Ross factions had grown out of the removal period, and factionalism continued into the period of the Civil War, with loyalties divided between the North and the South. Class divisions exacerbated this breakdown of the tribal community. The Cherokees were drawn into the war because of their geographical location and because many of them owned slaves. Thus, their choice of sides stemmed more from economic motives and old hatreds than from clan connections or from a concordance with Union or Confederate ideals.

Ross, who was principal chief of the Cherokee Nation for over forty years, attempted to maintain neutrality when the Civil War broke out. Albert Pike, who wanted the Cherokees on the Confederate side, wrote prophetically to Colonel John Drew on July 14, 1862, warning the Cherokees of the probable results of Union loyalty: "Surely the Cherokees are sagacious enough to know that soft as the paw of the panther may be, its treacherous nature will not long allow it to keep its claws concealed. The northern states will never forgive you. They may profess that until the war is over; but if they hold possession of your country they will punish you by parcelling out your lands; and licking their lips they will think they have done God good service."[17]

When the Cherokee Nation was surrounded by Confederate troops, the Union failed to offer any protection or support. All the other tribes in Indian Territory had signed treaties with the Confederacy, and factionalism among Cherokees was revived. Eventually, Ross was forced to abandon neutrality; on October 7, 1861, the council passed resolutions supporting a treaty of the Cherokees with the Confederacy. Troops were raised under Stand Watie and John Drew. When Union troops moved into Tahlequah in the spring of 1862, they arrested Ross and accompanied him to Washington in order to confer with Abraham Lincoln. In early 1863, Ross's faction declared their allegiance to the Union, freed their slaves, and repudiated the alliance with the Confederacy. Because Watie and his followers refused to accept this position, the Cherokee Nation was divided into "two nations" until the end of the war.[18]

For the most part, Cherokee women stood outside these battles over political loyalty. Most Cherokee women expressed no support for the ideals of either the Union or the Confederacy. These Cherokee women hated the war, wanted it to end, and often urged their husbands and sons to return home. Most of them spent the duration of the war at home with their families or as refugees, barely managing to survive. Yet a few Cherokee women were active participants as spies, raiders, and resisters during the Civil War. Delilah Falling, who was sixteen at the beginning of the war, recounted tales of her aunt, Margaret Brackett, who was a spy. Brackett, who was an accomplished horseback rider and who was adept at handling a gun, aided the Confederates in capturing a group of Northern soldiers carrying water to troops. Although their names are unrecorded, other women who provided necessary intelligence regarding troop movements have been mentioned in accounts of the war.[19]

In one incident, a woman aided in the execution of a notorious bushwhacker, Alf Bolin. A Federal soldier asked a Cherokee woman whom Bolin had been staying with to help capture him. She placed a coulter (an iron bar about two feet long and sharpened at one end like a knife blade, which farmers used on their plows) under a table by the wall on which she kept the water bucket. Bolin was seated with his back to the bucket. When the soldier went to get a drink of water, he grabbed the coulter and drove it into Bolin's skull. The soldier cut off Bolin's head and put it on a sixty-foot pole and left it there for three weeks.[20]

In addition to being spies, some Cherokee women resisted through argument and violence. Even in extreme danger, Cherokee women demonstrated heroism. One young woman confronted the troops when they threatened to hang her sister. She told them that they had better not put a rope around her sister's neck, but that they could hang her instead. This so amused the soldiers that they said they wouldn't hang either of them. After this young woman's mother and youngest brother had died, she and other refugees traveled to Fort Smith. On the way, they met Buck Brown and his bushwhackers, who threatened to burn their wagon. She said, "I told him if he treated a bunch of orphans and widows that way, he would surely be punished in some manner. He patted me on the head, and said I was a brave girl."[21]

When they could, Cherokee women fought back with more than words. Julius Pinkey Killebrew described another incident in which soldiers were in his house, and one of them started throwing hot coals around the room to set the house on fire. Killebrew's sister, Em, hit the soldier with a poker and knocked him down.[22] In another incident, when George Lloyd Payson and his sister witnessed the torture of an old Indian named Painter, his sister got a shot gun, waited until the men were bunched together, and shot into the crowd, bringing down three of the torturers. The others fled. "So the old man," Payson recalled, "was rescued by a shot fired by a woman."[23]

Some Cherokee women believed that the Civil War brought them together, whereas others believed that the war caused the breakdown of the women's community. Sallie Manus told a WPA (Works Progress Administration) interviewer, "During this bloody war, we women felt very near to each other because our troubles were the same."[24] Manus, the daughter of a Union supporter, noted that female relatives and neighbors sometimes banded together to weather the war, but class and racial differences often interfered with such gendered bonds. Because of factionalism within the tribe, the women's community showed signs of breaking down. Cherokee women could no longer count on one another for assistance; they no longer knew whom they could trust.

In addition to deprivation and violence, Cherokee women experienced wrenching changes to their status, authority, and sphere. This breakdown of the women's community became painfully obvious when women became raiders themselves, becoming active participants in pillaging. Ella Coody Robinson recalled an incident in which a group of women stopped to rob their house. Her mother told the women that she was Richard Fields's daughter and that her father had been a good friend to the traditional Cherokees. This deterred most of the group and they departed; but one woman took the new water bucket from the back porch before she left.[25] Susan Riley Gott told a similar story. Her grandparents owned slaves, but her father was pro-Union. In the last raid of the Pin Indians, they killed one of her mother's prized peafowls and decorated their hats with the feathers.[26] Gott contended, "The women belonging to the Pins were just as bad, if not worse than the men, as they ransacked the house."[27] Confrontations frequently arose between women in these situations. Emma Sixkiller recalled: "The third time they [the robbers] came there were several women in the gang and mother said to them, 'I know who you are. (They were painted and dressed so as to try to disguise themselves.) I have never done you any harm and I have these children here to feed,' etc. But they told her that they needed the things too so just went about helping themselves to anything that they found that they wanted and destroying what they thought we could use that they did not want."[28]

It is quite possible that women who were raiding did not regard their action as theft but simply a rightful redistribution of wealth in keeping with traditional values of sharing and hospitality. Their value system clashed with the assimilated, acquisitive values of elite women. However, going beyond taking what they needed for their own families, their destruction of the property of fellow Cherokees clearly reflected the breakdown of the women's community. Still, the motivations of the Cherokee women who pillaged must be observed in the context of intersecting conflicts. Many supporters of the Ridge Treaty party were also advocates of patriarchal gender roles, which may have intensified the hostility of more traditional, poor Cherokees. Racial and class distinctions thus became associated with acceptance of Euro-American gender roles, and these distinctions heightened the sense that such acculturated families could not carry out customary roles within a women's community.

Elite Cherokee women faced a crisis of identity when they were forced to perform unaccustomed duties and when they realized they could no longer be moral guardians of their families, as their husbands and sons were often absent and engaged in warfare. Traditional Cherokee women were no strangers to physical labor and viewed their experiences quite differently from their acculturated kin; the war reinforced the importance of traditional survival skills and the role of women as cultivators of the earth. These women thus witnessed the elevation of the importance of their roles in the community.

Many Cherokee women and men spent the duration of the war as refugees. The old, smoldering hatred between the factions (those who had supported the removal treaty and those who opposed it) led to "scorched earth" tactics and attacks on civilians throughout the war. When Opothleyoholo, the pro-Union Creek leader, was defeated in 1861, he and his followers fled north. They were joined by many Cherokees, Seminoles, and fleeing slaves, and they suffered bitterly through the winter of 1861–62.[29] George W. Collamore wrote to William P. Dole, the commissioner for Indian Affairs, on April 21, 1862, describing his visit to Opothleyoholo and his group of Indians who were loyal to the Union. In their flight from hostile troops, they were encamped on the Neosho River in the southern part of Kansas:

> Their march was undertaken with a scanty supply of clothing, subsistence, and cooking utensils, and entirely without tents, and during their progress they were reduced to such extremity as to be obliged to feed upon their ponies and their dogs, while their scanty clothing was reduced to threads, and in some cases absolute nakedness was their condition. Let it be remembered that this retreat was in the midst of a winter of unusual severity for that country with snow upon the prairie. Many of the ponies died from starvation. The women and children suffered severely from frozen limbs, as did also the men. Women gave birth to their offspring upon the naked snow, without shelter or covering, and in some cases new-born infants died for want of clothing, and those who survived to reach their present location with broken constitutions and utterly dispirited.[30]

The Indian Territory became a land of refugees. The Cherokee Nation appeared nearly abandoned as Confederate sympathizers fled south, sometimes as far as Texas, and Northern sympathizers fled north toward Kansas. Women in the Cherokee Nation faced backbreaking physical labor whether they remained at home or joined the refugees. Most of the Southern sympathizers remained undisturbed in their homes during the winter of 1862–63. However, after a second Union expedition from Kansas entered the Cherokee Nation during the summer of 1863, the country north and east of Arkansas lay in ruins. Southern refugee families who fled in 1863 first went to the Creek Nation and to the northern counties of the Choctaw Nation. Many women and children fled to safety in southern Indian Territory and Texas, where they stayed until the end of the war. Finally, in the summer of 1863, J. L. Martin of the Cherokee Nation took over the relief administration. Very few Southern families had remained in the occupied region by August 1863; it was estimated that there were six thousand Cherokee refugees.[31]

Watie wrote a desperate appeal to S. S. Scott, the Confederate commissioner of Indian Affairs, pleading with him to pay the delayed annuities. He closed with these words: "Shall I continue to encourage them, or shall I at once unveil to them the dread truth that our country is to be hopelessly abandoned, and that they are to receive the reward of poverty and ruin for their unswerving fidelity to the Southern cause?"[32]

Watie and some of his troops accompanied a number of destitute families to Texas. Although the weather grew quite cold after they started, he made the six-week journey without losing any lives. Refugee camps sprang up in Bonham, Sherman, and other northern Texas towns and in encampments on the Kiamichi, Boggy, Blue, and Washita Rivers in the Choctaw and Chickasaw Nations. Martin and Lucien Bell went across the Mississippi in the summer of 1864 to purchase cotton and wool cards to distribute to the refugees to enable them to make clothing. It was not until shortly before the end of the war that the Confederate government tried to meet its obligations to the Indians by paying annuities in cotton.[33]

Before the war, slaveholding women benefited from racial hegemony and the appropriation of slave labor. Without their slaves, or with only a few with them, these women were forced to perform many of these domestic tasks themselves. If their husbands were involved in the war, Cherokee women who had relied on slaves before the war suddenly had to become providers and protectors of their families. When the Civil War broke out, Sarah Watie, Stand Watie's wife, fled with her children first to the Red River and then to Texas to live with relatives.[34] Women such as Watie had become accustomed to relying on slaves to perform the most arduous labor, especially agricultural chores. Female slaves milked cows, made butter, cheese, candles, and soap, and did the spinning, weaving, and sewing. They cooked, gathered wood, hauled water, and washed clothes.[35] In her extensive correspondence with her husband, Watie wrote that she now had to spin every day in order to keep her children clothed. Because manufactured goods were generally unavailable, women's domestic drudgery increased dramatically. Watie spent much of her time trying to secure food and provisions, and she even had to plant crops herself. Because traditional Cherokee women were accustomed to this sort of labor, they did not experience the kind of psychological anguish that Watie did when she performed duties she believed were not her proper responsibility.

Unlike Watie, Mary Stapler Ross, the second wife of John Ross, did not have to "sow wheat"[36] or spin every day, but when she was driven from her home in Park Hill, she had to help care for thirty-six persons, including ten in her immediate family. The entire family, except those fighting in the war, moved east to Philadelphia. With limited money available, her physical labor increased, even though several house slaves accompanied the Ross family east.[37]

The Ross family had been accustomed to 50 to 100 slaves and considerable affluence before the war. However, when Ross died in 1866, he was in debt. Nevertheless, his wife epitomized true womanhood because of her wealth, education, gentility, and religious convictions.[38] Mary Stapler's letters to John Ross during their courtship in 1844 revealed these values along with a certain coquettishness.[39] Although she did not experience the physical deprivation or danger that Sarah Watie faced, she endured the loss of her beautiful home, Rose Cottage, which was burned, and lost a stepson, nephew, and other relatives in the war. However, from her extensive correspondence with her husband during the war, it does not appear that she experienced the severe challenges to her identity as a woman that Watie and other highly acculturated Cherokee women did. She had to expand her traditional role, but she did not have to step outside her sphere.

Unlike Ross, Hannah Worcester Hicks did not have the means to flee. The daughter of missionaries Samuel and Ann Orr Worcester, Hannah Worcester became a member of the Cherokee Nation in 1852 by marrying Abijah Hicks, who was the son of an early Eastern Cherokee chief. On July 4, 1862, her husband was murdered near Lee's Creek on his way back from buying supplies for his store, presumably by Pin Indians who had intended to kill another man and killed Hicks by mistake. Their daughter Edith remembered, "When they brought the little wagon home the front [was] all covered with blood."[40] The Pin Indians, members of the Keetoowah Society, opposed slavery and generally supported the Union. Their primary concern was tribal sovereignty, but the violence they perpetrated on Cherokee families had personal as well as political consequences.

Hicks vividly described the first night after her husband left for the last time. She had just gone to bed when she saw by a flash of lightning that a man was trying to raise the window of the corner room. She got a gun, and as she raised it, the trigger got caught and the gun went off, scaring away the man and startling Hicks, whose head had been inches from the gun. "That," she wrote, "was the beginning of terror & sorrow for me. I never saw my husband to tell him of it."[41]

Hicks began her diary on August 17, 1862, about a month after her husband's death. The first entry read: "On the 4th of July my beloved husband was *murdered*, killed, away from home, and I could not see him. So far from it—he had been buried twenty-four hours before I even heard of it. Buried without a coffin, all alone, forty miles from home. Alas, alas, my husband. Still the cry of my heart every day, and every hour, is, oh, my husband." Left alone with five children at the age of twenty-eight, her house was burned and her horses taken in August 1862. She then moved her family into the house of Dwight Hitchcock.[42] Nancy Hitchcock, Dwight's mother, regretted having to leave Hicks alone when she and her own family fled. In a letter to her friends, Brother and Sister Orr, she wrote:

> Poor Hannah we had to leave her with her *five* fatherless little ones because they could not come at that inclement season for want to suitable clothing & because she knew not where or to whom to go. She is still there living in Dwight's house with none to comfort her but her almost helpless children. . . . The whole country is *desolated and ruined.* The Secesh part of the nation have all gone South & the loyal Indians are all in the Federal army, who have not been killed & most of their families are broke up & encamped within Federal protection. A great many negroes were killed & many others taken off prisoners to Texas.[43]

From her diary entries, it is clear that Hicks was unaccustomed to physical labor. When she went to get a load of wood she "remembered her husband with renewed sadness" because he would never have allowed her to do such work.[44] Yet women's traditional work remained crucial to survival, as Hicks made clear in a letter to her sister, Ann Eliza: "Oh the losses, the losses we have had by the War. We get our living while Dwight is gone, by taking boarders, & Mary's making Butter. The Butter we have sold, besides all that we use at both places, has already amounted to more than 100 Dollars. But Mary works entirely too hard. I do fear she will soon be completely broken down. . . . And now our horse 'Stella' . . . was *shot,* in the pasture at Park Hill."[45]

Mary Scott Gordon told a WPA interviewer in the 1930s of another instance of the war's disruption of gender expectations. She recounted that during the Civil War her mother's sister's husband had died trying to preserve "appropriate roles." Gordon's aunt told her husband Arch not to return home again because he would be killed. He told her that he would have to come back and cut her some wood. Although her aunt's father, who also had been home, urged her to have a "negro by the name of Cicero cut the wood," Arch came back anyway. He brought a white man, Jim Goree, with him. When the Indians attacked, they killed both men and cut off Goree's head.[46]

Hicks, like so many other Cherokee wives and mothers, had to fend for herself. She had to travel eighteen miles to Fort Gibson for provisions, a three-day

Fig. 15. The children of Samuel A. and Ann Orr Worcester. *Left to right:* Leonard, Ann Eliza, Mary Eleanor, and Hannah. Robertson Studio, Muskogee, Indian Territory, no. 3174. (Courtesy Archives and Manuscripts Division, Oklahoma Historical Society)

trip. Edith Hicks Smith Walker remembered that the children—except Percy, the twelve-year-old boy—remained at home alone during these trips.[47] On September 24, Hicks wrote, "I begin to find out what is possible for me to do." She was empowered to perform nontraditional tasks in order to survive, but she experienced anxieties arising from a crisis of identity regarding her proper role.[48]

In addition to increased manual labor, women in the Cherokee Nation faced physical dangers and persistent psychological terror: raids were frequent. When Kansas Jayhawkers, plundering guerilla soldiers, came to George Mayes's house, they "pushed his mother out of the house and set fire to it, and burned the furniture, clothes, and everything. Mother stood like the Rock of Gibraltar and looked on, with not a sign of emotion on her face. Her heart was broken to watch the accumulation of sixteen years of married life vanish with the smoke."[49]

Sometimes families lost more than property in the raids. Lizzie Wynn saw her father murdered before her eyes. She recalled, "The Northern soldiers came to the door and I was standing at the head of his [her father's] bed. They told me to move but I thought if I stayed there they surely wouldn't shoot him. They shot him and blood and brains splattered all over me. I wasn't scared but I was mad." [50] Wynn's family had owned two families of slaves and three other slaves. Before his death, her father had freed all but one, a woman who accompanied them to Texas, and tried to remain neutral during the war. Neutrality, however, was nearly impossible given the battles that raged throughout the Indian Territory.

Family and friends who survived often related horrific tales of violence. Dwight D. Hitchcock, who married Hicks, described the violence that he witnessed in a letter of February 11, 1863: "Mrs. Hoyt & Mrs. Gunter died in bed, as did old Mr. Passor, I suppose. Abijah and Ann Ross were murdered—the latter & her oldest son by some roving Kechis. Willis was shot by a Federal picket guard for neglecting to answer his hail. These six I can think of, from our little number since the fourth of July last." [51] Hitchcock noted a story from his brother that was as chilling as any he recounted:

> David is perhaps at home. After being absent from his family for several months he ventured home in December; stayed but a day or two, as notice of his return was conveyed to Watie's men, then at the Falls; while making his way back to the Federal lines, in company with Judge Lewis Hildebrand, he was captured by a gang of "bushwhackers" & taken into a ravine to be stripped & killed, as the Judge was while standing so near that his brains were scattered over David's face; David instantly seized the gun of the man who was robbing him, & sank the barrel in his skull, & ran for life; one ball took effect in his left leg below the knee; but he continued to elude discovery by burying himself in the leaves, favored by the dusk of early evening. This was on Christmas day. . . . I think he is safe. [52]

Sarah Watie faced the frequency of sickness and death among her immediate acquaintances. After visiting a dying friend, she wrote poignantly, "She was my earliest friend. She was the friend of my childhood. It was long before either of us could speak. She says, 'You have come at last.' I told her, 'Yes' That was all I could say." [53] Hicks also faced numerous deaths among her family and acquaintances, and she felt despair because she did not feel that she was able to be the moral guardian of her family. On September 1, she confided her despair to the pages of her diary: "I am so cast down, so discouraged, I don't see how we are to live,—and my children—I am not training them up as I should. I do not pray half enough for that grace which alone can help me, and I fail every day and every hour." A week later she wrote, "I believe my heart is almost dead within me."[54]

After a skirmish with Opothleyoholo's party, W. P. Ross wrote to Colonel Drew, describing the brutality of the encounter. He wrote, "My men were fired on at their camp, as I learn, *first* two prisoners were taken and brutally murdered, having their brains knocked out with hominy pestles, and had evidently been tortured—their eyes having been punched out with sticks."[55] Other Cherokees commented on the brutality of the war. Jane [Ross?] wrote to her friend Sarah and described the grim conduct:

> For the last seven months the storm of war has howled so fearfully around us, that we have found it hard to compose ourselves sufficiently to write even to our best loved absent friends. . . . It were vain for me to endeavor to picture to you the terrors and trials we have passed through since last reported several times I kept a daily account of what was passing and then a new alarm would cause me to burn what might fall into the hands of our enemy more than once when our poor boys would venture home—they at a moment's warning would have to rush to the thickets and my feeble hands would then, unaided secrete saddles Saddle bags &c—One day just as Daniel, Lewis, Jim and others were making their way up from Gibson a party of Watie's men followed on a couple of horses behind, found a Drew man sitting by the road, killed him, and then placing a rope around his neck hauled him about as children would a sleigh— they occupied themselves long enough at this to give our folks time to get here.
>
> The Secesh have crossed at Webbers Falls and robbing at a terrible rate—Oh *why don't* our friends hasten along. The people are starving— and the Small pox has broken out on Caney—Are we doomed to destruction. . . . Katy and I cook, wash, make fires, work in the garden and even work an old mule in the cart when we get out of wood; Last week we put the children and a few shrubs &c into the cart and went up to our grave yard. I planted a few bulbs and a rose bush around your dead as well as ours.[56]

Bettie (Perdue) Woodall told a similarly grisly story of the Pin Indians' murder of her uncle. "Early the next morning the Pins rode into the yard, took Uncle Tom out in the yard and cut his heart out, and him alive. It was a horrible thing for us to see, and our only support was gone."[57]

Because of their location, families living in the northern and central areas of the Cherokee Nation were vulnerable to raids by both Confederate and Federal troops, as well as by Pins and bushwhackers. Sylvester Thornton described the results of the continuous raids:

> The first year of the Civil War, the soldiers took our two mules and we had to make a crop with one poor horse hitched to a home-made plow stock. I rode the horse and mother laid off the land. The second year the soldiers took our horse and we made a crop with a steer. The third year the Northern soldiers gave us a four-year-old mule that was so poor it could hardly walk. We never started our crop until the grass came as we had no feed for the stock. We only planted three acres of cotton, and two acres of oats. We did not break the land; we just planted in furrows.[58]

Hicks had to endure frequent raids. Her daughter recalled, "Every time the rebels would come we would hide under her dress. They were mean. My aunt had her little dead baby's picture in the brooch pin and they even took that, not because they wanted it but because they wanted to be mean."[59] On November 17, Hicks began her entry, "Today we have had experience in being robbed." She described the trauma: "As soon as it was light they came and begun. They took many valuable things, and overhauled every closet, trunk, box & drawer they could find. The leaders were Cherokees, those who have often eaten in my house, some of them."[60]

General James S. Marmaduke, a Confederate officer, heard about the incident, sent a guard, and ordered the vandals away. He also made them return some of Hicks's possessions. However, the robbers made away with the most valuable things.[61] Her daughter recalled many robberies: "We stayed there during the war and were robbed five different times. One time they got the livestock, the mules and horses, and then the next time they took our books not because they wanted them but because they thought they would annoy us. Stand Watie was always in the background."[62]

Stephen Foreman, a minister in Candies Creek before removal, kept an extensive journal throughout the war years. As he fled with his children, he often encountered Union troops. He described one especially harrowing incident:

> Wednesday, August 26, 1863,
> To our great surprise in about one hour after dark the Feds came upon us and surrounded our house. They rode up with their pistols drawn and cocked. When I first heard them coming I supposed them to be our men

and scolded the dogs and went to the gate of the yard fence. Pretty soon a number of them rode up where I was and asked several questions. The first was, Who are you? They then asked if we had seen any southern soldiers pass late in the evening. I replied, No. They said that was a lie, they knew better.

Foreman then went in the house and hid under a counter, and the troops came in with their pistols drawn and cocked. He left his hiding place and told them that he surrendered, that he had no weapons, and that he was not a soldier. The soldiers went into the room where his children were, and the children began to cry aloud and say, "They are going to kill Pa." His daughter Susie stood by him with her hand on his head, and the soldiers decided to spare him. He spent the night in the field near the house.[63]

In another robbery, a woman temporarily stopped the plunder of a house owned by Baptist missionary James Anderson Slover. While Slover was away, the home guard of Union men came to his house and carried away every article of clothing except what his family had on and took all the sheets and pillowcases from the beds. One Cherokee got a suit of the missionary's fine clothes, hat, and boots, and went to the barn, put them on, came into the house, strutted across the room, and said, "Slover Standwaity man." Slover's wife sent the oldest boy to a neighbor's house to tell her what was going on. The woman returned with the little boy and tried to make the Indians feel guilty for robbing a poor helpless woman; they simply took their loot and left.[64]

The woman who intervened in this robbery tried to reawaken the Indians' sense of decency. Most highly acculturated women, such as Watie and Hicks, grieved over the fact that they could no longer wield such moral authority. Perhaps this helps explain the identity crisis that they experienced. The more acculturated Cherokee women viewed themselves as moral guardians of their families. Watie's advice to her husband reflected this position: she always urged her husband and son to conduct themselves with honor and integrity and to remember their values.

Clearly many of Watie's entreaties went unheeded as her husband's raids across the Indian Territory became more and more numerous. Stand Watie burned Ross's home, Rose Cottage in Park Hill, but he did honor his wife's request to spare the life of William Ross.[65] Sarah Watie had written to her husband on June 8, 1863: "Tell my boys to always show mercy as they expect to find God merciful to them. . . . I am afraid that Saladin [the Waties' son] never will value human life as he ought." Then she made a special appeal for William Ross: "If you should ever catch William Ross dont have him killed. I know how

Fig. 16. Stand Watie. Phillips Collection, no.
1459. (Courtesy Western History Collections,
University of Oklahoma Libraries)

bad his mother would feel but keep him till the war is over. I know they deserve death but I do feel for his old mother and then I want them to know that you do not want to kill them just to get them out of your way. I want them to know you are not afraid of their influence. [A]lways do as near right as you can."[66]

Cherokee women had traditionally decided the fate of prisoners. Stand Watie's sparing Ross's life echoed this ancient practice.[67] Nevertheless, Sarah Watie was powerless to stop the violence and killing that her husband and his men engaged in almost daily. For instance, his troops killed Andrew Nave, who was presumably trying to escape. Sarah Watie lamented the corrosive effect that the war had on the Cherokee Nation:

I hope the war will close soon and we will get time to sit down in peace but it does look to me as if I could not contain my self any where. I am all out of sorts. [T]his war it will ruin a great many good people, they will not only lose all there property but a great many will lose there caracter which is more value than all their property. [Y]ou can hardly hear people speak of any of our people but something said that is against there

Fig. 17. Sarah C. Watie. Phillips Collection, no. 1453. (Courtesy Western History Collections, University of Oklahoma Libraries)

caracter. I am also most ashamed of my tribe. [I]t has got to be such a common talk that they all follow the army and that for bad purposes. I have long since lost all interest in my people. I sometimes feel that I will never be with them any more and it does not make any ods whether or not. I could not do them any good. I want to see the end of this war and then I will be willing to give up the ghost. [Y]ou will think that I got in the dumps befor I got done [with] my letter, well I do get that way when I think what they are and what they might be.[68]

Mrs. William P. Ross, who was homeless after enemies burned the family property in 1863, also wondered about the future of the Nation: "Where we will find another home I cannot say, but I still intend to go back to the Nation, but whether there will be peace, safety and pleasure living there for a long time to come is doubtful. At best things will be changed. Many of our friends have been scattered abroad upon the world. Others dead, yet others are estranged one from the other."[69] Watie's men had allegedly "robbed Mrs. Gunter's House when she was dying."[70]

Fig. 18. Rose Cottage, home of Chief John Ross at Park Hill, Cherokee Nation. Burned by Gen. Stand Watie, October 28, 1862. J. W. Morris Collection, no. 36. (Courtesy of Western History Collections, University of Oklahoma Libraries)

Hannah Hicks, Mary Stapler Ross, and Sarah Watie all shared a deep religious faith that helped them endure their suffering during the Civil War. They also shared fears about the future of the Cherokee Nation. Hicks longed for the war to end as she wrote, "Oh that this dreadful War may very soon be ended. That friends may dwell together in peace once more, and *the Sabbath* be again devoted to the Lord, to whom it belongs. We wait the time longingly." On her twenty-ninth birthday (January 29, 1863) Hannah wrote, "We have come to such *times* as I never thought to see—and no prospect for a living ahead. But I must try to *trust* myself and my children in the hands of Him who has preserved us hitherto."[71]

Cherokee women of all ages expressed a deepening sense of despair. Upon hearing of the destruction of their home, Ross wrote to her husband on December 3, 1863:

Thy very welcome letter was received this morn, containing the sad intelligence extracted from John Jones's letter about the desolation & distress in our Cherokee home. . . . I also note thee telling what a gloom was cast over our household by the sad news [of Andrew Nave's death]. O! may the hand of an Almighty Father & Ruler punish the guilty for their horrible wickedness. . . . [A]ll are moving about our duties with saddened hearts, but we are thankful when we think my loved Husband that thee is spared to us, & not permitted to fall into the hands of those wicked men.[72]

Ross expressed her sadness over the loss of Rose Cottage in a letter to her husband on December 4, 1863: "*Home,* my dear Husband we have no home there now, one we cherished so long & took so much trouble to beautify is now in ashes, all is ruin around. I do not think it safe for our loved ones to remain their any longer."[73] Like Watie, Ross experienced intense periods of loneliness. She wrote on March 19, 1864: "My beloved Husband, I take my seat this Eve at the Table where my dear Husband has been so often seated writing for the last week, now I am all alone & and my loved one is again far away & I am left to fill the void created by thy absence & although but a few hours have passed away I am sad & lonely so I feel like having a silent talk with thee." By spring 1865, Ross was in poor health, and she died on July 20, 1865, shortly after the end of the Civil War.[74]

Young Cherokee women also suffered as the Civil War seemingly robbed them of a future. Susie Foreman, who had courageously helped save her father's life during a raid by Federal troops, had attended the Fayetteville Female Seminary. In 1862, after completing her education, she began to teach at the Cherokee neighborhood school at Webber's Falls. After the incident with the Union troops, Susan and her father and brother made their way to the Creek Agency. While they were there she expressed her despair in a journal entry on December 6, 1863: "A beautiful day to those who can enjoy it, but I cannot. I have not the heart to enjoy anything. I am *miserable, wretched,* and almost tired of life. There is no enjoyment, no pleasure for me, nothing but a life of trouble and toil, before me. No bright future for me. One week after another passes away." The Foremans left the agency and went to Texas, where Susie died among the refugees from the Cherokee Nation in August 1864.[75]

Although she was not in such mortal danger, Watie faced real privation; in addition, her health worsened and her depression grew. Watie's son, Cumiskey, had died in 1863, and she feared for the life of her other son, Saladin. At only fifteen, he had joined his father's regiment.[76] On May 20, 1863, Watie wrote to her husband from Rusk, Texas: "I never could begin to tell you half as every thing seames to go wrong. . . . [I]t greaves me to think we are so far from each

Fig. 19. Chief John Ross and his wife, Mary Bryan Stapler Ross. OHS Glass Plate Collection, no. 19615.45. (Courtesy Archives and Manuscripts Division, Oklahoma Historical Society)

other if any thing should happen we are too far of[f] for to help each other. [B]e a good man as you always have been. [A]t the end a clear conscience before God and man is the advise of your Wife."[77]

Drew Gilpin Faust discussed the ways in which Confederate women in the South increasingly urged husbands and sons to desert in the later years of the war, demonstrating the conditional nature of their patriotism.[78] Writing on June 12, 1864, Watie urged her husband to withdraw from the war:

> I do wish you would leave the service and let them see whether they can do so well with out you as some seem to think. [A]s for me I want some to learn how well they will do for I dont feel as if they treat you right, so let them go where they want to go. [A]s for the Nation I believe it is bound to go to the dogs and the more one does to save it the more blame the[y] will have to bear. . . . I would rather die than always live in dread as we did, it is no pleasure. I would like to live a short time in peace just to see how it would be. I would like to feel free once in life again and feel no dread of war or any other trouble.[79]

Despite his wife's pleas, Stand Watie had no intention of deserting, even when his wife's letters became more and more desperate. In July 1864, she wrote, "I don't care if they never do get the old country back and if they do what good will it do such people, none only to fuss over it just let them have command and see what they will do we can live any where." She said that she could find more friends among strangers than she could among her own people. She concluded on a pessimistic note: "I do wish one could have peace once more but I fear that is not for me to see in my day."[80]

When husbands and sons came home on furloughs, Cherokee women urged them to stay. One woman told of her father's desertion from the Southern army. When he did not get a furlough, he deserted and joined his family in Parker, Texas. His wife dug a hole just long and wide enough for him to lie on his back, and then she placed a door over him. She kept him in this hiding place for several weeks.[81]

Like many other Cherokee women who experienced the consequences of a civil war within a civil war and who realized that neither women nor Cherokees shared a communal vision, Watie did not like what she saw. Finally, she received her husband's letter of June 23, 1865, stating, "Have agreed upon the cessation of hostilities."[82] Near Doaksville, the capital of the Choctaw Nation, on a blazing hot day on June 23, 1865, General Watie surrendered to Lt. Colonel A. C. Matthews. Watie was the last Confederate general to surrender his command in the American Civil War. When the Confederate Chickasaw and Caddo warriors officially surrendered on July 14, almost three months after Appomattox, the Civil War in Indian Territory had finally ended.[83]

As they returned home, the Cherokees, who had already survived the Trail of Tears, dispossession of their eastern lands, years of intratribal violence, marauding guerrilla bands, and the plundering of both sides of the war, had to begin again. It took the Cherokee Nation at least a decade after the end of the Civil War to recover from the devastation. William P. Ross, John Ross's nephew, who was elected twice as principal chief of the Western Cherokees and who served as the first editor of the newspaper, the *Cherokee Advocate,* described in 1864 the devastating effects of the war:

Everything has been much changed by the destroying hand of War . . . but few men remain at their homes. . . . [N]early all the farms are growing up in bushes and briars, houses abandoned or burnt . . . some idea of the great and melancholy change which has come over our once prosperous and beautiful country . . . livestock of all kinds has become very scarce. . . . We have not a horse, cow or hog left that I know of. Condition of a great many . . . though some few have a yoke of oxen or a mule . . . great increase in the number of wild animals. The wolves howl dismally over the land and the panther's scream is often heard. Bears have often been seen in the Bayou Manard mountains within ten miles of here.[84]

As Cherokee women returned home, they confirmed Ross's worst fears. Mary E. James described her return home to Hudson Creek to find everything gone or destroyed. Her parents had to start over without slaves to work for them. They arrived back at their homes in the spring, and they camped that summer while they were building a house. They subsisted on fruit from the orchard and wild game.[85] Mary Cobb Agnew, whose family supported the Confederacy, returned home to similarly deplorable conditions. She recalled that the house and cabins had been burned and that the fields were all grown up with thick underbrush. Most of the animals had been killed, and those that had survived were living wild in the woods. Agnew described how everyone had to start all over again, building their homes, clearing the ground, and planting their crops.[86]

More than one-third of adult Cherokee women were widows at the close of the Civil War, and one-quarter of Cherokee children (1,200) were orphans. For these survivors, the cessation of hostilities left deep scars. The loss of so many husbands and fathers was a devastating blow to the society. From psychological, economic, and political perspectives, the implications were tremendous. Widows were forced to eke out a living in the midst of a shattered Nation, which had lost four thousand people. Many husbands who did return from the war were disabled or seriously wounded. The war casualties came on top of the loss of a fourth of the Cherokee population during and following removal.[87] Clearly, women would have much work to do, whatever their beliefs about gender roles.

Through the eyes of wealthier, highly acculturated women such as Watie, Ross, Hicks, and the Cherokee women who gave their oral histories in the 1930s, we have seen that women discovered "what they could do" in an emergency. They had to expand their roles as wives and mothers to encompass what were considered male responsibilities in a Euro-American framework of values. Cherokee women had to raise crops; haul wood and supplies; care for the sick; bury the dead; spin, weave, and sew if they were to have any clothes; and endure the psychological terror of robberies, violence, and the destruction of their homes and property. They endured the death of many loved ones. These women showed remarkable strength, resistance, and courage whether they remained at home, became refugees, or lived in exile. Some of them relied on their religious faith to sustain them, and they all abhorred the war. They never perceived it as an occasion for honor or glory but as the result of men's passions. For the women who had accepted white notions of women's proper sphere, the Civil War caused them to question their identities as women and as Cherokees. However, traditional Cherokee women saw the ancestral gender values reinforced and validated. Ironically, the Civil War provided Cherokee men, whose roles as hunters and warriors had been seriously undermined for decades, the opportunity to become warriors again; instead of hunting, however, they pillaged. But those who had fought for the Confederacy experienced defeat, not the glory of victory. Thus, although the Civil War forced into the open the debate over meanings of gender, political and class divisions kept any consensus from emerging.

Traditional Cherokees achieved political victory after the Civil War. When John Ross died, William P. Ross was selected to finish out his term. Later, Lewis Downing, a traditionalist who had been acting chief in 1866, became principal chief in 1867.[88] Although this gave traditional Cherokees political power, the more acculturated and wealthy Cherokees continued to dominate the social and cultural life of the Nation. Class and racial divisions that emerged during the war persisted after the fighting ceased.

Cherokee women's responses to altered gender roles during the Civil War raised larger questions about how crises affect women's identities and status over both the short and long term. If the transformation of gender roles is viewed as a temporary expedient because of an emergency, fundamental changes may not follow. However, when women become empowered in crises and choose to exercise their independence—regardless of how painful the experience—their view of themselves often changes. They may become ambivalent about returning to their previous roles or, in some cases, embrace them more zealously. We have seen how profoundly class and caste shaped women's views of themselves in the Cherokee Nation both before and during the Civil War. These elements would also shape the ways in which they reconstructed their social and psychological identities after the conflict.

5
Reconstruction

The Cherokees were able to live effectively in the Cherokee world as well as the white world. To white society, that meant our people were the most acculturated, although we still were not—and never would be—placed on the same level as the whites.

Wilma Mankiller, *Mankiller: A Chief and Her People*

After the horrors of the Civil War, the western Cherokee Nation once again began to rebuild its institutions of government and education. The crises of removal and the Civil War forced into the open the debate over meanings of gender. In some ways, removal legitimized both male political power and women's exclusion from the process; because divisions generally followed economic rather than clan connections during the Civil War, the authority of the clans diminished. Continuity with traditional values had characterized the prewar period, but the majority of Cherokees, who embraced the traditional values, found themselves confronting a small but influential group of highly acculturated, often intermarried Cherokees who embraced the values of white society. After the war had ended, no consensus emerged regarding what it meant to be a woman in the Cherokee Nation. Conversions to Christianity increased dramatically after the Civil War. Moreover, the Cherokee Female Seminary became the primary educational institution for Cherokee women, and it strongly promoted acculturation to white values.

During the late nineteenth and early twentieth centuries, women in the western Cherokee Nation attempted to construct a new gender system that drew upon traditional ideas, even as they adapted to dramatically changing conditions. They all faced the daunting challenge of reconstructing their lives after the war. Their experiences, however, varied across class and race and in response to their relationship with other constituencies within the Cherokee Nation. Cherokee women in the elite class adopted many of white society's values. In the pre–Civil War period, they had relied on slave women to perform domestic labor, thus enabling them to perform their roles as ladies. In the aftermath, they had to find other ways to maintain status and respectability. Meanwhile, traditional Cherokee women were in the majority, but they were generally poor and were increasingly viewed as backward for their resistance to civilization.

Within the context of political and social turmoil, survival itself in the western Cherokee Nation seemed to hinge on acculturation. In spite of this, not all Cherokee women embraced acculturation. Fierce struggles occurred within the Nation over Cherokee meanings of gender, identity, assimilation, and cultural survival.

Because many Cherokees supported the South during the war, the U.S. government punished the entire Nation during Reconstruction. They demanded access for railroads through Indian Territory, failed to remove intruders, insisted that the Indian nations give citizenship and land to their freed slaves, and thwarted their sale of neutral lands and the Cherokee Outlet (a piece of land in Indian Territory owned by the Cherokees and leased for cattle grazing). The U.S. government also stalled payments owed to the tribe. The federal government's refusal to remove white intruders allowed the intruders to become both numerous and disruptive, leading to severe destabilization within the Nation. By the late nineteenth century, the Cherokee Nation was threatened with eradication.[1]

Thus the period from Reconstruction to the turn of the century marked an accelerated period of often forced assimilation for Cherokees in Indian Territory. Cherokee schools and Christian churches promoted assimilation as a strategy for survival. The Cherokee male and female seminaries, established in 1850, reopened after the Civil War and continued to train the future leaders of the Nation. English was the official language of the schools. However, assimilation was not strictly imposed on the Cherokees; they selectively adopted those aspects of white society that they considered necessary for survival.[2]

Women who attended the Cherokee Female Seminary saw the adoption of white American values as necessary for survival. In the federal boarding schools such as Chilocco and Carlisle, as well as in the Cherokee seminaries, American Indians took what they needed, but they did not abandon their traditional cultures. They appropriated knowledge and became familiar with white American values and morals. Some used this knowledge to defend tribal interests and identity. Like African American women in the late nineteenth century who aspired to middle-class gentility and respectability, they saw education as a vehicle of mobility and considered white values as something to be learned and then used to benefit their own interests.

Fig. 20. Members of the junior class, Cherokee Female Seminary, 1898. Piburn Collection, no. 4. (Courtesy Western History Collections, University of Oklahoma Libraries)

Some Cherokee women who attended the seminary genuinely embraced many white values, abandoned speaking Cherokee, and adopted Christianity. However, most of these women were from families who were already highly assimilated. Traditional, full-blooded women rarely attended the seminary in large numbers. Nonetheless, the Female Seminary exerted a positive influence on many of its students and enabled them to become physicians, business-women, educators, and prominent social workers. In addition, the educated women contributed tremendously to the survival of the Cherokee Nation. At the same time, the social atmosphere at the school contributed to tensions and rifts between progressive Cherokee girls of mixed heritage and those from more traditional, uneducated backgrounds. Only two full-bloods attended the Female Seminary the first year it opened, in 1851. Only 160 full-bloods eventually enrolled in the seminary, about 9.6 percent of the seminary population.[3]

Isabel Cobb, perhaps the first Cherokee woman trained as a physician, attended the Female Seminary. Her life revealed the ways in which women who attended the seminary went on to become professional women and community leaders. Of mixed Cherokee and white ancestry, she served as a bridge between the traditional Cherokee culture and white middle-class culture. Born on October 25, 1858, in a double log cabin near Morgantown, Cobb—the eldest child

Fig. 21. Group of students at Cherokee Female Seminary at Tahlequah after it was rebuilt in 1889. T. L. Ballenger Collection, no. 7. (Courtesy Western History Collections, University of Oklahoma Libraries)

of five siblings—moved with her parents, Joseph and Evaline Clingan Cobb, to a farm near Cleveland, Tennessee.[4]

Cobb's written reminiscences focus on her childhood in Tennessee, and her doctor's journal focuses on the years 1893–1927. She practiced medicine until 1930, when she fell and broke her hip. Cobb recalled that her father served in the Civil War in Nashville, working in the Union commissary department in 1863. Thus her mother, like Hannah Hicks, had to manage alone and try to survive amidst the frequent raids on her chicken roosts and pigpens.[5]

As the train pulled out of the station in Cleveland, Tennessee, in 1870, twelve-year-old Cobb had tried to imagine her new life in Indian Territory. She and her family traveled for days over lush mountains and desolate stretches, finally arriving in Fort Scott only to learn that they had to go the rest of their way in two covered wagons to Tahlequah and on to what is now known as Wagoner, Oklahoma.[6]

When Cobb and her family arrived in Indian Territory the Cherokee Nation was still recovering from the tremendous loss and devastation imposed by the Civil War. Cobb's family settled about five miles southeast of what became

Wagoner, Oklahoma, ten miles north of Fort Gibson. This farm, located on a prairie in Cooweescoowee district, consisted of "10 plus acres of land in cultivation, a log cabin for a kitchen and bed and living room; another log cabin chicken house, a log spring house and the hull or frame of a new cabin with roof extending over for a porch and kitchen (we made them)."[7]

Cobb began attending the Cherokee Female Seminary in 1879, and she was among the first to graduate. While she attended the seminary, she pursued a rigorous academic program, simultaneously encountering training in becoming a "lady." The curriculum was modeled on that of Mount Holyoke and focused on preparing the girls to become wives and homemakers. The education, however, was empowering for a bright young woman such as Cobb. She wanted to pursue further education after graduation, and her Uncle Sam Cobb helped her to attend Glendale Female Seminary near Cincinnati, Ohio. When she graduated from there in 1880, she returned to the Cherokee Female Seminary and taught for several years. In the fall of 1888, Cobb began her studies at Woman's Medical College in Pennsylvania, graduating in June 1892.[8] She became one of the first women—and certainly one of the first American Indian women—to become a physician. Female shamans and healers were quite common in the Cherokee Nation, especially before European contact. In the late nineteenth century, however, there were few women doctors of any background. By the late part of that century, women physicians were becoming more acceptable in obstetrics and gynecology (at least in the urban areas), but many white Americans considered female doctors deviant and generally untrustworthy. Among the Indians, virtually no formally trained female physicians practiced, although American Indian women continued as traditional healers. Cobb adopted white dress, gentility, and many Euro-American values. Yet, remaining single, she resembled the first white female doctors, such as Elizabeth Blackwell, who felt that they had to choose between marriage and a profession. She never opened an office, but she centered her practice on relatives and neighbors. Cobb stayed busy performing house calls for all kinds of ailments, attending women in labor (sometimes for as long as two weeks), and performing surgeries.

Cobb's medical journal lists her patients, the nature of their illnesses, her fees, and the deaths among those she treated. She does not note any of the traditional Cherokee ceremonies and rituals surrounding childbirth. The absence of such information probably means that Cobb's patients were highly assimilated, although we cannot be sure of this. Certainly, her patients had confidence in her abilities as a physician.

On March 29, 1893, Cobb recorded the first entry in her doctor's journal.

Writing about Mrs. A. B. Parkinson, she noted that the call was obstetrical in nature, commenting that her patient had "a hard, first labor." She recorded the twenty dollars she received for her services, which became her standard fee for a long attendance. Two rather chilling one-line entries follow the next year on January 16, 1894 (Mrs. William Harrison), and February 3, 1894 (Mrs. James B. Cobb Jr.): "Confinement, child dead and macerated." The terse entry does not convey the sorrow of the frequent infant mortalities that fill her journal. She recorded on January 30, "Mrs. V. Berry, Abortion 3 mo. + tubs. + Uterus. Adherent plac." Because other entries note miscarriages, and this is the only entry regarding abortion, she evidently meant that she or someone else had performed an abortion procedure. No fee was recorded.[9] Cobb recorded approximately 441 female patients, although some of these involved repeated visits by the same patients, and ninety-nine male patients, which meant that 77.56 percent of her practice was female and 22.44 percent was male. Her yearly income ranged from a high of $329.55 in 1896 to a low of $20 by 1915, with an average between 1893 and 1915 of $190.42. The entries end around 1915, with entries as well as income becoming sparser after 1909.[10]

In her role as physician in the late nineteenth and early twentieth centuries, Cobb represented a Cherokee professional "new woman." She epitomized women's agency and acculturation on her own terms. In the context of Cherokee culture, her status as a female doctor was extremely rare, but her nurturing behavior resembled female healers and shamans who had performed similar functions for hundreds of years. This remarkable woman survived the Civil War, the first and second world wars, and the institution of Oklahoma statehood, performing the duties of her chosen career and serving as a mediator between Indian and white culture.

Thus the Female Seminary and its students functioned as agents of change in the Cherokee acculturation to white values. In addition to schools, churches served as one of the primary vehicles of the assimilation process. Cherokee conversion to Christianity was a crucial influence in formulating gender identities. The Christian churches appear to have experienced an increase in the number of members in the post–Civil War era. The Northern Baptists remained the most numerous representatives in the Cherokee Nation after the Civil War. Before the war, 25 percent of the Cherokee population was Baptist. Southern Methodism was popular with the Confederate sympathizers, but the ABCFM missionaries did not return after the war.[11]

Just as their predecessors did before removal, Indian Territory missionaries attempted to convert the Cherokees to Christianity and to middle-class, patriarchal family values. White women missionaries sought to model gentility and teach patriarchal gender roles; but because of their location on the frontier, they were also, in a sense, pioneer women. Their decision to go to Indian Territory was a bold move for women of their class, and this decision brought them both hardships and adventure. Thus they could escape some strictures of white middle-class gender expectations because of the unusual conditions, but at the same time gender hierarchies were retained within the mission families. Women in these families were generally highly educated and could not have failed to see Cherokee women's exercise of property rights, autonomy, and strength.

Reverend Joseph Leiper, his aunt, Margaret (an accomplished scholar of theology), and his wife, Fanny Leiper, were Presbyterian missionaries to the Cherokees from 1889 to 1893.[12] They reinvigorated the mission at Park Hill a few years after its closure during the Civil War. Joseph Leiper served the mission as pastor, led school classes, and ministered to Cherokees in outlying areas of Park Hill. He also restarted the Cherokee Press. His wife, who was an accomplished artist, gave art lessons and devotional chalk talks. She also taught a general education class to men and boys, and she managed the parsonage. Margaret (Maggie) Leiper taught Cherokee students but spent much of her time educating black children living in the area who had no schools.[13]

The Leiper home at Park Hill greatly resembled their residence back East, complete with a piano, wallpaper, and furniture. Joseph Leiper wrote to his aunts back home, telling them that they tried to create a beautiful example of family life in the mission: "We try to make our home as bright & pretty as we can & have the people enjoy it with us. Outside of distinctive Bible teaching nothing is more needed by these people than to teach them how to live."[14] The Leipers threw themselves into their work. Leiper conducted his classes and services in English with occasional assistance from a Cherokee interpreter. This was a dramatic shift from pre–Civil War services, which had relied heavily on interpreters, and the increasing number of Cherokees who spoke English was an indication of how extensive acculturation was becoming.[15]

As before the Civil War, the Baptists were highly successful in attracting Cherokee members because of Evan and John Jones, who were devoted to revitalizing Cherokee traditional values, defending tribal sovereignty, and converting the Cherokees to Christianity. They were involved in helping to found the Keetoowah Society, a radical group loosely associated with Christianity. This group formed in the 1850s among a group of Baptist Cherokees, especially in the Flint district. Among the prominent leaders were Lewis Downing, Budd Gritts, and Gasannee (Smith Christy).[16] The Keetoowahs blended Christianity with traditional Cherokee ceremonies and beliefs. Many Cherokees belonged

Fig. 22. Cherokee men, women, and children outside a home, Cherokee Nation, c. 1890. Faux Collection, no. 104. (Courtesy Western History Collections, University of Oklahoma Libraries)

to both the Keetoowah Society and a Christian church. From 1859–89, the Keetoowah membership was very strong among Cherokees settled in Indian Territory. Within their troubled Nation the Cherokees sought reassurance and community.[17]

The economic and political dislocations caused by the crisis of the war exacerbated already existing tensions over gender meanings and whether the Cherokees would retain traditional values or become assimilated. After the Civil War, the Cherokee Nation experienced severe problems of violence (including domestic violence), extensive intermarriage with white Americans, and attacks on tribal sovereignty. Cherokee families and the gender relations within and between them became a lightning rod for many of the stresses that Cherokee society confronted. Cherokee women responded through legal action, out-marriage (intermarriage), and other strategies. They also succeeded in acquiring significant amounts of property and improvements. Pages of faded nineteenth-century handwritten court records reveal murders, rapes, estate settlements, citizenship battles, wills, permits for white workers, marriages and divorces—the intimate lives of Cherokees who left no diaries, letters, or other personal accounts. The court records reflect manifestations of the arena of

Fig. 23. Cherokee woman with child, Cherokee Nation, c. 1890. Faux Collection, no. 100.
(Courtesy Western History Collections, University of Oklahoma Libraries)

struggle and the resulting disharmony. Domestic violence arose directly from
the disruption of gender roles. Court records also reveal the persistence of
Cherokee values regarding both communal and women's ownership of property as they faced the further encroachment of white people in their territory
and families.

These internal stresses weakened their ability to develop a united strategy
to confront the country's most powerful corporations and a U.S. government
bent on destroying Cherokee sovereignty. Several themes emerge in the Cherokee Nation's judicial records. The court records reveal numerous cases involving
theft in the 1880s. Horse theft and hog stealing were common. An enormous
number of intermarriages between white Americans and Cherokees occurred
in the late nineteenth century, the majority of which were between white men
and Cherokee women. At the same time, Cherokee women continued to own
property and improvements, and they controlled significant wealth within the
Nation.[18]

A gendered analysis of the Cherokee court records reveals many contradic-
tions. The Supreme Court and the lower courts had no female justices or
judges. No female lawyers practiced before the courts, and no women served

Fig. 24. Cherokee family outside their home, Cherokee Nation, c. 1890. Faux Collection, no. 101. (Courtesy Western History Collections, University of Oklahoma Libraries)

on juries. The Cherokee courts resembled the judiciary of the U.S. government in that it was a male preserve. However, the absence of women in official positions was not consistent with the very powerful economic and marital power they wielded in the court records. Unlike white women, Cherokee women had historically owned property and held large and small estates of improvements. The records of the Cherokee Supreme Court consistently upheld this principle:

> The law of the Cherokee Nation gives to woman the same rights as it does to man and the law protects her in the means to defend her rights to the same extent, and in the same manner as it does the man—and the marriage relation does not change her relation to the law. She can hold her property separately, she can acquire and dispose and control her property after marriage as well as before, she can sue and be sued. The husband therefore cannot assume or imperil any of her rights and ought not to be allowed to annul any of her obligations by assuming such rights.[19]

In the case of *Audry Esky vs. J. L. Bigby [Bigbey?]*, March 21, 1890, the court ruled that a husband could not imperil his wife's rights. The judges reiterated the rights of Cherokee women to hold and dispose of their own property. The case was eventually dismissed at the plaintiff's cost. Land naturally was held in common, but all Cherokee citizens owned their own improvements (houses, farms, barns, livestock, fences, ferries, etc.). The court records reflect lively activity among women bringing suits against men and against other women.

Although the statistics are approximate because of the illegibility of many entries, the pattern of intermarriage between white men with Cherokee women is quite striking. In fact, intermarriages often appear to outnumber marriages among Cherokee citizens in the years from 1867 to 1895. The following table illustrates the upward trend of these intermarriages:[20]

White American men and Cherokee women (Cooweescoowee district)

1867: 3	1868: 8	1869: 7	1870: 7	1871: 8	1872: 7
1873: 10	1874: 12	1875: 4	1876: 4	1877: 5	1879: 9
1880: 13	1881: 10	1882: 10	1883: 12	1884: 11	
1885: 24 (1 "colored U.S. citizen" listed)		1886: 31	1887: 26	1888: 17	
1889: 19	1890: 31	1891: 27	1893: 2	1894: 21	1895: 61

Cherokee men and white American women

1894: 1	1895: 4	1896: 1

During the years 1884 and 1885 the number of intermarriages between white men and Cherokee women more than doubled in one district, and the rate remained high throughout the following decade. When a white man wished to marry a Cherokee woman, he had to have ten male Cherokee citizens sign a petition attesting to his good character. Upon his marriage, he would become a Cherokee citizen, and the tribe understandably wanted to be cautious regarding whom they admitted to their membership. Much less common was the marriage of a Cherokee man to a white American woman. For example, only six such marriages were recorded in the years 1894–96 in the Cooweescoowee district, compared to more than eighty-two involving white men and Cherokee women. Intermarriage with white American citizens generally led to more accelerated assimilation of their children into American and patriarchal values. Not all Cherokee women who married white men gave up Cherokee ceremonies and traditions or adopted their husbands' values in toto. However, their children often grew up speaking English as a first language, and many adopted Christianity as well.

Intermarriage sometimes led to disputes over citizenship and property ownership. From May 12, 1891, to February 25, 1895, in the Cooweescoowee district alone, twenty-three divorce suits were brought to the court, thirteen by women. One case involved a white American citizen, Robert Skinner, who was married to a Cherokee woman, Jemima Skinner. She sued him for divorce on February 14, 1889, complaining that:

> He got mad about her objection to his niece following them home from Missouri and he was upset about her Board Bill and he wanted his grandson-in-law to open a farm here to which she objected and told him he was the only one would get a right through me in the Cherokee Nation. Then he said he wouldn't make her any farm—They had a fight—He was asleep in the chair and she said he might as well get some rest—that he looked so uncomfortable . . .
>
> Jemima said, "I went in to go to bed and knelt down beside the bed to pray—while I was praying to God to relieve the Burden he jumped out of bed and said are you praying to God to relieve the Burden of your heart and says I will relieve it—and walked out in the front room. . . . [A]s he was leaving he raised his fist and said, 'I will never sleep in that Room again as long as my head is hot.'" She went upstairs to sleep. He left and came back with his wagon for his things and she said, "[I]f you go you will never come back." We bid each other friendly Good Bye and he got in his wagon and drove off.

Robert Skinner told a different story. He said that his wife refused to sleep with him and locked him out of their room. The unhappy couple received the divorce with no damages awarded.

In this case, tensions arose over Skinner's objecting to her husband bringing in his relatives to occupy Cherokee Nation land. Realizing that intermarriage might disrupt matrilineal traditions and lead to greater acculturation, some Cherokees resisted. Intermarriages raised these sorts of issues because the husbands were citizens by marriage not by birth, and thus the tribe faced the possibilities of even more "intruders" setting up improvements and farms. Moreover, if the intermarried couple divorced, the white man might lose his citizenship in the Cherokee Nation, which could have significant economic consequences.[21]

Domestic disputes frequently arose over property matters or suspected infidelities, and they were sometimes fueled by alcohol. Alcohol exacerbated domestic violence and frequently led to fights and even, at times, to murder. One such case resulted from a domestic dispute in 1893. Jim Williams and his wife

Charlotte (Sixkiller) presumably were "having a Racket about her baby. They were all drinking. Dick [Boggs] intervened when he [Jim] was going to whip her. Jim knocked her down and Dick tried to stop him." Williams pulled out his knife, and then Boggs pulled his out and gave it to Sixkiller. Williams somehow got hold of Boggs's knife and killed him. Just two months later, Williams was convicted and sentenced to death by hanging.[22]

Cherokee women also could be violent, and in the case of *Cherokee Nation vs. Polly Muskrat*, a jealous rage appears to have fueled the conflict. Betsy Sawney gave the following testimony: "Polly Muskrat came to my house . . . she hit me with a rock. She just hit me one lick with the rock and dropped the rock and let in on me with her fist. When she got through beating me she got up and jerked my sack off of me and tore it up. She picked up the rock and struck with both and I went in the house and she hit me two licks in the house with the sack. She was jealous of me." Although no verdict was recorded, Sawney sought $150 in damages for the physical harm she suffered.[23] Jealousy also played a part in the divorce case of *Annie Mayfield vs. John R. Mayfield*. Annie Mayfield brought the suit for divorce and division of property on August 19, 1892. The property was worth $5,000—a large estate for residents of the Nation. Annie Mayfield asked for damages amounting to $2,000 "for defamation of plaintiff's good name, also one half of boarding, clothing, and education of their three children." Annie claimed that her husband had for several years lived adulterously with Nelly Phillips in nearby Sand Town and in other locations. Meanwhile, Phillips asserted that she was Nelly Mayfield. In addition to adultery, Annie Mayfield argued that John Mayfield had treated her in an "extremely cruel manner." Annie Mayfield further alleged that around July 1, 1890, John Mayfield publicly showed a letter that accused her of infidelity. She claimed that he "seeks thereby to destroy her character and as a wife and mother of his children and to bring her into disrepute in the community in which she lives." She requested custody of the children and property acquired during their marriage. The judges did not grant an appeal, and Annie Mayfield presumably won her case.[24] Charges of women's infidelity appear in numerous divorce cases of the period, revealing that expectations regarding Cherokee women's morality had significantly shifted from earlier periods when they had sexual freedom and autonomy. Because no penalties had previously existed for adultery, the criminalization of adultery marked a decided shift in the Nation's intervention in personal life.

Divorces were fairly common among Cherokees throughout the post–Civil War era, and disputes often arose over alimony, damages, custody, and ownership of improvements. Sometimes these disputes escalated into violence. In earlier periods, divorce had traditionally been a simple matter. One member of the couple essentially put the other one out of the household. As the Cherokees adopted a more elaborate legal system in the nineteenth century, more attention was given to disposition of joint property. In addition, the custody of children became more complicated because the kin systems had been attenuated. Reliance on the courts to resolve marital disputes was a relatively recent development during this period, and the legalization of domestic relations marked a further departure from clan control. Formerly the clans sought retribution for violent acts, regulated marital partner choices, and controlled many other aspects of social relationships. The adoption of the Cherokee Constitution in 1827 did not immediately eliminate clan traditions and practices, but the authority of the clans began to steadily diminish. Therefore, by the post–Civil War period, the Cherokees were increasingly turning to the courts to handle marriage and divorce issues, criminal punishments, and property and domestic disputes.

In the period from September 1887 to October 1894, there were forty-one suits filed for divorce, twenty-two of which were brought by women. Desertion and adultery were the two most common reasons presented for seeking a divorce. In one divorce, the couple was more imaginative in framing their reasons. In the case of *Adam Wilson vs. We le nou Wilson,* the clerk wrote on May 16, 1888, "This suit brought for a divorce. They are supposed to be tired of one another and want new fields to wander over in the future." They were granted their divorce and presumably entered the aforementioned "new fields."[25]

Adultery figured prominently in many divorce cases, but few were recorded in such detail as that of *Louisa Schable vs. Simon Schable.*[26] Settled on September 27, 1886, Louisa Schable received custody of the children. Her husband had evidently abandoned her and failed to turn over any proceeds from the sale of stock and tools belonging to their shoe shop. Simon Schable had previously brought a divorce suit against his wife, accusing her of adultery. He eventually withdrew the charge, but his wife claimed that her reputation had been seriously damaged. She also alleged that he had committed acts of extreme cruelty against her. The court persuaded Louisa Schable to withdraw the suit, and the defendant paid her four hundred dollars. In addition, she got their house in Tahlequah, the ground upon which it stood, most of the household goods in the little house, and some articles from their other house. They mutually agreed to divorce on September 29, 1886.[27]

On November 22, 1886, a white woman, Melissa Dawson, sued her Cherokee husband, W. A. Dawson, for divorce and alimony with two thousand dollars in damages. She alleged extreme cruelty and desertion by her husband. He had deserted her a year previous to the case. She claimed that harsh and abusive words had passed between them. Apparently, scenes of abuse and anger would be followed by periods of mutual forgiveness, and they lived thus until separating in November 1884. Then in July 1885, they occupied the same bed for two consecutive nights, "renewing their marriage relations and condoning all past offenses. Her husband provided full food, clothing, and medical attendance and with provisions ample for her maintenance until mid-summer." Afterward, however, he apparently abandoned her again, and she sued. Ultimately, the judges ruled in favor of her husband; she was even required to pay court costs.[28]

When a Cherokee woman brought a divorce suit against her husband who had previously been a U.S. citizen, she could request or stipulate that he not lose his Cherokee citizenship. Frequently husbands did lose their citizenship, but it was possible to maintain it. When M. C. Wood sued her husband, Henry Wood, for divorce, she agreed that a decree of absolute divorce would be granted, that she would be granted custody of their three children, and that the citation to revoke Henry's citizenship would be withdrawn. The property settlement revealed the division of rather substantial property. As the agreement read:

> Wife gets one dwelling house and lot, one half of all the furniture, one upright piano, half of the horses and mules, wagons, buggies, hack and harness of equal value, head of hogs, 2,000 ft. of fencing on building lumber of whatever kind or character desired by M. C. Wood. The home farm on the Tahlequah and Fort Gibson wagon road 2 miles SW of town farm and improvement and tools and to pay her a $1,000-pay all outstanding debts and mercantile creditors on stock of merchandise and all costs of indebtedness on said stock and store of whatever kind and character. Pay one-half of all debts accrued or may accrue in the above styled case, except attorney debt. She gives up all future support from him for herself and child. He gets farm machinery and tools, cattle, wheat, stock.[29]

Henry Wood's economic standing perhaps protected his citizenship rights. The Nation might have been unwilling to lose such extensive resources.

As reflected in the statistics of divorces in all the Cherokee districts, women brought half or more of all divorce cases; however, of the sixteen divorces recorded in the Tahlequah district from 1884 to 1891, women initiated only five.[30]

Another case in which the husband faced forfeiture of his citizenship in the Cherokee Nation involved violence. The case was *Lizzie Lipsey vs. William Lip-*

sey in the Cooweescoowee district, which was decided on June 10, 1898. They had been separated since 1894. Lizzie Lipsey testified that her husband objected to her hiring a girl to help her with the housework. While he was drunk, he dismissed the girl, which precipitated a fight. Lizzie said that he had struck her on the head with a six-shooter and knocked her down. On another occasion he had allegedly struck her with a billiard cue that was filled with lead, causing serious injury and infection. She pointed out the scar that remained on her forehead.

Her husband testified that he suspected his wife of infidelity with a man named Doherty who was currently living with her. He reported that in their argument his wife had threatened to shoot him, taunted him by saying that their child was not actually his, and then kissed him and said the child really was his.

Lipsey continued his testimony: "Later—In the morning bout five o'clock I saw Al Doherty in the bed with my wife in the act of adultery. The next night I went to the barn and hitched up my team and drove peaceably off. She would never allow me to come and see the children or allow them to accept any presents from me." The divorce was granted for the plaintiff on June 10, 1898.[31]

The divorce records reveal that Cherokee women were highly assertive and sometimes even combative. Their matrilineal, matrilocal tradition survived in many ways, even into the late nineteenth century. They frequently were the plaintiffs in divorce suits and in suits over improvements, and they jealously guarded their sexual and economic autonomy and rights.[32] In the case of *Nancy Clay vs. Nicholas Clay,* the plaintiff sued for divorce and damages of three hundred dollars, one wagon and team, and harness. The court granted Nicholas Clay the farm and improvement on White Water, the court costs to be equally paid by both parties. Nancy Clay had been a widow when she married her husband, who was a citizen by adoption. Nancy Clay claimed her husband was "incompetent to perform sexual intercourse. He couldn't sleep with nobody— that he couldn't do anything in the way of family duty." Her husband strongly objected to his wife's testimony. Nancy Clay also alleged abusive violence: she cited a fight they had had during which blood had flowed down both of their faces. The court granted the divorce on May 5, 1887.[33]

Just as divorces created internal stresses in the Cherokee Nation during the nineteenth century, acts of violence weakened their ability to resist threats to their sovereignty. The murder trial of *Cherokee Nation vs. Willis Pettit* involved a woman, Margaret Bird, who was murdered by her son-in-law. The transcript reads: "He shot her in the eye after a quarrel. She had told him he was mean to his wife. He [Pettit] had presumably said his wife had quit him and he wanted to sell his hogs and place. He had said he was going to kill Margaret. She had threatened to have him killed before Monday morning and he said Monday morning is passed. Margaret was his mother-in-law." Pettit was found guilty on March 10, 1882, and sentenced to hang.[34]

In another case, a wife sought legal redress because of domestic violence. Eugenia Davison wrote to J. M. Bell in 1884 requesting his legal services to secure a divorce for her as a result of her husband's violence against her. She wrote:

> I will take the plesher to drop you a few lines in the regards of getting me a divorce from Mr. W. A. Patezold. We have bin apart ever since last March the 1st, I cannot live with him any longer he slapes and cuffes me around like a dog and threatens my life and all so some of the Cherokees down there[.] [H]e said they was 4 or 5 he is going to kill before he leave the Nation and I know the ones to and that ain't all I know bout him. Pleas put this in next cort[.] [W]rite as soon as you get this and let me know if you can assist me.[35]

These incidents of murder and domestic violence were lightning rods for internal struggles. Another indication of a stressed Cherokee society was the increased occurrence of rape. The court records describe some rape cases in detail, and an analysis of these cases reveals a pattern in the attacks and the convictions. The patterns of harsh convictions were quite distinct from those of similar suits in U.S. courts during this period. The Cherokee courts only had jurisdiction over those offenders who were Cherokee citizens. Judge J. B. Mayes presided over a rape case on November 8, 1876, that resulted in a conviction and a sentence of fifteen years in prison. The prisoner had waylaid the plaintiff and caught her by the river. As she tried to cross the river, the prisoner caught her and led her out of the water. Chow yee kah testified in court regarding the attack: "He said you have been refusing my advances, and says now I am going to have it my way. Prisoner then took his leg and tripped me down, and then I fell and he then fell on top of me. He violated my person and committed a rape on my person. He done what he started to do. He had been in the habit of staying all night at my house, and crawling to bed to me at night, and I would tell him to go away and he would go away."[36]

The other rape case that is discussed in some detail was brought by Patsy Johnson. The victim testified:

> I was going home in the evening. Willie overtook me and halted me but I did not stop and he overtook me and catched hold of me and having a

stick in my hand I wore it out over him and then he catched me and throwed me down. I kept on fighting him[.] [F]inally he got hold both of my hands and he let go one hand and struck me with the other hand twice when he throwed me down. He hurt me in the side and the right side and from the bruises I received I was unable to do any work for one week after. I done all I could. He overpowered me and committed the crime of rape. He told me not to cry and he came on toward Nivenses. And I went on home that's all.

When questioned, Willie Riley, the defendant, admitted to having had sexual intercourse with Johnson more than once. He said that he was not married to her, and he had never heard that Johnson was a common prostitute. He told the judges that previously she had freely consented to have sex with him. The court ruled in her favor and convicted Riley, sentencing him to ten years in prison and hard labor.[37]

Another rape case, *Cherokee Nation vs. Fox Daugherty,* was reported in some detail, although its outcome is uncertain. The woman testified: "I was laying on the bedstead when he [Fox Daugherty] committed this rape. When he committed the rape upon me he did not get through. When I cried he ran off. Fox was in between my legs when I waked up and he got into me and I knew it." Then as she got up, she recognized him. No verdict is recorded.[38]

In the collection of highly detailed records, there are five rape cases and two attempted rape cases. In two high-profile cases, the defendants were found guilty and sentenced from ten to fifteen years in prison. One defendant was found not guilty, and three were dismissed. The disposition of one of the cases is not recorded. The harsh penalty for rape indicated how heinous the Cherokees considered the crime. Yet the small number of cases suggests that Cherokee women may have been reluctant to bring such charges to public attention. Another complication involved jurisdictional problems, because Cherokee courts did not have the authority to try U.S. citizens, and those offenses would thus have had to come before a federal court. For this reason, if a U.S. citizen were accused of raping a Cherokee woman, he would be tried before a U.S. court.

Cherokee women often responded to rape, domestic violence, desertion, and adultery through legal action. Because they had lost political power since the passage of their constitution and because the Civil War had further undermined the traditional clan functions, the Cherokee women's resort to the legal system was essential. Fortunately, the courts delivered verdicts that reflected an evenhanded approach to both men and women. Cherokee women maintained their property rights and custody rights; however, the courts did not give preferential treatment to mothers in disputes. The court records often reveal contested meanings of gender arising from the crises of removal and the Civil War.

The matrilineal kinship structure of the Nation was gradually shifting to a patrilineal structure. This was reflected in the fact that men were working more in the fields, people were not always adhering to clan marital restrictions, and biological fathers were beginning to assume the roles previously performed by the mothers' brothers. Yet many Cherokees resisted these changes as seen in the growth of traditional societies such as the Keetoowahs.[39] We have seen examples of the pressures within the Cherokee Nation for women to adopt white middle-class respectability, gentility, and language. On one side of this struggle were Cherokees who retained to a large extent traditional values regarding gender, sexuality, and spirituality. On the other side of the struggle were individuals who became nearly totally assimilated into the white culture. In addition, there were black Cherokees and former slaves who embraced white values such as Christianity, in part to distance themselves from their bondage. Joseph Epes Brown described this continuum of change: "Within this spectrum of multiple possibilities there are examples across groups as well as within particular groups, of near-total retention of traditional values at the one end of the scale to near-total assimilation at the other end. The vast majority of groups or individuals, however, probably lie in the mid-range and generally represent a more or less synthetic reassemblage of Indian and American values, always with the retention, however, of a remarkable degree of traditional Indianness."[40]

Cherokee women who were in the upper class increasingly viewed education as a vehicle of survival and adopted many of white society's Victorian values of morality, culture, and progress. They cultivated the domestic arts and outward symbols of gentility and respectability from their style of dress to the ways in which they furnished their houses. However, just as the earlier adoption of spinning wheels and calico dresses did not mean that Cherokees stopped strongly identifying with their own culture, so too, this later acculturation did not indicate an eradication of traditional ways. However, after the Civil War Cherokee women could no longer depend on black women to do their domestic work, and they lacked the wealth to afford gentility. African American women confronted discrimination and destitution and fought for their share in the Cherokee Nation's land and treasury. In the post–Civil War period no consensus emerged within the Cherokee Nation regarding meanings of gender. At the same time, the U.S. government's concerted campaign to dispossess the Cherokees of their land and tribal sovereignty continued unabated, testing as never before the resiliency of tribal identity and values.

III
Crisis of Allotment

6
Allotment

Though every treaty, including the Hopewell treaty of 1785 to the 18th treaty of 1866 were repudiated and treated as a scrap of paper, the greatest outrage of all time was committed by Congress in 1893 when it passed the Act authorizing the Dawes commission.

Daniel Coodey Ross, Indian-Pioneer History Collection

After a generation of systematic reduction of the Indians' property by robbing through the courts and consumption through the Bureau, and progressive degradation of the Indian spirit by the destruction of native institutions and the substitution of a benevolent despotism, it began belatedly to dawn upon those who were responsible for the policy that the Indians were not exactly prospering under its execution.

Angie Debo, *And Still the Waters Run*

On June 16, 1906, Oklahoma Territory and Indian Territory were jointly admitted to the Union as the state of Oklahoma. On November 16, 1907, in Guthrie, a symbolic marriage occurred as part of the inaugural ceremonies for the new state government. A nearly white Cherokee woman in a stylish dress "wed" a white businessman of Oklahoma City.[1] Governor Haskell applauded the union of the Indians, the original owners of the land, and their white neighbors into the new state. The red and white stripes of the American flag symbolized, he said, "the red and white man under the azure sky." Ironically, the seal of the Oklahoma Territory portrayed a frontiersman holding the hands of an Indian, an industrial scene and a hunting scene in their respective backgrounds. The figure of justice and her balanced scales appeared between them. Despite the imagery of joint ownership of statehood, according to a census in 1907, Indians numbered only 101,228 persons in the Five Civilized Tribes out of the state's population of 1,414,177 residents.[2]

The crises of removal and the Civil War had exacerbated tensions over meanings of gender. Moreover, Cherokee women had always been closely tied to the land because, traditionally, they owned and farmed the land. By the time of removal, Cherokee women had already been expanding their roles by adopting new technologies such as the spinning wheel and loom, and Cherokee men, whose hunting lands had been drastically reduced, were participating more in the farming activities with the women. When they arrived in Indian Territory they established small farms that were worked by both women and men.

During the Civil War, Cherokee men became soldiers, and the Cherokee Nation became a community of primarily women and children. Thus Cherokee women who did not have to become refugees were able to reestablish their ties with the land as farmers out of necessity. Some were assisted by their slaves or former slaves. In the aftermath of the Civil War, the U.S. government abrogated their treaties with the Indian nations in their desire to acquire more Indian land for white settlements and economic development by railroad, coal, and mining companies. The abolition of the Cherokees' communal ownership of land and the official termination of tribal government caused the most profound change of the three crises, further revealing contested meanings of gender.

Prior to the admittance of Oklahoma into the Union, eastern philanthropists had joined with railroad and mining officials to push for allotment of Indian land and to promote the Dawes Act, which was passed on February 8, 1887. The chief provisions of this act were to grant "160 acres to each family head [male], eighty acres to each single person over eighteen years of age and each orphan under eighteen, and forty acres to each other single person under eighteen." In addition, "a patent in fee would be issued to each allottee," which would be held in trust by the U.S. government for twenty-five years. This was a measure intended to prevent its being sold or encumbered during the period of twenty-five years. Moreover, allottees could receive citizenship if they abandoned their tribes. American Indian women in tribes covered by the Dawes Act who married white men received allotments. The Dawes Act did not apply to the Cherokees, but the U.S. government planned the allotment of Cherokee land and began the process with the later passage of the Curtis Act in 1898.[3] Thus the legislation codified Indian men as heads of households, and although married Indian women eventually were given allotments, profound changes occurred regarding gender identities. This discrepancy between men and women's allotments ran counter to matrilineal traditions. The policy of viewing Indian men as heads of households was a conscious effort to encourage patriarchal family structures, undermining women's power. Under the amendment, married women received the same allotment as single older children over eighteen. In both cases, the allotment policies severely destabilized Indian families. For example, theoretically, children could take their allotments and seek to become independent of their parents. However, children ceased to be a responsibility and became sources of revenue through their allotments.[4] Although the

Dawes Act did not apply to the Cherokees, the general U.S. policy was to extend allotment to all the "Civilized Tribes."

The implementation of the allotment policies and the Curtis Act, which officially abolished tribal governments, undermined women's traditional association with the land and severely disrupted clan and familial relationships. The enforcement of these policies occurred in the midst of fierce resistance by many Cherokee women and men. However, a surprising number of women, especially elite Cherokee women, supported allotment and statehood, because they thought that the Cherokee Nation could not effectively deal with the problems of violence and alcohol.

The Report of the Commissioner of Indian Affairs, October 1, 1889, presented the federal government's policy of allotment:

> The Indians must conform to "the white man's ways," peaceably if they will, forcibly if they must. They must adjust themselves to their environment, and conform their mode of living substantially to our civilization. This civilization may not be the best possible but it is the best the Indians can get. They can not escape it, and must either conform to it or be crushed by it. . . . The tribal relations should be broken up, socialism destroyed, and the family and the autonomy of the individual substituted. The allotment of lands in severalty, the establishment of local courts and police, the development of a personal sense of independence, and the universal adoption of the English language are the means to this end.[5]

Powerful interests such as homesteaders, land companies, and railroad companies supported this position, seeing allotment as a means to gain large areas of Indian land by legal means.[6]

Debo characterized the general effect of allotment as an "orgy of plunder and exploitation probably unparalleled in American history."[7] What difference did gender make in the allotment process? Why was common ownership of land central to Cherokee identity and survival? What were the goals and consequences of allotment on Cherokee traditional values, gender relationships, and sovereignty? The crises of removal, the Civil War, and allotment of Cherokee land in Indian Territory undermined tribal sovereignty, destabilized gender and family relationships, and led to impoverishment and dispossession. Moreover, allotment failed to accomplish its stated goal of assimilating Cherokee people into white society. The policy aimed to substitute individualism and individual autonomy for the Cherokees' ethic of harmony and communal land ownership. The Cherokees resisted allotment through a variety of ways: by stalling and refusing to negotiate with the Dawes Commission, by refusing to enroll in the program, and by revitalizing their traditional ceremonies. Nevertheless, through the Dawes Act, the U.S. government relieved the Indians of almost two-thirds of their land between 1887 and 1930, even requiring the tribes to pay for surveying and allotting.[8] The rationale for the policy of allotment was to civilize the Indians; the true motive was greed and its aim was to dispossess them of their land.[9]

Reformers supported the allotment of Indian land because they believed that the virtue of hard work could only be taught through the individual labor needed to maintain private homesteads.[10] The Women's National Indian Association was formed in 1879 to help the plight of the American Indians. Within a decade, they had seventy local branches and were closely affiliated with the Women's Christian Temperance Union and the Protestant churches. In addition to their educational and missionary activities, they became focused on political reform and presented a petition with one hundred thousand signatures to Congress, urging the strict observance of treaties with the Indians. They also began to endorse allotment of lands in severalty. Likewise, Helen Hunt Jackson, author of *A Century of Dishonor*, advocated dividing Indian lands into individual or family plots. She also supported the establishment of schools to prepare the Indians to manage their property wisely.[11]

In 1883 an eastern humanitarian group began to meet annually at Lake Mohonk, New York. Senator Henry L. Dawes, who later authored the allotment bill, gave an address at the third meeting. The conference, organized by Albert K. Smiley, a Quaker, strongly lobbied for the abolition of tribal governments, the granting of U.S. citizenship to Indians, and the division of communal land holdings.[12]

The Indian Rights Association, an outgrowth of the Lake Mohonk group, adopted a platform for the uplift of Indians that included allotment. Eastern humanitarians, then, rather than greedy western interests, were responsible for pushing through the Dawes Act. They fervently believed that communal landholding was an obstacle to the civilization of the Indians.[13] Notwithstanding, when the Board of Indian Commissioners asked forty-nine Indian agents about the allotment policy in 1885, not a single one believed that the Indians in their areas were ready for allotment, and more than half doubted that such a policy could be successful.[14]

On January 17, 1881, principal chief D. W. Bushyhead, an opponent of allotment, reiterated the importance of Cherokees' holding land communally when he said: "The Constitution and laws of the Cherokee Nation make its domain the common property of the Cherokee people, wisely intending that the benefits from the same, and making the homes of our people inalienable. There is no doubt but this is the true system of government for the protection of the poor and helpless in the continued possession of their homes—[h]ence we have no paupers. There is not a citizen of the Cherokee nation but who can have a piece of land that he and his posterity can hold in perpetuity."[15] Their concept of "use ownership" prevented destitution within the community because it ensured an equitable distribution of property. Although the tribe held the land in common, individual tribal members could control the use of a plot of land by clearing it. So long as they continued to use it, the property was removed from the communal domain. Still, the remaining lands were open to all for hunting, fishing, and gathering wood.[16]

Despite the Indians' commitment to communal land ownership, the commissioner of Indian Affairs, John D. C. Atkins, insisted: "They must abandon tribal relations; they must give up their superstitions; they must forsake their savage habits and learn the arts of civilization; they must learn to labor, and must learn to rear their families as white people do, and to know more of their obligations to the Government and to society."[17] Still, the delegates of the Chickasaw, Creek, and Cherokee nations continued to oppose allotment and support communal land tenure. They appealed to the president of the United States when the Dawes Act was being considered and continued to embrace the logic then expressed:

> Ownership of lands in common has been a part of tribal policy of the Indian from time immemorial. It is with them a religion as well as a law of property. It is based upon peculiarities and necessities of the race, which cannot be ignored without the gravest perils to the people. In the transition of any race from the savage state to civilization, the highest welfare of the people can be secured only by a common ownership of the soil. Ownership in severalty must necessarily result in the acquisition of the great body of the lands by a few strong and unscrupulous hands, with poverty and misery for the masses of the people.[18]

After years of apprehension and delay, the Cherokees in Indian Territory had no choice but to respond to allotment. Even though the Dawes Act did not directly affect the Cherokee Nation, the commission began its operation to enroll Cherokees as early as 1896.[19] Because Cherokee women did not assume public roles in the struggle, we must look to oral histories to discover their views and actions during the period of allotment. They were not passive victims; many of them opposed and resisted allotment. Minnie L. Miller characterized some of their reactions: "Many Cherokees were grieved, many never enrolled, and many did enroll who were not entitled to do so. This was another time in the history of the Cherokees where the white man laid the foundation to take from them their lands, their homes and all that they held dear and their tribal laws under which they had lived for a century."[20] Mary Cobb Agnew recalled white people calling the Cherokees barbarians and half-wits and remembered white men coming to enroll everyone because, presumably, the Indians did not have the capacity to attend to their own business. At the same time, she recalled resenting the giving of land to freedmen.[21] Mary J. Baker recalled that some Indians who received land should not have and that some who were entitled to allotments never got them. "Many times," she said, "this was the fault of the fullbloods because they didn't enroll, but they did not approve of the enrollment and could not be made to understand it and did not believe that it would ever be done." Through their resistance, many of the more traditional Cherokees thus ended up landless.[22]

Others were ambivalent about whether to enroll. For example, Harvey Chaplen recalled that his two surviving brothers, Daniel and Thomas Chaplen, headed to Muskogee in order to enroll for their allotments. After traveling for two days, they returned home without enrolling.[23] Nick Comingdeer said that allotment renewed the hatred that existed when the treaty Cherokees joined the Confederacy during the Civil War. After the war, the treaty Cherokees joined the Downing Party, the group that supported the law to begin allotment among the Cherokees.[24] Bird Doublehead claimed, "At the time allotments were made each Indian on the roll was allotted three hundred and twenty dollars worth of land." Doublehead received $360 in 1896 at Muskogee as an old settler's payment; his strip money for the sale of the Cherokee Strip in 1893 was $265.75.[25] Mary Gott claimed that the Cherokee land was appraised at $.50 to $6.00 per acre.[26] Running through the interviews of the Indian-Pioneer History Collection is the sentiment voiced by Benjamin Knight: "The Cherokees never were in favor of the railroads or the allotment of land. The railroad bill was passed by the legislature without the consent of the majority of the common people." Knight claimed that when allotment was put to a general vote of the Cherokee Nation, the dissenting Nighthawks did not vote, and thus the bill passed.[27]

Traditional Cherokee men and women opposed the allotment policy. Members of the Keetoowah Society were especially active in their resistance. The Keetoowah Society was very strong from 1859 to 1889. Only full-blooded Cherokees could be members, and they had to withdraw from any other society or lodge. The February 15, 1876, resolution stated their main objective: "The intention . . . we should not become citizens of the United States." The Keetoo-wahs peacefully resisted the allotment of land in severalty at the turn of the century. Central to the Keetoowah Society were the Sacred Fire, brought to the West on the Trail of Tears and believed to have never died out; the White Path, the path of peace; Cherokee traditional spirituality and ceremony; and the an-cient Sacred Wampum belts, woven from wampum shells telling the history and traditions of the Keetoowahs and the Cherokee Nation.[28] The Creek, Chero-kee, Choctaw, and Chickasaw "irreconcilables" established the Four Mothers Society that had as many as twenty-four thousand members at the time. Be-ginning perhaps as early as 1895, the Four Mothers Society remained active in 1906. Monthly dues of one dollar for men, twenty-five cents or more for the women, and five cents for the children supported the organization. At least some of the members kept paying dues from 1895 to 1915, and most likely a long time after that.[29] Both the Four Mothers Society and the Keetoowah So-ciety sought to return to the traditional matriarchal and matrilineal traditions and ceremonies of the Cherokee Nation. Thus they sought to restore Cherokee women's power and gender equivalence within the Nation. These goals were inextricably connected with their resistance to abolishing communal owner-ship of land.

The Four Mothers Society was formed at Sulphur Springs in the Illinois dis-trict, and, like the Keetoowah Society, it was based on ancient ceremonial tra-ditions practiced by the southeastern tribes. The name of the organization is highly significant as it honors the mothers of the tribes. Cherokee mothers were believed to be direct descendents of Selu, the Corn Mother. The Sacred Fire is the physical manifestation of the life-giving Sun, the Creator. The members who were from the Natchez, Cherokee, and Muscogee (Creek) Nations orga-nized to fight the allotment of tribal lands and assimilation into the non-Indian world. Redbird Smith, who had been an important member of the Kee-toowahs, became involved with the Four Mothers. They revived the Green Corn ceremony, the Cementation ceremony (Friends Made), New Moon cere-monies, and held stomp dances. As we saw earlier, the Green Corn ceremony honored Selu, and the stomp dance reinforced the authority of the clans and the traditional power of Cherokee women.

The stomp dance is very heavily gendered. Seven shelters, representing the matrilineal clans of the Cherokee Nation, are set up, and women cook and serve food to all who come. This practice expresses the traditional hospitality ethic. Women and men alternate in the dance around the fire, with the men singing and the women setting the rhythm of the dance. Thus, the dance cannot take place without the presence of both sexes. The Four Mothers are still active in their ceremonial grounds in the Muskogee (Creek) Nation. The Four Mothers Society has existed along with the Keetoowah Society for more than a century. The main stomp dance ceremonial center of the Four Mothers Society was at Wauhillau Mountain in Adair County, Oklahoma, as late as 1990.[30]

Despite their common goals and their desire for unity, factionalism plagued the Keetoowah Society and the Four Mothers Society. Disagreements arose over whether the societies should be primarily religious or political. Factionalism was especially intense between 1891 and 1901. When the Keetoowahs met at Moody's Spring near Tahlequah many of them were resigned to the fact that allotment was the only choice they had. Redbird Smith refused to give in, and he and other members of the Keetoowahs broke away to form the Nighthawks.[31]

The Keetoowah Society officially incorporated without the Nighthawks in 1905. As many as five thousand Cherokees had resisted enrollment with the U.S. government by 1902, and the Indian agents began arresting the leaders, including Smith. In 1902 the Nighthawks broke with the Four Mothers, because Smith wanted them to be more Cherokee and less Natchez in practice.[32]

Smith, a Cherokee full-blood, showed the U.S. senators a photograph of the original patent to his tribe and presented an eagle feather that his great-grandfather had received at the negotiation of the removal treaty. He said:

> I say that I never will change; before our God, I won't. It extends to heaven, the great treaty that has been made with the Government of the United States. Our treaty wherever it extends is respected by the Creator, God. Our nations and governments all look to our God. . . . I can't stand and live and breathe if I take this allotment. Under the allotment rules I would see all around me—I see now all around me and all the Indians—people who are ready to grab from under us my living and my home. If I would accept such a plan I would be going in starvation. To take and put the Indians on the land in severalty would be just the same as burying them, for they could not live.[33]

Smith, among other resisting Cherokees, did eventually enroll with the U.S. government.

Cherokee women played a vital role in resisting allotment, but they did not participate in the formal negotiations. Yet, because Cherokee women were members of the Keetoowah and Four Mothers societies, they had a voice in the struggle against allotment. However, Cherokee men filled the leadership positions, even in these traditional organizations. Despite this, the organizations were influential in restoring women's traditional respect and power within the Cherokee Nation through the revival of ceremonies.

Sometimes resistance brought impoverishment. When Indians refused to register their choices, the Dawes Commission selected land for them. When they were sent their certificates and patents, a number of Indians sent them back. Even as late as 1912, approximately two thousand Cherokees, primarily full-bloods, refused to claim their allotments. They lived in the "Cherokee hills" in extreme poverty but refused per capita payments that represented their share of the final division of their property.[34]

James Muskrat of Vinita, a Cherokee full-blood, served as an interpreter for an enrolling party sent into the hills by the Dawes Commission. In 1905 he told an interviewer for *The Vinita Chieftain* that about two hundred Indians had been found who had not filed on land and who were not on the current tribal rolls. He said that many others refused to enroll and were opposed to both allotment and the destruction of tribal relations. They opposed the federal government at every step. The paper gave an account of a full-blood who owned a fine farm but refused to file on it. When a freedman went to the land office and filed on the place, the full-blood refused to enter a contest, and after nine months the freedman took possession of the Indian's home. The Indian police ejected the former owner and carried his household goods to an adjoining hillside. The reporter wrote, "The fullblood is now living in a tent with his family while the negro occupies his home." The article reflected the continuing tensions over freedmen's rights as well as the dilemma faced by traditionalists regarding whether to enroll or not.[35]

Not all full-bloods opposed allotment. In a notorious case, Red Bird Sixkiller, father of Captain Sixkiller, who won fame as captain of the Indian police, was the first full-blood to advocate allotment. He was a prominent man and a member of the Cherokee Council. He introduced a bill providing for a division of the lands, and it nearly cost him his life; the only reason that he escaped was that he virtually stood alone in his support of allotment.[36]

In contrast to Sixkiller, Daniel Gritts, a leader of the Keetoowahs, was one of the best-known leaders of the full-blood element in the Cherokee Nation, and one of the six leaders who opposed the allotment of lands to the Indians. He and the other leaders were arrested and put in jail because his followers would not enroll and because they presumably intimidated their tribespeople who wanted to do so. When they were arrested, the six Indians vowed they would stay in prison and die before they would sign the white man's roll or advise their people to do so. One Sunday afternoon, however, the commission brought them from the jail and enrolled them. Exactly why they changed their minds remains a mystery.[37]

In fact, the Snakes (Creek resisters to allotment) and Nighthawks continued underground and held a Cherokee convention in 1923 at Fort Gibson. Its goal was to restore common title of their land.[38] The irreconcilables were the most adamant opponents of allotment, but the Cherokees as a whole opposed the policy. Despite the difficulties of opposing allotment, in addition to the Keetoowahs, Nighthawks, and Four Mothers Society members, many other Cherokees tried to resist the abolition of communally-held land. The Cherokee Commission initially refused to negotiate with the Dawes Commission in 1897, but eventually, like all the other tribes, they were coerced into a meeting. No Cherokee women were present during the eighteen days of the meeting. Just as Cherokee women were not present in these negotiations, they were not members of the delegation sent to Washington, D.C., to protest the legislation. The absence of a formal role for women did not mean that they had no influence concerning the controversy, but we have little evidence that they politically asserted themselves in a public fashion as they had during the removal controversy.[39]

However, Cherokee women did agitate to preserve the capitol in Tahlequah, with its contents and grounds. An editorial titled "A Monument to Greatness," in the *Nowata Advertiser* of November 25, 1904, contained notice of the campaign being waged: "The women of the Cherokee nation are demanding that there be no forgotten past. When the rush of homeseekers from the north and east reach the Territory and a new government reigns, the Cherokee women do not want their nation forgotten. They would have the past remembered and revered."[40] Cherokee women had historically served as conservers of culture. This public expression by Cherokee women was one way in which they struggled to preserve traditions.

Because Cherokee women experienced a loss of political power with the passing of their Nation's constitution in 1827, and the authority of the clans had been lost during the subsequent years, it is understandable that they aggressively utilized the Cherokee Nation's court system in the post–Civil War period. The records reveal constant disputes over improvements on their land, indicating the pressures on Cherokees as they faced a shrinking land base and the aggressive attempts by the railroad and mining companies to seize more land. Although wills, probate records, and property disputes are less dramatic than cases involving divorce, adultery, domestic violence, and rape, they reveal details regarding the material culture of the Cherokees and insights into their economic status. Both men and women held estates of varying wealth, and an

analysis of their property sheds light on the gender dimensions of the ownership. In the 1868 case of *Betsy Pettit vs. Curry Pettit,* for example, Betsy Pettit
sued the defendant for ownership of livestock rated at the aggregate of $335.00.
In this case the court found that plaintiff Betsy Pettit had clearly established
her ownership to the property that included a yoke of oxen and eighteen head
of cattle. The court ruled accordingly and instructed the defendant to pay court
costs.[41]

Of the cases recorded from October 5, 1868, to December 3, 1875, the disposition was recorded for seventy-four; women brought eighteen suits against
men and seven suits against other women; men brought eighteen suits against
women and twenty suits against other men. In some cases, clues about the sex
of the litigants were indeterminate. But clearly during this period, women were
as likely to sue men as men were to sue women, even though overall men
brought thirty-eight suits whereas women brought only twenty-five. The majority of these cases revolved around disputes over improvements. In some
cases, confusion resulted because of the Civil War or because the owner of an
improvement left the country.[42]

The estates of Cherokee men and women tended to range in value from five
hundred dollars to one thousand dollars. For members of the elite class the
estate could have been evaluated at four thousand dollars or more. In the majority of the documented wills, the wife would leave her estate to her husband,
making provisions for her children, and the husband would do the same. W. P.
Adair's will, filed on June 2, 1881, directed his wife to provide a home and education for his daughter and to distribute the claims money (from claims made
after the war's destruction of his property) in order to provide the other children (his deceased brother Bruce's sons) with as good an education as possible.

In another case, special attention was directed to the woman's daughters.
Belle Stevens, who owned three houses, filed her will on July 9, 1896, requesting
that $5 be left to her only son and "the remainder of her estate to her three Girl
children-viz. Laura Stevens, Carrie L. Stevens, and Mary E. Stevens, and that
the same shall be held in trust for them by the executor of the will until the
said Mary E. Stevens shall become of age unless otherwise disposed of as herein
provided and then either divided between said Girls or sold by the executor and
the proceeds divided between them." She directed that the girls were to be kept
together and sent to a good school, and she further directed that her property
be sold if necessary in order to defray this expense or provide for their welfare.
She stipulated that if any of the girls married before Mary E. Stevens came of
age, that daughter's right of maintenance or education would cease. Consequently, she would have no further interest in the estate until it was finally

divided. This attentiveness to the education of daughters and other female relatives characterized many of the Cherokee women's wills. For example, in another case, on September 11, 1896, Mary E. McDaniel requested that her husband Oscar B. McDaniel pay the expenses of a college education for her niece Pemmie Cummins in a good U.S. school of record after she finished her primary education at the Female Seminary.

Peggy Rogers's estate illustrated the nature of the property and improvements of a wealthy Cherokee woman's considerable estate. Her estate's value totaled $981.75 on December 1, 1867. The inventory shows a house and a farm on the Grand River, a wagon, three featherbeds, two quilts, pillows, a bedstead, a hand saw, and a considerable number of livestock including sheep, lambs, a sow, six pigs, five bay mares, two bay studs, an iron gray horse, one mule, a mare mule, two cows, two calves, a small field, houses and farm on the east side of the Grand River, one brown sorrel horse, and the amount sold for a place on the west bank of the Grand River over the original valuation ($300). Taking into account debts, the estate amounted to $906.19.[43]

In contrast to Peggy Rogers, other women's estates were more modest, such as that of Nancy Wildcat. Her estate included two mare ponies, one mare colt, a bay horse, a bay pony, one cow, a calf, one cow, a steer, and another cow and a heifer. Her estate amounted to $270.00. Similarly, Peter Proctor's estate represented a typical example of a Cherokee's improvements. Proctor left his modest estate worth $460.00 to his wife, Nancy. It included three houses and two farms, a mule, a saddle and pots, a rifle, and a pistol.[44]

Thirty years after these probate cases and eleven years after the Dawes Act passed, the Curtis Act destroyed tribal governments in Indian Territory and abolished tribal courts.[45] Thereafter, Cherokee women and men had to resort to U.S. courts, which were composed of all white judges and juries. Even though their property rights had remained intact throughout removal and the Civil War, after allotment of Cherokee communal lands and the dissolution of their judicial system, they faced an uncertain future. After the passage of the Curtis Act on June 28, 1898, the Cherokees bargained for more favorable terms. The tribal delegates tried to secure a provision that all land would be nontaxable for thirty-five years. While the federal commissioners modified their proposal, the Cherokees obtained for their individual allottees more protection against alienation than other tribes were able to. They also stipulated that only forty-acre allotments would be given to former slaves, and they would not share in the distribution of the tribal funds.[46]

The same factionalism and class divisions that characterized the crises of removal and the Civil War emerged again as many descendants of the Treaty party's supporters favored allotment. Because some Cherokees supported the Confederacy during the Civil War, the U.S.-Cherokee treaty of 1866 was puni-tive, undermining tribal sovereignty, opening Indian Territory for the building of railroads, and coercing the Cherokees into giving land to freed slaves. When the Radical Republican goal of giving land to freedmen was realized in Indian Territory, allotment began to exacerbate racial tensions.[47]

Another major source of internal stress in the Cherokee Nation involved the opening of Indian Territory to economic development after the Civil War. The Treaty of 1866 only granted right of way for the railroad, but the Cherokees feared that, with allotment, the railroad would claim land as public domain for building roads through the Cherokee Nation. W. A. Duncan, a Cherokee, ob-jected strenuously to any land grant to the railroad. He said, "That railroad has the Cherokees in its jaws; its very teeth are dripping. Now I say let the Govern-ment of the U.S. get it out of the way." He added:

> That very request on the part of the railroad attorney makes me feel still a greater degree of dread of the tremendous paws of the beast that crushes and grinds to powder the rights of all people, not only of the Cherokee Nation and the U.S., but all the world! And then look how un-reasonable it is; their coming here in an hour when we are on the point of utter destruction—when we are now quivering at the very point of total annihilation and eternal demolition.
>
> Gasping for a breath to try to whisper a word in defense of our rights; then that great railroad comes—that indestructible monster of total dissolution—and tells us not to do anything that will embarrass their rights; that we must bend our opinions and wishes to suit theirs. They cannot fool us in any way like that. With all due deference and respect to the Chief, I would say that the railroad Co. cannot fool me like that.[48]

The Cherokees had reason to fear supporters of the Dawes Commission such as the railroads. When the railroad corporations entered Indian Terri-tory, they had been granted rights-of-way for two railroad routes, one north to south, one east to west, under the 1866 treaties.[49] The Missouri, Kansas and Texas Railroad and the Atlantic and Pacific Railroad companies crossed into the Cherokee Nation in 1870. In addition to the rights-of-way, the railroads received a land grant of twenty feet in width, as specified in the post–Civil War treaties. Although the railroads were supposed to be subject to the Cherokee trade and intercourse laws, the railroad towns that sprang up were perennial sources of trouble. The coming of the railroads increased the incidences of trespassing, theft, disease, and the building of saloons.[50]

The struggle began between corporate power and tribal sovereignty. Congress decided in 1882 to grant the Frisco Railroad a right-of-way through the Choctaw Nation on a route not stipulated in a treaty. This was a significant watershed of U.S. Indian policy in post–Civil War history. No longer would the U.S. government negotiate formal treaties with Indian tribes. Railroad building concomitantly brought a rush for mining. During the 1880s, corporate ventures dramatically escalated in cattle, oil, and mining. The corporations benefited from intertribal conflicts, inadequate enforcement of laws against trespassing on Indian land, and the federal government's unwillingness to take a stand. In addition, white settlers ignored Indian law.[51] To mount a campaign against some of the most powerful corporations was nearly impossible given the financial straits of the Cherokee Nation following the Civil War: the Cherokee Nation had $97.83 in its tribal treasury in 1866.[52]

As Indian Territory was opened up to economic development, the majority of the Indians in the region subsisted on small farms, deriving income from leasing land or from small businesses. Lawyers, doctors, and teachers composed a small professional class. More than thirty thousand persons claimed membership in the Five Civilized Tribes. From 1898 to 1907 the Dawes Commission recorded 101,506 persons on the roles. Eventually 19,526,966 acres of the Five Civilized Tribes were surveyed and 15,794,400 were allotted to tribal members. The rest was reserved for public purposes such as town sites and schools. The coal and mineral lands were reserved for tribal benefit. This process left little surplus land in the Five Civilized Tribes area to be homesteaded by whites.[53] In 1881 Indians held 155,632,312 acres of land; in 1890, 104,314,349; in 1900, 77,865,373, of which 5,409,530 had been allotted.[54] On April 2, 1903, Chief T. M. Buffington signed the first title to real estate in the Cherokee Nation.[55]

The allotment policy was a failure because it hurled the Indians into a monetary economy without the educational and technological means in which to survive. The policy of division of land with little regard for comparability in quality led to the likelihood that a family could not survive on a single plot alone. Thus they were more willing to sell a plot if they were unable to farm it profitably. Cherokees also sold allotments if their land was not arable or if the taxation burden was too high. Not surprisingly, of the 155.6 million acres the Indians held in 1881, they held only 77.8 million acres by 1900 (of which 5.4 million acres were allotted). From the passage of the Dawes Act to the New Deal policies of 1934 (which sought to reverse the policy), Indians lost an estimated

83 million acres, about 60 percent of their original 138 million acres of reservation land (a land base promised to be theirs forever). Moreover, almost half of this remaining land was arid or semiarid and lacked any irrigation.[56]

Just as in earlier crises, the Cherokee Nation was divided along class and family lines; they disagreed over allotment, economic strategies, and whether to become acculturated to white values. As the Indian Territory was opened to economic development, a small but vocal minority championed allotment, statehood, and capitalist economic policies. The allotment controversy thus awakened smoldering tribal factionalism and exacerbated racial and class tensions.

Along with most of her relatives, Sarah Watie supported allotment. Many wealthy, highly acculturated Cherokee women saw allotment as inevitable and, indeed, desirable. Her nephew, E. C. Boudinot, son of Elias Boudinot, who had been murdered because he signed the Treaty of New Echota, strongly supported allotment and saw himself as a new Indian capitalist. He edited the *Cherokee Advocate* and served as a delegate to Washington, D.C. In 1881, Boudinot received a threatening note that said, "If you remain longer than Sixty days you will do so at your own Peril. Remember the fate of the Ridge Family."[57]

Boudinot's life cruelly demonstrates the ironies of the so-called civilization program and the layers of deception practiced by the federal government. For someone who believed in the promise of the American dream of success, individualism, private property, and capitalism, it must have been disillusioning to discover that the dream was not meant for Indians. When Boudinot tried to set up a Cherokee railroad company, and again when he started a tobacco factory, the very government that demanded he embrace white values stopped his efforts. In 1867 he opened a tobacco factory in the Cherokee Nation and did not pay taxes, because he believed that an act of treaty exempted Cherokees from all taxes. But the commissioner of internal revenue seized and confiscated the factory on February 2, 1870, maintaining that tobacco manufactured in Indian Territory was liable for tax when it was taken out of that territory for sale. Fifteen years later Congress authorized the court of claims to make settlement for damages suffered by Boudinot.[58]

Boudinot's dream of Indian capitalism was not destined for fruition; the U.S. government wished to keep the Indians economically dependent, and larger interests such as the railroad and mining companies had a significant role in congressional and presidential politics. The Supreme Court had decided against Boudinot, arguing that an act of Congress could nullify a prior treaty. Boudinot was out of step with the majority of his fellow Cherokees.[59] Native-run railroads would have been a healing compromise, but the federal government wanted to destroy tribal governments as well as guarantee transportation throughout Indian Territory. Thus the railroad companies came into Indian Territory in the 1870s, followed by the coal corporations. The cattle corporations came in the 1880s, and oil companies arrived in the 1890s.[60]

From the end of the Civil War to the admittance of Oklahoma into the Union in 1907, Cherokees in Indian Territory struggled to preserve tribal sovereignty in the face of dramatic economic and political changes. Cherokee women faced the possibility of losing their property rights and being forced to comply with white moral codes and legal statutes. Nevertheless, they attempted to reconstruct a system of gender that retained many traditional values and at the same time adapted to the drastic changes in the Cherokee Nation. They lost their judicial system in addition to control and administration of their school system; they became vulnerable to economic control by the railroad and mining corporations. The major challenges in the late nineteenth and early twentieth centuries revolved around allotment, freedmen's rights, intruders, sale of the Cherokee Outlet, and the power of railroad and coal corporations. Ultimately, all efforts failed to preserve the Cherokee Nation's political institutions. However, just as they had fought relentlessly against removal, the Cherokees fiercely defended their autonomy.

The Cherokee Nation was one of the last to be allotted. All Indians, regardless of class, suffered financial loss during the allotment period. The rich lost their excess holdings, and poorer Indians experienced financial hardship from the expenses incurred for the selection of their allotments. An act of 1908 removed restrictions from 70 percent of the minors who had received allotments directly, along with any land that they had inherited from deceased allottees. Corrupt guardians and unprincipled parents sold the children's land. Many children were kidnapped right before they reached their majority and were forced to sign deeds over to relatives.[61]

In 1929, even the Board of Indian Commissioners, which had been chiefly responsible for the shattering of communal holdings, admitted that the Dawes Act had been a failure and that its overall impact had been the loss of Indians' property.[62] As in previous periods when the Cherokees confronted white society, Cherokees attempted to retain cultural structures and beliefs. Communal ownership of land was an especially crucial infrastructural underpinning on which balance within the community rested. A corollary for the white American society would have been for a foreign nation to abolish private property throughout the country and make all land communally owned.[63]

Struggles within the tribe and external political, economic, and social pressures contributed to the weakening of Cherokee sovereignty. Intermarriage became much more extensive in the post–Civil War era. In 1809, Cherokees numbered 12,395, with estimates that half of their population were of mixed ancestry. A total of 341 whites had married into the Cherokee Nation at this juncture. By 1860, there were 13,821 Cherokees by blood and 716 whites. Then, by 1890, according to a census of Indian Territory, there were 29,166 whites and 22,015 Indians in the Cherokee Nation as calculated by appearance. Naturally, appearance is an unreliable way to determine the population, but it does indicate the tremendous influx of whites into Indian Territory.[64]

Along with intermarriage, another persistent and daunting challenge facing Cherokee society was the freedman's issue. In the 1866 treaty, the U.S. government mandated that the Cherokees adopt their former slaves as members of the Nation. Although the Radical Republicans in Congress could not force the South into giving land to freedmen and freedwomen, they had the political power to do so in the Indian Territory. The Cherokees held a greater number of slaves than any of the other tribes in Indian Territory. In 1835, before removal, the Cherokees owned 1,592 slaves, and by 1860 they owned 2,511. Alone of all the slaveholding tribes in Indian Territory, the Cherokees freed their slaves during the war.[65] List after list attempted to accurately record Cherokee freedmen and freedwomen, and each roll was challenged and revised. When the Cherokee tribal rolls finally closed, Cherokee freedmen had already fought forty years to receive their rights.

By 1910, five years after the official deadline, allotment in the Cherokee Nation was practically completed. At that time, allottees had not all received their deeds. Yet 4,346,145 acres of Cherokee land had been allotted to 41,824 individuals.[66] Allotment failed on every count. Remarkably, the Cherokees survived allotment and attempted to retain aspects of their traditional culture amid the encirclement of white society and the accelerated evangelism by white churches. The division of the land promoted economic individualism, whereas federal policies continued to discourage Indian capitalist ventures. Wilma Mankiller, who was the first woman to ever hold the office of principal chief of the Cherokee Nation, wrote, "Of all the things that happened to our people at the turn of the century, I think the individual allotment of land had the most profound effect on the way we view ourselves, and on the social system of our people."[67]

The consequences of allotment for the Cherokee Nation were profound. Allotment of land in severalty further destabilized families and gender identities and ultimately impoverished many Cherokees, dispossessing many of land altogether. Loss of communal land holdings made them dependent on guardians if they were orphans or full-bloods, and this state of affairs opened up a period

of unparalleled greed and graft. The U.S. government had assured the Cherokees that if they "removed" from the Southeast and their ancestral lands, they
would hold the western lands in perpetuity without white encroachment. Thus
the symbolic marriage of the Cherokee woman and the businessman at the inaugural ceremonies of Oklahoma's statehood must have seemed especially
poignant for Cherokees, most of whom had no interest in becoming citizens
of the United States.

Conclusion

Many Native Americans felt utterly violated and compromised. It seemed as if the spiritual and social tapestry they had created for centuries was unraveling. Everything lost that sacred balance. And ever since, we have been striving to return to the harmony we once had. It has been a difficult task. The odds against us have been formidable. But despite everything that has happened to us we have never given up and will never give up. There is an old Cherokee prophecy which instructs us that as long as the Cherokees continue traditional dances, the world will remain as it is, but when the dances stop, the world will come to an end. Everyone should hope that the Cherokee will continue to dance.

Wilma Mankiller, *Mankiller: A Chief and Her People*

In 1984 at Red Clay, Tennessee, a few miles from where my sister lives, a reunion of the Cherokee Nation of Oklahoma and the Eastern Band of Cherokees occurred. This was the first time the two groups had come together since removal in 1838. In an emotional ceremony the two Cherokee groups lit the eternal flame, ignited by torches that had been lighted a few days earlier at Cherokee, North Carolina. Eastern Cherokee runners carried the torches along 150 miles of mountainous roads.[1] Before they returned to Red Clay, 146 years after their last council meeting in the East, the Cherokees had endured three crises: removal, the Civil War, and allotment of their lands. Still, Cherokee language and culture survive.

Rayna Green told me that she imagined writing a story in which eighteenth-century Cherokee women meet to plan their survival. While under siege by white intruders, they recognize the impending assaults on their communities and form a plan to intermarry and spread their genes to ensure that the future will be filled with Cherokees. Then someday—yes, someday—everyone will be Cherokee. Green's story reminds us that, in order to begin to understand Cherokee women in the nineteenth century and in the contemporary United States, we must see that their survival has stemmed from their sense of humor, a deep spirituality, and a strong will, as well as their extraordinary ability to simultaneously change and remain the same. Vine Deloria spoke about Indian humor in his memorable, passionate book *Custer Died for Your Sins*. He captures the subversiveness of Indian laughter and its spiritual, healing magic. Although there is a dimension of humor in the story, it is also a serious commentary on Cherokee women's history. Green pointed out that the intent of her story is twofold: to explain why currently everyone claims to be Cherokee and to have a Cherokee grandmother (but cannot explain their relationship) and to reinforce the eighteenth-century women's understanding that being Cherokee is contingent only on maternal/female ties, not on Euro-American male courts that confer standing based only on paternal/male ties. Moreover, she stated that the story rejects the implication of traitorous betrayal by women inherent in historical accounts of Cherokee women's intermarriage as well as the implied racialist discussion of "blood" and the "dilution" of Cherokee culture by intermarriage. The story rejects the nineteenth-century racialist insistence on "blood" as a quantifier of "Cherokeeness" and returns control of who is and who is not Cherokee to the mothers.[2]

Several years ago, when Bill Anderson organized a symposium for the North Carolina Humanities Council on Cherokee women, many scholars attended, including a large group of Cherokee women who composed a long row. As scholar after scholar gave splendid papers, a ripple of giggles ran across the row of Cherokees. This wave of laughter was wonderfully enigmatic. My hope is that this book will call forth not only giggles, but also some tears, even a laugh or two, and provide some insights into those remarkable ones who call themselves the Ani´-Tsa´lăgĭ´, or the Ani´-Yû ñ´wiyă´.[3]

When Cherokees met Europeans, the Europeans assumed that one of the reasons the Cherokees were uncivilized was because the women had so much power. Their power was tied to their role as producers and mothers. The Cherokee and Euro-American worldviews differed dramatically regarding appropriate gender roles, marriage, sexuality, and spiritual beliefs. As we have seen, Cherokee women were farmers, and Cherokee men were hunters. Their society was matrilineal and matrilocal, which meant that the women owned their residences and the fields they worked. Cherokee women were healers, producers, warriors, traders, wives, and mothers. They taught their daughters to cook, prepare game, do beadwork, and make baskets, pottery, and clothing. They enjoyed sexual freedom and easy divorce, but the clans maintained strict incest taboos, and in all their actions tribe members had to take the welfare of the community into account. Cherokees believed in a sexual division of labor, but the difference was associated with complementarity and equality, not hierarchy or domination. Their religious beliefs differed greatly from Christian theology. Because the public and private spheres were not highly differentiated, Cherokee

Fig. 25. Cherokee woman making basket. (Courtesy Museum of the Cherokee Indian, Cherokee, North Carolina)

women enjoyed a higher status than in those societies in which there is little permeability.

Throughout this book we have seen how Cherokee women have lost and gained power in a variety of ways but have always exercised their agency. Intended to impress the U.S. government—and especially Georgians—that the Cherokees were civilized and democratic, the Cherokee Constitution of 1827 politically disenfranchised women but preserved their property rights. Although these political changes were pragmatic, strategic moves, they also stemmed from the economic shift from horticulture and hunting to more intensive agriculture and from adoption of patriarchal values by influential elite Cherokees who drafted the legislation. Cherokee women protested removal, as they were more tied to the land than Cherokee men, but they were excluded from formal political decisions. No Cherokee women were lawyers, judges, or members of juries. Cherokee women still retained covert political power, but their formal power had diminished. We have seen that in the period from 1838 to 1907 the meanings of gender in the Cherokee Nation were contested because of differing responses to wars, economic and political transformations, adoption of new technologies, Christian evangelism, and U.S. governmental policies. Although all of these are interrelated, the economic transformations appear to be the driving force in the adaptations in gender relationships.

Cherokee adaptive strategies changed from the precontact period to 1907. We have seen that at the time of first contact with Europeans, Cherokee women were primarily the farmers and Cherokee men were the hunters. Therefore, each was essential in feeding their families. Fluctuations in either area might periodically mean more protein derived from one source or the other. Thus their adaptive strategy included the elements of both horticulture and hunting. In the eighteenth century the deerskin trade became a major aspect of their economy. A capitalist economy was emerging, but they still relied on the women's farming. A series of wars in the eighteenth century forced the Cherokees to cede a significant portion of their hunting lands. After the American Revolution, the U.S. government sought to implement change within the Cherokee Nation with a civilization program, and the government agents and missionaries became the intended implementers of change. The government helped finance the missionaries in setting up schools and missions and issued spinning wheels, looms, and plows to the Cherokees in an effort to convert the women into housewives and men into farmers.

This book has sought to uncover the ways in which Cherokee women experienced three crises in their history—removal, the Civil War, and allotment. These crises prompted changes in the role of Cherokee women, how they defined appropriate behavior, and how they related to men. Just as they fought over what it meant to be a woman, so too have historians produced contested versions of the broader story. The official story during this period was that the American colonies threw off the tyranny of England and began to fulfill its "manifest destiny" of occupying the entire continent to become a "city on the hill," an example of democracy to all the world as God's new chosen people. They brought Christianity and civilization to the Native people of the continent. This interpretation dominated the literature of Indian-white relations until the last fifty years with few exceptions. In fact, at the recent Winter Olympics in Utah, the opening ceremony included a pageant that re-created this mythic account of the settlement of the West. It began with a very beautiful, romanticized portrayal of the Indians before contact with the Europeans, and then there was an equally heroic portrayal of the courageous pioneer settlers.

On the other hand, the devil theory of Cherokee history reads very differently. An evil U.S. government forced the poor, helpless Indians to change or die. The government stole their land and made them walk to Indian Territory.

Fig. 26. Seliyeni, a medicine woman, and son, Walker
Calhoun, by Frans Olbrechts, ethnologist with the BAE
1926–27; published in Swimmer Manuscript. Negative no.
996-d-4. (Courtesy National Anthropological Archives,
Smithsonian Institution)

Although battered, they managed to rise Phoenix-like in the West. By the time
they arrived in Indian Territory, they had lost one-fourth of their tribe and had
experienced violent divisions because of the enmity between the members of
the Ross and Ridge factions. Still bitter over the Treaty party's signing their
eastern lands away, some tribal members assassinated Elias Boudinot and John
Ridge. Just as the Cherokees were recovering from removal, the Civil War began. Cherokees split over backing the North or the South. Once again, their loss
was great. Their country was devastated, homes burned, animals killed or run
off, farms grown up, and their population greatly diminished.

Then the devils returned in great numbers—intruders, homesteaders, the
railroad, mining, and coal companies, and a U.S. government voracious for
more of their land. In order to complete that civilization—and steal as much
more land as possible—the government, aided by reformers, passed the Dawes
and Curtis Acts to allot Indian land and break up communal land holdings.

Although many of these events did actually occur, all the Indians in this version are victims who are acted upon and have no agency. Change is imposed. It also proposes a neoromantic view in which only the traditional is desirable: acculturated Indians are not real Indians but are little worse than the white devils. The official story of the brave pioneers who conquered the wilderness and the tragic tale of the victimized Indians both lack ambiguity and nuance. Any model of culture change that views such a subtle process as resembling Manichean dualism misses the truth. These transformations are dialectic; they occur over time and are fought over and contested. Sometimes a new consensus is reached, but tensions remain. Acculturation was not coerced but negotiated. This does not mean that Cherokees have not suffered or been brutalized or been dispossessed of their lands. However, they have always been actors, and they have disagreed on how best to resist. Sometimes these differences were not recognized until times of crisis. They fought over gender identities; sexual division of labor; whether to remove or not; the provisions of the removal treaty; slavery; whether to side with the Ridge or the Ross group; signing the Treaty of New Echota; religious beliefs and morality; and over land, language, and education.

Continuity, not dramatic change, characterized the period before and during removal. Cherokee women were extremely skilled in adopting the new technologies of spinning wheels and looms. They employed new techniques to clothe their families. They continued to farm with more assistance from the men. With a reduced land base, Cherokee men had less game to hunt. They began to domesticate animals, utilize plow agriculture, and to develop their horticultural practices.

Regardless of the Cherokees' adaptations and acculturations, they still faced removal. But because the Cherokees were highly effective in lobbying Congress and obtaining generous support from Northeastern reformers, they were one of the last tribes to be removed from the Southeast. White women and Cherokee women had an interesting connection during this period. White women funded mission societies, which sent missionaries to the American Indians. White female missionaries attempted to convert Indian women who already had more freedom and equality than they did.

When the Cherokees arrived in Indian Territory and rebuilt their social institutions and structures, women still farmed and men cleared fields and hunted. Often slaves provided much of the labor for the reconstruction of the Nation. Because of the reduction of their land base and absence of major wars, Cherokee men's roles had changed more than women's in the period before the Civil War.

The Civil War was a watershed for cultural adaptation and struggle because of its divisiveness and its destruction of life and property. Slavery ended, which meant that freedmen and freedwomen had to become subsistence farmers or sharecroppers and that Cherokees had to adapt to the opening of Indian Territory to economic development. The railroad, mining, and coal companies might have brought new opportunities for the Indians, but the U.S. government discouraged and sometimes prevented Indian entrepreneurship. Therefore, the Cherokee Nation remained predominantly rural, agricultural, and internally involved in reconstructing their homes and institutions.

Allotment dealt the most serious blow to Cherokee women's power, their identity, and identification with the land. Intermarriage and conversion to Christianity in the twentieth century also led to more acculturation for the Cherokee Nation. Theodore Roosevelt called the Dawes Act "a mighty pulverizing engine to break up the tribal mass." Many Cherokees considered land a spiritual domain, not a possession. Therefore, they were extremely resistant to abandoning the traditional view of common ownership of land. Even as late as the 1940s and 1950s, traditional Cherokees lived in rural communities in Oklahoma.[4] Traditional Cherokees, who speak the Cherokee language and observe traditional ceremonies and rituals, still live in the mountains of North Carolina and in remote communities in Oklahoma.

Many questions come to mind at this point in the discussion: Is gender an appropriate category of analysis for Cherokee history after 1907? What did it mean to be a Cherokee woman in 1907? Have notions of gender become so diverse that there is really no such thing? What importance does this have for gender history? Is fragmentation essential to reformulation of gender? Are modern Cherokee women, who bring together diverse gender roles, the product of this process? After 1907 the Cherokee women's experiences varied. Traditional Cherokee women still lived in rural, agricultural settings of allotted land. Many Cherokee women continued to observe ancient ceremonies and participate in stomp dances. Clan affiliations were strong or weak depending on the extent of intermarriage within the families. Class, education, and religious differences shaped the Cherokee women's experiences. However, continuities persisted. For example, Cherokee women still focused on being wives and mothers, continuing a key role in production for the family. A small professional class of Cherokee women developed: those who were of the "talented tenth" and graduates of the Female Seminary. These women became teachers, nurses, doctors, lawyers, and community leaders. The Curtis Act ended the official recognition of Cherokee sovereignty by the U.S. government and officially abolished institutions of tribal government. Cultural sovereignty, however, has continued to persist, as has the Cherokees' belief in their political sovereignty as a nation. The struggle to be recognized by the U.S. government has been ongoing, and only with the Wheeler-Howard Act (Indian Reorganization Act) of 1934 was the allotment policy reversed and tribal organization again encouraged for many tribes.[5] Identities were contested and fragmented as a result of adaptations to economic and political changes, formal statehood, and presumed citizenship in the United States.

Still, by 1907 gender was an appropriate category of analysis for Cherokee history: gender was contested and fragmented by class, education, religious beliefs, and race. In many ways, contemporary gender roles within the Cherokee Nation, as represented by Wilma Mankiller and Joyce Conseen Dugan, reflect the ways in which gender meanings are reconstituted into a new synthesis of traditional and diverse gender roles: mother, wife, producer, professional, and political leader. These women bring traditional values to the position of chief, previously held by men. They rose to prominence through their work within the communities. A major insight into gender history in the 1980s and 1990s revolved around both the impossibility of grouping all women together and a growing sensitivity to women's differences: race, class, and ethnicity. The Cherokee case reveals further complexity and variation within a single tribe. This does not mean that women, by virtue of their sex, did not share experiences such as marriage, motherhood, and political and economic discrimination. Sometimes being Cherokee was more determinative than being female. In other cases, gender might eclipse ethnicity as more determinative in a particular situation.

Through the experience of three crises, the Cherokee people redefined what it meant to be a Cherokee woman. Remarkably, although they adapted to white society, they preserved their language, traditions, dances, and ceremonies. Approximately 10 percent of the tribe at the time of removal was highly acculturated; these people were often intermarried with white Americans and converts to Christianity. Yet adoption of European dress and language did not necessarily imply loss of Cherokee identity and culture. Often, their perceptions were that survival itself as a Nation hinged on selective acculturation and the appearance of civilization. Removal and the Civil War reinforced older Cherokee values and beliefs, whereas allotment dealt a serious blow to Cherokee women's power and tribal sovereignty. Equality, complementarity of gender relationships, and communal land ownership were crucial to maintaining equilibrium within the Cherokee Nation. However, even after extensive intermarriage, the allotment of Cherokee land, and a significant number of conversions

Fig. 27. Joyce Dugan, chief of the Eastern Band of
Cherokees, 1995–99. (Courtesy Museum of the
Cherokee Indian, Cherokee, North Carolina)

to Christianity, many Cherokees continue to speak their own language and observe ancient ceremonies and rituals.

In her autobiography, Mankiller spoke of her personal challenges in trying to maintain a Cherokee approach to life. The Cherokee elders called it "being of good mind." As she explains, it means one has to think positively and turn all that is handed out into a better path. For example, at the beginning of some Cherokee traditional prayers and healing ceremonies, everyone is asked to remove all negative things from their minds and to have a pure mind and heart.[6] Mankiller contended that the strategy of adopting white culture backfired. An appeasement policy failed to satisfy anyone. She wrote: "As a result, the strength of our people diminished especially given the increased influence of the mixed blood population, which also greatly changed the status of Cherokee women. The clan system and time-honored practice of descent through maternal lines began to erode. The Cherokee Constitution further limited women's rights by excluding them from government offices and prohibiting them from voting. Cherokee women were expected to become subservient and domesticated like white women who were home oriented."[7] In the areas of production

Fig. 28. Wilma Mankiller, chief of the Cherokee
Nation of Oklahoma, Tahlequah, Okla., October 12,
1991, C. R. Cowen Collection, no. 19687.IN.FC.1.1.11.
(Courtesy Archives and Manuscripts Division,
Oklahoma Historical Society)

and reproduction Cherokee women adapted to challenges from white society,
the government, and missionaries, and cultural persistence outweighed the loss
of Cherokee identity during the period from 1838 to 1907. Nevertheless, meanings of gender changed and were contested.

Only in the late twentieth century, with a return to Cherokee women's original position of visibility at negotiations, have we seen a return to formal power
as well as covert power. Cherokee women have reclaimed their power, as the
elections of Mankiller and Dugan demonstrate so brilliantly. Beloved women
such as Nancy Ward might also be war women, because war women probably
became beloved women after menopause. Beloved women were elders who
were revered for their wisdom and spiritual power. Mankiller and Dugan did
not come to their power in exactly the same traditional ways as the beloved
women, but they came to their power metaphorically. They sought to reestab-

lish balance and harmony for men and women. Mankiller and Dugan reflect the contemporary "negotiated response" to varying meanings of gender within the Cherokee Nation. As leaders, they also reveal the fact that even today Cherokee women have a different status than in mainstream American society. They combine traditional roles of women as wives and mothers with the roles of producers and leaders in the public sphere. Again the private and public spheres are not highly differentiated.

Both Mankiller and Dugan won the admiration and respect of their constituents through their dedicated work in the community. Before being elected as principal chief of the Eastern Band of Cherokees in 1995, Dugan was the director of education in the Qualla Boundary. Although there had never been a female chief of the tribe before, Dugan said that when she ran for chief she did not think very much about the fact that she was a woman. She believed that survival issues were more central to her than gender oppression. She believes fervently in cultural preservation, and she has promoted the study of Cherokee language and the reclamation of Cherokee lands. She called for "healing within the Cherokee community" in her inaugural speech on October 2, 1995. The community was divided over whether to pursue the venture. Dugan has worked tirelessly for better health care during her term: she was instrumental in acquiring a diabetes wellness center for the tribe, which opened on August 27, 1999. One tribal member out of three has diabetes. She spoke personally with President Bill Clinton about the urgency of action in this area. When she participated in a roundtable discussion on race at the White House she expressed her dismay that the president had not appointed an American Indian to his Initiative on Race commission. Serving as principal chief from 1995 to 1999, she faced tremendous challenges over the gambling issue. On November 13, 1997, Harrah's Cherokee Smoky Mountain Casino on the Qualla Boundary opened.[8]

In 1817 and 1818, groups of Cherokee women protested the loss of their land and removal from their ancient homeland. This was the last formal political protest against the U.S. government made by Cherokee women. On October 11, 1997, the Eastern Band of Cherokees, the Keetoowah Band of Cherokees, and the Cherokee Nation of Oklahoma came together in a moving ceremony. They were commemorating the return of sacred land. Chief Dugan was instrumental in recommending the purchase of land originally known as Kituwah, or Mother Town, a site containing burial mounds dating back to 5,000 to 6,000 B.C.E.. The purchase price of more than 3.5 million dollars for 309 acres that included Kituwha was derived largely from the gambling enterprises. Dugan spoke on that occasion about the meaning of cultural continuity: "The significance of place is not something we have learned, for we have not lost our homes because of removal. We are indeed fortunate that our ancestors worked so hard to preserve this heritage for us."[9] This land that lies east of Bryson City was occupied continuously for more than 10,000 years. Among other artifacts found there is a soapstone bowl that is over 8,000 years old. Here the Cherokees' ancestors received the clan laws and sacred ceremonies.[10] Cherokees have thus come full circle with a new configuration of gender meanings based on traditional Cherokee values of placing the good of the community above that of the individual and of honoring Cherokee women as wives, mothers, producers, and now public leaders. The private and public spheres again have merged. Another connotation of that gathering at Kituwah was the extraordinary resilience of the Cherokee people who endured removal, the Civil War, allotment of their land, and countless efforts to abolish their sovereignty. Yet, present at the occasion were representatives of the Eastern Band of Cherokees, the United Keetoowah Band of Cherokees, and the Cherokee Nation of Oklahoma, standing together at the same site as their ancestors of thousands of years, reclaiming their Mother Town.

Elie Wiesel begins his novel *The Gates of the Forest* with the following story:

When the Great Rabbi Israel Baal Shem-Tov saw misfortune threatening the Jews it was his custom to go into a certain part of the forest to meditate. There he would light a fire say a special prayer, and the miracle would be accomplished and the misfortune averted. Later, when his disciple, the celebrated Magid of Mezritch, had occasion, for the same reason, to intercede with heaven, he would go to the same place in the forest and say "Master of the Universe, listen! I do not know how to light the fire, but I am still able to say the prayer." And again the miracle would be accomplished.

Still later, Rabbi Moshe-Leib of Sasov, in order to save his people once more, would go into the forest and say: "I do not know how to light the fire, I do not know the prayer, but I know the place and this must be sufficient." It was sufficient and the miracle was accomplished. Then it fell to Rabbi Israel of Rizhyn to overcome misfortune. Sitting in his armchair, his head in his hands, he spoke to God. "I am unable to light the fire and I do not know the prayer; I cannot even find the place in the forest. All I can do is to tell the story, and this must be sufficient."

And it was sufficient.

God made man because he loves stories.[11]

The history of the Cherokees has resonance with Elie Wiesel's loving tribute to memory and the importance of stories. Cherokees have continued to tell their tales of despair and lamentation, but they also tell stories of cultural persistence and survival. The extraordinary courage and strength of the Cherokee people are sources of celebration. In my search for Caldonia, she came to represent Cherokee women's tenacious ability to survive. She was married to a white man, somehow avoided having to leave Tennessee on the Trail of Tears, and lived five more years. The mystery of her life remains, and one must imagine those five years after her kin left for the West. She may have been able to live at her husband's sawmill without being threatened. But upon her death she had to be buried outside the regular cemetery and not beside her husband. A small mountain stone inscribed, "A Cherokee Indian" marks her grave in the country cemetery and the wind blows through the wildflowers and rustles the grass above the ground where she lies.

Notes

Abbreviations

ABCFM Papers   American Board of Commissioners for Foreign Missions Archive, Houghton Library, Harvard University

CN Papers   Cherokee Nation Papers, WHC and OHS

GFC   Grant Foreman Collection

IPHC   Indian-Pioneer History Collection, Indian Archives, OHS

JHP Papers   John Howard Payne Papers, Newberry Library, Chicago

OHS   Archives and Manuscripts Division of the Oklahoma Historical Society, Oklahoma City

RG   Record Group

WHC   Western History Collections, University of Oklahoma Libraries, Norman

WPA   Works Progress Administration

Introduction

I have retained original spellings throughout the following chapters and have made no attempt to indicate errors or irregularities, as this would be distracting to readers.

1. David H. Corkran, *The Cherokee Frontier: Conflict and Survival 1740–1760* (Norman: University of Oklahoma Press, 1962), 110–11.

2. Richard White, *The Middle Ground: Indians, Empires, and Republics in the Great Lakes Region, 1650–1815* (New York: Cambridge University Press, 1991), ix.

3. David Rich Lewis, *Neither Wolf Nor Dog: American Indians, Environment, and Agrarian Change* (New York: Oxford University Press, 1994), 5. Lewis has pointed out, "Change is not just something that happens *to* someone or something, it is a negotiated *response* to the situation."

4. See especially the works of Ruth Landes, Michelle Rosaldo, Nancy Chodorow, Ruth Underhill, and Sherry Ortner. Eleanor Leacock advanced a Marxist perspective regarding Native peoples. See *Women and Colonization: Anthropological Perspectives*, ed. Mona Etienne and Eleanor Leacock (New York: Praeger, 1980). An extensive body of anthropological scholarship exists on matrilineal traditions beginning with the work by Lewis Henry Morgan. See Lewis Henry Morgan, *League of the Iroquois* (1851; reprint, New York: Corinth Books, 1962); Morgan, *Systems of Consanguinity and Affinity of the Human Family* (Washington, D.C.: Smithsonian Institution, 1870); Morgan, *Laws of Descent of the Iroquois* (n.p., [1858?]); Morgan, *Ancient Society* (New York: Henry Holt, 1877). See also Engels's classic work, *The Origin of the Family, Private Property, and the State* (1884; reprint, New York: Pathfinder Press, 1972). The ethnographies on Native women are quite extensive; for an imaginative analysis of the shift from a patrilineal to a matrilineal system, see Fred Eggan, "Historical Characteristics of Choctaw Kinship," *American Anthropologist* 39 (1937): 34–52.

5. Gerald M. Sider, *Lumbee Indian Histories: Race, Ethnicity, and Indian Identity in the Southern United States* (New York: Cambridge University Press, 1993), 280. Sider writes, "The notion of culture as 'shared values' should not be taken to be a simple fact of social life; rather, it delineates a terrain of necessary struggle. Just as the notion of class is historically meaningless unless it is understood to point toward processes of struggle and change, so also the notion of culture, of shared values, must be understood to be about who is going to share what sorts of values, in what ways, why, and with what effects." His view of culture includes "an arena of struggle not just between but within ethnic groups and classes" (285, 287). Sider pointed out that "Native peoples must continue to struggle and that these struggles must continue to divide native peoples, partly antagonistically, from one another. One reason why this is so is that none of the available strategies for coping with domination can possibly be very effective, or effective for very long. Isolation, confrontation, accommodation, opposition: all have their partial successes and their costs, their adherents and their opponents" (280).

6. Sally Roesch Wagner wrote about a similar culture that greatly influenced the early suffragists; they were able to envision gender equality by observing the Iroquois Nation in which women had autonomy and power. See her *The Untold Story of the Iroquois Influence on Early Feminists: Essays* (Aberdeen, S. Dak.: Sky Carrier Press, 1996).

7. Michelle Zimbalist Rosaldo pointed out that "perhaps the most egalitarian societies are those in which public and domestic spheres are only weakly differentiated, where neither sex claims much authority and the focus of social life itself is the home" ("A Theoretical Overview," in Michelle Zimbalist Rosaldo and Louise Lamphere, *Woman, Culture, and Society* [Stanford: Stanford University Press, 1974], 36). See also Henrietta L. Moore, *Feminism and Anthropology* (Minneapolis: University of Minnesota Press, 1988), 32, and the work of Eleanor Leacock, *Myths of Male Dominance: Collected Articles on Women Cross-Culturally* (New York: Monthly Review Press, 1981).

8. Linda Alcoff developed an insightful notion regarding "positionality" in order to rehistoricize women's experiences. See her "Cultural Feminism versus Poststructuralism: The Identity Crises in Feminist Theory," *Signs* 13, no. 3 (1988): 405–36.

9. Sherry Ortner, a prominent feminist anthropologist, argued that women's association with nature has been a source of their oppression. She claimed that since men have sought to control nature, they have also tried to control women. Moreover, Simone de Beauvoir's monumental work, *The Second Sex* (New York: Alfred A. Knopf, 1952) adopts an

existentialist, socialist approach to explain women's oppression. In de Beauvoir's view, a woman's oppression stems from her position as "the other." She implies that male roles and values are the norm, and to the extent that women diverge from them, they will be oppressed. Thus the female body is not valorized, and marriage and motherhood are seen as oppressive. De Beauvoir's endorsement of Engels's work on the role of the development of private property in explaining women's subordination has salience in the Cherokee case, as well as her emphasis on the necessity of women's economic independence as a prerequisite for liberation. Judith Butler's "performance theory," as she develops it in *Gender Trouble: Feminism and the Subversion of Identity* (New York: Routledge, 1990), is imaginative but has limited relevance for Native women, and the same holds for her "queer theory." The only aspect in Cherokee women's experiences illuminated by Butler's approach is the permeability of gender constructs as represented by "war women," women who assume masculine roles. Berdache (transsexual dressing and assumption of roles) in other tribes might be closer to her paradigm of "performing gender." For a full discussion of the major feminist theorists and feminist transformations in the United States, see Carolyn Johnston, *Sexual Power: Feminism and the Family in America* (Tuscaloosa: University of Alabama Press, 1992).

10. In describing recent research about American Indians, Nancy Shoemaker focuses on works that document their "agency." Nancy Shoemaker, ed., *American Indians* (Malden, Mass.: Blackwell, 2001), 6–7. In her splendid collection of articles on American Indian women, Shoemaker points out that recent literature acknowledges that "gender differences were crucially important in Indian cultures for organizing behavior and activities but gender was also flexible and variable." See Nancy Shoemaker, ed., *Negotiators of Change: Historical Perspectives on Native American Women* (New York: Routledge, 1995), 5. For a review of recent literature, see Carolyn Ross Johnston, "In the White Woman's Image? Resistance, Transformation, and Identity in Recent Native American Women's History," *Journal of Women's History* 8, no. 3 (1996): 205–18. For additional information on the literature in the field of Indian women's history see Rayna Green, *Native American Women: A Contextual Bibliography* (Bloomington: Indiana University Press, 1983), 199; Gretchen M. Bataille and Kathleen Sands, *American Indian Women: A Guide to Research* (New York: Garland, 1991); Ruth Landes, *Ojibwa Woman* (New York: Norton, 1971), 191; Michelle Zimbalist Rosaldo and Louise Lamphere, *Woman, Culture, and Society* (Stanford, Calif.: Stanford University Press, 1974); Patricia Albers and Beatrice Medicine, eds., *The Hidden Half: Studies of Plains Indian Women* (Washington, D.C.: University Press of America, 1983); Carolyn Niethammer, *Daughters of the Earth: The Lives and Legends of American Indian Women* (New York: Macmillan, 1977); Laura F. Klein and Lillian A. Ackerman, eds., *Women and Power in Native North America* (Norman: University of Oklahoma Press, 1995); Theda Perdue, ed., *Sifters: Native American Women's Lives* (New York: Oxford University Press, 2001); Wilma Mankiller and Michael Wallis, *Mankiller: A Chief and Her People* (New York: St. Martin's Press, 1993); Henrietta L. Moore, *Feminism and Anthropology;* Carolyn Thomas Foreman, *Indian Women Chiefs* (Muskogee, Okla.: Hoffman Print Co., 1954); Etienne and Leacock, *Woman and Colonization;* Joan M. Gero and Margaret W. Conkey, *Engendering Archaeology: Women and Prehistory* (Oxford: Basil and Blackwell, 1991); Nancy Shoemaker, ed., *Clearing a Path: Theorizing the Past in Native American Studies* (New York: Routledge, 2002); Rachel A. Bonney and J. Anthony Paredes, eds., *Anthropologists and Indians in the New South* (Tuscaloosa: University of Alabama Press, 2001); and J. Anthony Paredes, ed., *Indians of the Southeastern United States in the Late Twentieth Century* (Tuscaloosa: University of Alabama Press, 1992).

See also the works of Carol Karlsen, James Axtell, Raymond Fogelson, William Cronon, Katherine Osburn, John Demos, Fred Hoxie, Francis Paul Prucha, Mary Young, Gerald Sider, and Neal Salisbury. The works of Charles Hudson, William G. McLoughlin, and James Mooney are absolutely essential in understanding the history of Native women.

11. See J. Anthony Paredes, "Paradoxes of Modernism and Indianness in the Southeast," *American Indian Quarterly* 19, no. 3 (1995): 341–60. In this imaginative article, Paredes analyzes the misconceptions stemming from the "ethnographic present fallacy" of much scholarship. He cautions against ignoring or minimizing intra-group variations: "Where intra-group variation is acknowledged it tends to become oversimplified and moralized into such distinctions as traditionalists vs. modernists, conservatives vs. progressives, full-blood vs. mixed-blood. The full panoply of the complexity of culture change is easily lost in such binary oppositions." Paredes also reminds us that when the indigenous cultures of the Southeast first encountered the Europeans they were themselves the products of tremendous cultural changes over thousands of years. Thus indigenous people constantly constructed their cultures and were involved in ongoing negotiations with one another.

12. Theda Perdue, *Cherokee Women: Gender and Culture Change, 1700–1835* (Lincoln: University of Nebraska Press, 1998), 195.

13. Ibid., 9–10.

14. Sarah H. Hill, *Weaving New Worlds: Southeastern Cherokee Women and Their Basketry* (Chapel Hill: University of North Carolina Press, 1997), xix.

15. Ibid., xvii–xix, 321.

16. The Henry G. Bennett Distinguished Service Award Winner (presented in 1990 to Chief Wilma P. Mankiller) <http://www.library.okstate.edu/about/awards/winners/mankill.htm> (June 2002).

17. Mankiller and Wallis, *Mankiller*, 243–45, 272–73. For more on her election in 1987 see The Henry G. Bennett Distinguished Service Award Winner (presented in 1990 to Chief Wilma P. Mankiller) <http://www.library.okstate.edu/about/awards/winners/mankill.htm> (June 2002).

18. Wilma Mankiller, "Rebuilding the Cherokee Nation" (speech at Sweet Briar College, Lynchburg, Virginia, Apr. 2, 1993) <http://gos.sbc.edu/m/mankiller.html>, 12–13 (June 2002).

Chapter 1

1. William G. McLoughlin, *Champion of the Cherokees: Evan and John B. Jones* (Princeton: Princeton University Press, 1990), 35; Raymond D. Fogelson, "On the 'Petticoat Government' of the Eighteenth-Century Cherokee," in *Personality and Cultural Construction of Society*, ed. David K. Jordan and Marc J. Swartz (Tuscaloosa: University of Alabama, 1990), 170. The primary focus of this work is the Cherokees who went to Indian Territory. Some attention focuses on early accounts and studies of the Eastern Band of Cherokees because their works are invaluable in understanding traditional Cherokee myths, ceremonies, and gender expectations. I have gratefully relied on the works of scholars such as James Mooney, the most well known anthropologist to do fieldwork with the Eastern Cherokees in the late nineteenth century, Frans Olbrechts, Charles Hudson, Fred Gearing, John Finger, as well as collections in the Museum of the Cherokee Indian, Cherokee, North Carolina, and oral his-

tories of Cherokees. My sources for descriptions of Cherokee traditional beliefs also include John Howard Payne, who collected the stories and myths of the Cherokees in the nineteenth century. The Cherokee landscape of mythic space remains elusive. However, we can discern certain basic patterns of belief, ritual, and ceremony that seemed crucial to Cherokee identity for hundreds of years.

2. JHP Papers, 4:92. Members of each clan could not intermarry on pain of death (JHP Papers, 4:65, 4:270, pt. 2). Payne recorded the names of the clans as Wolf, Blind Savannah, Paint, Long Hair, Bird, Deer, and Holly. See Philip Reid, *A Law of Blood: The Primitive Law of the Cherokee Nation* (New York: New York University Press, 1970), 37. See also Harriet J. Kupferer, *Ancient Drums, Other Moccasins: Native North American Cultural Adaptation* (Englewood Cliffs, N.J.: Prentice Hall, 1988), 217–40. As Kupferer noted, the Cherokee kinship system was of the "Crow Type." The mother's lineage was the most important, but the father's lineage, mother's father's lineage, and father's father's lineage were also very significant (231). Thus they extended the kinship terms used for identifying people in the four matrilineages to all the members of the four clans (232).

3. John Ridge, Washington City, Feb. 27, 1826, JHP Papers, 8:109.

4. Reid, *A Law of Blood*, 37–48; 131–35; William Harlen Gilbert Jr., *The Eastern Cherokees*, Bureau of American Ethnology, Bulletin 133 (Washington, D.C.: GPO, 143) 245–53, Anthropological Papers, 19–26.

5. John P. Brown, *Old Frontiers: The Story of the Cherokee Indians from Earliest Times to the Date of Their Removal to the West*, 1838 (Kingsport, Tenn.: Southern Publishers, 1938), 18.

6. James Adair, *Adair's History of the American Indians*, ed. Samuel Cole Williams (1775; reprint, Johnson City, Tenn.: Watauga Press, 1930), 146–47.

7. Charles Hudson, *The Southeastern Indians* (Knoxville: University of Tennessee Press, 1976), 197–98. During the marriage ceremony, the bride and groom might also have exchanged beanpoles (cane or wood entwined with vines) to symbolize sexual union. Here Hudson is referring to southeastern Indians generally and does not specifically mention the Cherokees. In Cherokee marriage ceremonies, both the man and the woman carried blankets that were tied together during the ceremony.

8. Fogelson, "On the 'Petticoat Government,'" 166.

9. Reid, *A Law of Blood*, 117.

10. Fogelson, "On the 'Petticoat Government,'" 166–67.

11. William Bartram (1739-1823), "Observations on the Creek and Cherokee Indians," *Travels and Other Writings* (New York: Literary Classics of the United States, 1996), 544. Bartram was writing on the Creeks and Cherokees in this section; see also Fogelson, "On the 'Petticoat Government,'" 168–69. On the friendship dance, see Frank G. Speck and Leonard Broom, in collaboration with Will West Long, *Cherokee Dance and Drama* (1951; reprint, Norman: University of Oklahoma Press, 1983), 65-68.

12. Fogelson, "On the 'Petticoat Government,'" 169. Because there were no formal penalties for adultery among the Cherokees, infidelity might be punished through conjuring. When men were jealous of their wives they might seek out a medicine man for assistance. He would set his crystal and pray for information. If the woman was innocent, it never changed; if she was guilty, two persons would appear in the crystal. The medicine man would then take some flies that he had previously killed for this purpose. He then pronounced the evil that would come to the woman if she was guilty. He declared if upon open-

ing his hand one of the flies came to life, it would fly to her and bore into her abdomen. After seven days she would feel the fly's gnawing into her heart and she would die (JHP Papers, 1:36–37).

13. Ibid.

14. Rayna Green, *Women in American Indian Society* (New York: Chelsea House, 1992), 47, 51.

15. Hudson, *Southeastern Indians,* 260, 319–20.

16. Daniel Sabin Butrick, ABCFM Papers, ABC 18.3.1, vol. 11:205. Reprinted with permission of Wider Church Ministries of the United Church of Christ and the Houghton Library, Harvard University.

17. Adair, *History of the American Indians,* 131; Fogelson, "On the 'Petticoat Government,'" 174–75.

18. Mary Douglas, *Purity and Danger: An Analysis of Pollution and Taboo* (1966; reprint, London: ARK Paperbacks, 1984), 115, 138, 142.

19. This chapter relies heavily on Hudson's classic work, *The Southeastern Indians.* Recently, a lively exchange occurred between Hudson and Mary C. Churchill. See Churchill, "The Oppositional Paradigm of Purity versus Pollution in Charles Hudson's *The Southeastern Indians," American Indian Quarterly* 20, nos. 3–4 (1996): 563–93; Charles Hudson, "Reply to Mary Churchill," *American Indian Quarterly* 24, no. 30 (2000): 494–502. Approaching her critique of Hudson's work from a postmodernist point of view, Churchill claims that Hudson's interpretation is seriously flawed. According to Churchill, Hudson's oppositional paradigm fails to acknowledge the concept of complementarity as well as the positive dimensions of "pollutants." Ultimately Hudson has the last word: although he acknowledges that he regrets using the term *abominations* for *anomalies,* he never thought of them as "detested and loathsome" (496). Hudson vigorously denies that he conceived of the oppositions as "good" and "bad," and did not impute moral content to them (498). Moreover, Churchill's argument is itself seriously flawed as she does not offer a convincing alternative interpretation. The fact that Hudson draws on early observers of Cherokee culture such as James Adair, John Lawson, William Bartram, John R. Swanton, and James Mooney does not discredit but supports his interpretive framework. Douglas, whose work *Purity and Danger* informed Hudson's work, revised her analysis of purity and pollution in 1975 when she remarked that she "came to doubt that the Hebrew response of rejecting anomaly was the normal one." She began to emphasize that anomalies could be regarded as "favorable or horrifying." See also Douglas, *Implicit Meanings: Essays in Anthropology* (London: Routledge and Kegan Paul, 1975). Churchill regards this refinement of Douglas's approach as fatal to Hudson's interpretation. However, Hudson had already revealed this insight in his work when he described the ways in which the Cherokee feared and revered anomalies such as the Uktena.

20. Frank G. Speck and Leonard Broom, in collaboration with Will West Long, *Cherokee Dance and Drama* (Berkeley: University of California Press, 1951), 24–39.

21. J. P. Evans, "Sketches of Cherokee Characteristics," JHP Papers, 6:221–22.

22. Hudson, *Southeastern Indians,* 406–8; Speck and Broom, *Cherokee Dance and Drama,* 33–34.

23. Speck and Broom, *Cherokee Dance and Drama,* 38. As Speck reported after his visits in eastern Cherokee communities from 1928 to 1931 and 1934 to 1935, his informant, Will West Long, said that the Cherokees performed the dance prior to the actual appearance of Europeans.

24. Raymond D. Fogelson and Amelia B. Walker suggested another interpretation. The Booger Dance may have acted out a basic tension between old men and young men in which each fears and desires the power of the other. The masked figures may have represented travelers seeking hospitality from the assembled Cherokees, and the Booger Dance brought together old and young men so that they could experience the characteristics of one another. Moreover, the performance parodied what was foreign to Cherokee ethics. They write, "This masked drama highlights certain problematics of Cherokee life: the uncontrolled excessiveness of young men, the nagging moral authority of the elders, and the inappropriate behavior of non-Cherokees." See Raymond D. Fogelson and Amelia B. Walker, "Self and Other in Cherokee Booger Masks," *Journal of Cherokee Studies* 5, no. 2 (1980): 88–102. For an account of J. P. Evans's descriptions of Cherokee dances, see his "Sketches of Cherokee Characteristics," *Journal of Cherokee Studies* 4, no. 1 (1979): 16–20 (prepared in 1835, originally in JHP Papers, vol. 6). See also Carol[yn] Johnston, "Burning Beds, Spinning Wheels, and Calico Dresses: Controlling Cherokee Female Sexuality," *Journal of Cherokee Studies* 19 (1998): 3–17, and Sharlotte Neely, "Adaptation and the Contemporary North Carolina Cherokee Indians," in *Indians of the Southeastern United States in the Late 20th Century*, ed. J. Anthony Paredes (Tuscaloosa: University of Alabama Press, 1992), 43.

25. Frans M. Olbrechts, "Cherokee Belief and Practice with Regard to Childbirth," *Anthropos* 26 (1931): 18–19. Olbrechts continued the work of James Mooney on the Cherokees in North Carolina. The Cherokees used contraceptive measures such as *Cicuta maculata*, L.; Spotted Cowbane; Musquash Root; Beaver's Poison. A woman who wanted to put an end to her procreative abilities chewed and swallowed the roots for four consecutive days. Some informants hinted that promiscuous women used this drug, especially if they were married. One of Olbrechts's informants, Will West Long, told him that they had not heard of abortion, and the informant was horrified at the idea. See also Fogelson, "On the 'Petticoat Government,'" 173–174. For a splendid discussion of the multiple-soul concept, see John Witthoft, "Cherokee Beliefs Concerning Death," *Journal of Cherokee Studies* 8, no. 2 (1983), 68–72.

26. Ibid., 19–20. For analysis of color symbolism, see Nancy Shoemaker, "How Indians Got to Be Red," *American Historical Review* 102 (June 1997): 625–44; and Christopher Miller and George R. Hamell, "A New Perspective on Indian-White Contact: Cultural Symbols and Colonial Trade," *Journal of American History* 73 (Sept. 1986): 311–28.

27. Olbrechts, "Cherokee Belief and Practice with Regard to Childbirth," 20–21.

28. Ibid., 21–22; Adair, *History of the Cherokee Indians,* 129–30; JHP Papers, 4:280, pt. 2. Recent research tends to emphasize the taboos surrounding menstruation as indicative of women's strength. See Martha Harrison Foster, "Of Baggage and Bondage: Gender and Status among Hidatsa and Crow Women, *American Indian Culture and Research Journal* 17 (1993): 142. See also Gregory Evans Dowd, "North American Indian Slaveholding and the Colonization of Gender: The Southeast before Removal," *Critical Matrix* 3 (1987): 11–15, and Richard A. Sattler, "Women's Status among the Muskogee and Cherokee," in *Women and Power in Native North America*, ed. Laura F. Klein and Lilian A. Ackerman (Norman: University of Oklahoma Press, 1995), 218–19, for very different interpretations of gender relations in other tribes.

29. Olbrechts, "Cherokee Belief and Practice with Regard to Childbirth," 21–24.

30. Douglas, *Purity and Danger,* 69.

31. Olbrechts, "Cherokee Belief and Practice with Regard to Childbirth," 22–24. Ol-

brechts noted that some practices survived and were observed by the more conservative members of the tribe.

32. Ibid., 24–25; JHP Papers, 4:271–72, pt. 2.

33. Olbrechts, "Cherokee Belief and Practice with Regard to Childbirth," 25–29.

34. Ibid., 29–31.

35. Ibid.

36. Fred O. Gearing, *Priests and Warriors: Social Structures for Cherokee Politics in the Eighteenth Century,* vol. 5, no. 5, pt. 2, memoir 93 (Menasha, Wis.: American Anthropological Association, 1962) 2–3.

37. James Mooney, *Myths of the Cherokee and Sacred Formulas of the Cherokees* (Nashville: Cherokee Heritage Books, 1982), 242–49; Hudson, *Southeastern Indians,* 149–56; JHP Papers, 2:51–62.

38. Mooney, *Myths of the Cherokee,* 242–49; Hudson, *Southeastern Indians,* 149–56.

39. Ibid., 242–49; Hudson, 151–55. See also Fogelson, "On the 'Petticoat Government,'" 174, 176.

40. Hudson, *Southeastern Indians,* 174–75, 357, 363–64. Hudson contends that "Jealousy and ambiguity lie at the heart of witchcraft."

41. Ibid., 121, 149, 155.

42. Ibid., 366–67; Adair, *History of the American Indians,* 101–17; JHP Papers, 1:32, 43, 51, 53, 84–86; JHP Papers, 3:87–88, 94–97, 100–4; JHP Papers, pt. 2, 4:219, 227–28, 231; JHP Papers, 6:222–24.

43. Charles Hicks and Calvin Jones, "Manners and Customs of the Cherokees" *Niles's Register,* supplement to Vol. 16, Indian Nations, Baltimore, Oct. 13, 1818, CHN 095, reprinted from the *Raleigh Register.* Digital Library of Georgia Database, Galileo-Southeastern Native American Documents, 1730 1842 <www.galileo.usg.edu> (June 15, 2001). See also JHP Papers 2:85 for information on Charles Hicks.

44. For a full description of the New Moon ceremony, Green Corn ceremony, and Ripe Corn ceremony, see JHP Papers, 1:49–53, and Thomas Lewis and Madeline Kneberg, *Tribes That Slumber: Indians of the Tennessee Region* (Knoxville: University of Tennessee Press, 1958), 176–77, 180–81. Hudson described the Green Corn ceremony as practiced by the southeastern tribes generally, especially the Chickasaw and Natchez. However, the Cherokees conducted the ceremony in a similar fashion. He relies primarily on James Adair's account of the ceremony (Hudson, *Southeastern Indians,* 226–27, 365–75 (inclusive), 368, 373); Europeans called it the "black drink" because it had a dark color. However, the Indians called it "white drink" because it symbolized purity. The drink was made from leaves of a kind of holly (*Ilex vomitoria Ait.*) and drunk only by mature men. It contained a great deal of caffeine and was used as an emetic or purgative in ceremonies. See also Adair, *History of the American Indians,* 101–17.

45. JHP Papers, 1:49–53; Lewis and Kneberg, *Tribes That Slumber,* 176–77, 180–81.

46. Hudson, *Southeastern Indians,* 318, 319, 365, 368–75; Adair, *History of the American Indians,* 101–17.

47. Hudson, *Southeastern Indians,* 126; Mooney, *Myths of the Cherokee,* 256–57, 240–42. For a discussion of the proper treatment of fire in the hearth as related by Will West Long, see Witthoft, "Cherokee Beliefs Concerning Death," 72.

48. Mooney, *Myths of the Cherokee,* 319–20. For a description of the *Ulûñsû'tĭ* of the Uktena, see pages 297–98.

49. Ibid., 316–19; Hudson, *Southeastern Indians*, 175–76. Some Cherokees believed that Stone Coat and Spear-finger were the male and female manifestations of the same monster that could shape shift. See also Mooney, *Myths of the Cherokee*, 252–54. Circe Sturm presents an imaginative discussion of the meaning of blood in Cherokee culture; see her *Blood Politics: Race, Culture, and Identity in the Cherokee Nation of Oklahoma* (Berkeley: University of California Press, 2002).

50. See James Mooney, "The Cherokee Ball Play," *American Anthropologist* 3 (1890), 105–32. Mooney described the ball game as the Cherokees played it in the late nineteenth century. J. P. Evans wrote, "This is a favorite amusement with the Cherokees, and to excel in it is considered a proof of manhood, and adds greatly to a man's respectability & standing in society" (J. P. Evans, JHP Papers, 6:221–22). See also Raymond David Fogelson, "The Cherokee Ball Game: A Study in Southeastern Ethnology" (Ph.D. diss., University of Pennsylvania, 1962).

51. Hudson, *Southeastern Indians*, 408–9, 411, 418; all of Hudson's account is taken from Mooney, "The Cherokee Ball Play," 105–32. See also JHP Papers, 4:61–65, 87.

52. Ibid., 411–12.

53. Ibid., 411–14.

54. Ibid., 414–16.

55. Ibid., 416–20. See also Mooney, "The Cherokee Ball Play," 105–32.

56. Henry Timberlake, *Lieut. Henry Timberlake's Memoirs, 1756–65*, ed. Samuel Cole Williams (1927; reprint, Johnson City, Tenn.: Arno Press, 1971), 102. Timberlake appears to be the first to record women in the Cherokee stickball game. For an excellent description of the ball play and women's and men's participation, see also Fogelson, "Cherokee Ball Game."

Chapter 2

1. Moody Hall to Jeremiah Evarts, Apr. 5, 1825, ABCFM Papers, ABC 18.3.1, vol. 5:2.

2. Alice Taylor-Colbert, "Cherokee Women and Cultural Change," in *Women of the American South: A Multicultural Reader,* ed. Christie Anne Farnham (New York: New York University Press, 1997), 49–52.

3. Theda Perdue, *Slavery and the Evolution of Cherokee Society, 1540–1866* (Knoxville: University of Tennessee Press, 1970), 49, 58. Although Joseph Vann owned 110 slaves, only two other planters owned more than fifty slaves.

4. Taylor-Colbert, "Cherokee Women and Cultural Change," 49–52.

5. Reid, *A Law of Blood,* 129; Tom Hatley, *The Dividing Paths: Cherokees and South Carolinians through the Era of Revolution* (New York: Oxford University Press, 1993), 97, 220.

6. Perdue, *Cherokee Women,* 72, 75–81. A subject of debate in the literature on Indian women concerns their changing economic status. Kathryn E. Holland Braund argues that in the case of the Creek Indians, the idea of the deerskin trade's making women dependent on men is overstated. She sees Creek men and women as equal participants in the trade and does not think that it led to Creek women's subordination. She points out that before the deerskin trade, women were dependent on men for clothing because they relied on male hunters to provide leather and furs. However, men also depended on women to make the cloth into clothes and process the leather. For a splendid analysis of the impact of trade on Creek culture and gender roles, see Braund's *Deerskins and Duffels: The Creek Indian Trade with Anglo-America, 1685–1815* (Lincoln: University of Nebraska Press, 1993) and her ar-

ticle "Guardians of Tradition and Handmaidens to Change: Women's Roles in Creek Economic and Social Life during the Eighteenth Century," *American Indian Quarterly* 14, no. 3 (1990): 239–58. Claudio Saunt tends to agree that during the 1760s, Creek men and women participated equally in the deerskin trade, but he argues that when demand for raw deerskins increased dramatically in the 1780s, the young warriors took over the trade and began to exclude women, whose work was no longer essential. Creek women then began to lose economic power. Still, women farmers in the Creek Nation provided the bulk of their families' food. So, even though they may have become shut out of the deerskin trade, they remained essential to the tribal economy. See Saunt, *A New Order of Things: Property, Power, and the Transformation of the Creek Indians, 1733–1816* (Cambridge: Cambridge University Press, 1999), 143–44, 150. Karen Anderson and Mary C. Wright agree that market participation altered women's economic roles and eventually resulted in their subordination to men. See Anderson, *Chain Her by the Foot: The Subjugation of Women in Seventeenth Century New France* (New York: Routledge, 1993) and Wright, "Economic Development and Native American Women in the Early Nineteenth Century," *American Quarterly* 33, no. 5, Special Issue: American Culture and the American Frontier (1981): 525–36. Varied interpretations provide insights into the complexity of determining male and female economic status. Lucy Eldersveld Murphy challenges a declension interpretation in her work on Sauk, Mesquakie, and Winnebago women. See her "Autonomy and the Economic Roles of Indian Women of the Fox-Wisconsin River Region, 1763–1832," in *Negotiators of Change,* ed. Nancy Shoemaker (New York: Routledge, 1995), 72–89.

7. See Theda Perdue, "Women, Men, and American Indian Policy: The Cherokee Response to 'Civilization,'" in *Negotiators of Change,* ed. Nancy Shoemaker (New York: Routledge, 1995), 90–114. For an intriguing study of Indian women in the Great Lakes region, see Carol Devens, *Countering Colonization: Native American Women in the Great Lakes Missions, 1630–1900* (Berkeley: University of California Press, 1992).

8. In her highly imaginative book, *The Age of Homespun: Objects and Stories in the Creation of an American Myth* (New York: Alfred A. Knopf, 2001), Laurel Thatcher Ulrich reminds us that the ubiquitousness of homespun, the everyday textiles that ordinary women made in their households, became a sustaining cultural myth.

9. Ibid., 413–14. See also Laurel Thatcher Ulrich, *A Midwife's Tale: The Life of Martha Ballard Based on Her Diary, 1785–1812* (New York: Alfred A. Knopf, 1990).

10. Michael Paul Rogin, *Fathers and Children: Andrew Jackson and the Subjugation of the American Indian* (New York: Alfred A. Knopf, 1975), 179–80.

11. Wade Alston Horton, "Protestant Missionary Women as Agents of Cultural Transition among Cherokee Women, 1801–1839" (Ph.D. diss., Southern Baptist Theological Seminary, 1992), 15, 20–24, 32. See also William G. McLoughlin, "Who Civilized the Cherokees?" *Journal of Cherokee Studies* 13 (1988): 65.

12. See Request for Federal Road 1805, Oct. 27, 1805, Box 1, Folder 17, Document PA0002, Penelope Johnson Allen Collection, University of Tennessee, Knoxville. Johnson was a local historian of the 1930s. Ostensibly, this document was from an unidentified source directed to the Cherokees.

13. Rogin, *Fathers and Children,* 179–80, 4.

14. Roy Harvey Pearce, *The Savages of America: A Study of the Indian and the Idea of Civilization* (Baltimore: Johns Hopkins University Press, 1967), 92–93.

15. Jeremiah Evarts, "Memorandum," Apr.–May 1822, ABCFM Papers, quoted in

William G. McLoughlin, *Cherokees and Missionaries, 1789–1839* (Norman: University of Oklahoma Press, 1995), 139. See also Kupferer, *Ancient Drums, Other Moccasins*, 227, 229. Kupferer recalled the explicitly sexual content of the songs sung during the friendship dances, citing Speck and Broom who collaborated with Will West Long in research on Cherokee dance and drama. They recorded bawdy lyrics to the songs. In one such song, the dancers were interpreted as singing, "We are going to touch each other's privates." Moreover, exchanges among women in the same clan were openly sexual. They routinely commented on such subjects as sexual prowess or observations on genitals. Missionaries who spoke the Cherokee language may have been shocked by their open discussions about sexuality as well as by their behaviors.

16. Colonel Return J. Meigs to Mr. Trott, Answers to inquiries relating to the Cherokees, Aug. 1817, Galileo-Southeastern Native American Documents, 1730–1842, Document PA0001, Penelope Johnson Allen Collection.

17. McLoughlin, "Who Civilized the Cherokees?" 65.

18. See William G. McLoughlin's *Cherokees and Christianity, 1794–1870: Essays on Acculturation and Cultural Persistence*, ed. Walter H. Conser Jr. (Athens: University of Georgia Press, 1994), 67–68, and his "An Alternative Missionary Style: Evan Jones and John B. Jones among the Cherokees," in *Between Indian and White Worlds: The Cultural Broker*, ed. Margaret Connell Szasz (Norman: University of Oklahoma Press, 1994), 99–102. McLoughlin's many splendid books on the Cherokees provide a rich, textured view of their responses to Christianity. See especially his *Champion of the Cherokees, Cherokee Renascence in the New Republic* (Princeton: Princeton University Press, 1986), and *After the Trail of Tears: The Cherokees' Struggle for Sovereignty, 1839–1880* (Chapel Hill: University Of North Carolina Press, 1993).

19. Penelope Johnson Allen, "History of the Cherokee Indians," Manuscript, 1935, p. 432, Special Collections, Chattanooga Hamilton County Library, University of Tennessee, Knoxville. Throughout this book I use the terms "full-blood" and "mixed blood" as McLoughlin and Finger do. Perdue strongly objects to the continued use of these terms because they might convey racist or racial overtones. I am in no way trying to perpetuate such a meaning of these terms, but I find them descriptive of the ways in which Cherokees themselves characterized blood quantum. The terms are in no way precise, however, in determining who was progressive and highly acculturated and who was traditional.

20. Allen, "History of the Cherokee Indians," 441. After removal, Boot continued to preach in the West. Allen described the establishment of the Methodist Missions in the nineteenth century: "Wills Valley: Dixon C. McLeod; John Spears, interpreter, John F. Boot, a Cherokee; Conesauga: Green M. Rogers; Young Wolf and Edward Graves, interpreter; Valley Town; Robert Rogers; William McIntosh, Turtle Fields, interpreter; Chatooga: Joseph Miller; Mt. Wesley and Asbury: James J. Trott; Coosawatee: Jacob Ellenger, Joseph Blackbird, interpreter; Selacon: Greenbury Garrett; The Agency: William M. McFerrin; Lookout: Nicholas D. Scales" (Allen, "History of the Cherokee Indians," 435).

21. William W. Crouch, "Missionary Activities among the Cherokee" (master's thesis, University of Tennessee, 1932), 96–99, 107, 111–12, 130, 144, 153, 155–56.

22. Rufus Anderson, ed., *Memoir of Catharine Brown: A Christian Indian of the Cherokee Nation*, 3rd ed. (Boston: Crocker and Brewster, 1828), 13–15.

23. Robert Sparks Walker, *Torchlights to the Cherokees: The Brainerd Mission* (1931; reprint, Johnson City, Tenn.: Overmountain Press, 1994), 178.

24. Ibid., 118, 179, 182.

25. Anderson, *Memoir of Catharine Brown,* 26.

26. Ibid., 28, 39, 41, 48.

27. Daniel Sabin Butrick, Journal, Jan. 27, 1820, ABCFM Papers, 18.3.3, vol. 4–5, written shortly after Catharine and her brother David arrived.

28. Walker, *Torchlights,* 183; Anderson, *Memoir of Catharine Brown,* 100.

29. Anderson, *Memoir of Catharine Brown,* 107, 111.

30. Ibid., 98, 111, 132, 177.

31. For this perceptive interpretation of Brown, see Perdue, "Catharine Brown: Cherokee Convert to Christianity," in *Sifters: Native American Women's Lives,* ed. Perdue (New York: Oxford University Press, 2001), 77–91.

32. Bernard Sheehan, *Seeds of Extinction: Jeffersonian Philanthropy and the American Indian* (Chapel Hill: University of North Carolina Press, 1973), 165–67; Walker, *Torchlights,* 97, 118, 138, 176.

33. "Who Is a Beautiful Woman?" *Cherokee Phoenix,* Apr. 1, 1829, 4. Buck Watie changed his Cherokee name to Elias Boudinot when he converted to Christianity.

34. On May 27, 1829, readers also opened the pages of the Cherokee Nation's newspaper to read the qualification for a wife: "A bride should have nine qualifications, beginning with the letter p. viz.: Piety, Person, Parts, Patience, Prudence, Providence, Privilege, Parentage, and Portion—but that which should be the first of all, and most of all in consideration, which is Piety, is now the least of all, and with many none at all." (*Cherokee Phoenix,* May 27, 1829, 4).

35. Ralph Henry Gabriel, *Elias Boudinot: Cherokee and His America* (Norman: University of Oklahoma Press, 1941), 60–61, 65, 91. See also Dale Van Every, *Disinherited: The Lost Birthright of the American Indian* (New York: William Morrow, 1966), 46–61.

36. McLoughlin, *Cherokees and Missionaries,* 25.

37. Walker, *Torchlights,* 312. See also Narcissa Owen, *Memoirs of Narcissa Owen* (Washington, D.C.: n.p., 1907), 36.

38. Samuel A. Worcester to David Greene, Park Hill, May 10, 1846 [1847], ABCFM Papers, ABC 18.3.1, vol. 13.

39. Wade Horton, "Protestant Missionary Women," 212–13. For an imaginative study of women Protestant missionaries to China, see Wayne Flynt and Gerald W. Berkley, *Taking Christianity to China: Alabama Missionaries in the Middle Kingdom, 1850–1950* (Tuscaloosa: University of Alabama Press, 1997), 191–237. Flynt describes the ways women missionaries both transformed Chinese gender roles and were profoundly changed and empowered by their experiences.

40. McLoughlin, *Cherokees and Missionaries,* 249.

41. Hannah Moore to David Greene, Sept. 10, 1844, ABCFM Papers, ABC 18.3.1, vol. 5.

42. Marion Starkey, *The Cherokee Nation* (1946; reprint, New York: Russell and Russell, 1972), 67.

43. Sophia Sawyer to David Greene, May 1, 1820, ABCFM Papers, vol. 10:B2. For additional correspondence with Greene, see ABC 18.3.1, vol. 10. For Samuel Worcester's comments on Sawyer's unruliness, see Worcester to Greene, May 28, 1834, ABCFM Papers, ABC 18.3.1, vol. 7.

44. Sophia Sawyer to David Greene, Dec. 27, 1838, ABCFM Papers, ABC 18.3.1, Box 2,

vol. 10. See also Carolyn Thomas Foreman, "Miss Sophia Sawyer and Her School," *Chronicles of Oklahoma* 32, no. 4 (1954–55): 395–413, esp. 397.

45. Foreman, "Miss Sawyer," 398. See Sophia Sawyer to David Greene, Newark, Oct. 18, 1837, ABCFM Papers, ABC 18.3.1, vol. 10.

46. Starkey, *Cherokee Nation*, 303. Sawyer was born in Fitchburgh, Massachusetts, on May 4, 1792, and began her career as a missionary for the ABCFM in Nov. 1823. Kimberly C. Macenczak, "Sophia Sawyer, Native American Advocate: A Case Study in Nineteenth Century Cherokee Education," *Journal of Cherokee Studies* 16 (1991): 26–37, esp. 26.

47. Macenczak, "Sophia Sawyer," 34–35.

48. Alice Taylor Colbert, Manuscript, 2002; Foreman, "Miss Sawyer," 399.

49. Foreman, "Miss Sawyer," 402.

50. Horton, "Protestant Missionary Women," 6–7, 64–65.

51. Robert F. Berkhofer, *Salvation and the Savage: An Analysis of Protestant Missions and American Indian Response, 1787–1862* (Lexington: University of Kentucky, 1965), 38–39.

52. Walker, *Torchlights*, 17; ABCFM, *First Ten Annual Reports of the American Board for Foreign Missions, 1810–1819* (Boston: Crocker and Brewster, 1834), Sept. 10, 11, 1818, p. 9, on girls' work.

53. Moore to Greene, Aug. 4, 1842, ABCFM Papers, ABC 18.3.1, vol. 10. See also Michael Coleman, *American Indian Children at School, 1850–1930* (Jackson: University Press of Mississippi, 1993), 40, 112, 118, 192, 195.

54. *Annual Reports*, ABCFM, Hartford, Conn., Sept. 20–21, 1820.

55. Berkhofer, *Salvation and the Savage*, 15.

56. Susan Taylor, Brainerd, to Jeremiah Evarts, Feb. 23, 1839, JHP Papers, 8:55.

57. Nancy Reece to "Dear Madam," May 16, 1828; Nancy Reece to Mrs. Louisa Sanborn, June 17, 1828; Nancy Reece to Miss Abigail Williams, June 19, 1828; Nancy Reece to Mrs. Connor, 1828; Nancy Reece to Mrs. Elizabeth Preston, July 27, 1828, Brainerd, JHP Papers, 8:1, 6, 8, 10, 12, 17–30.

58. Nancy Reece, Brainerd, to "Dear Madam," May 16, 1828; JHP Papers, 8:1.

59. Christiana McPherson to the president of the United States, Brainerd, n.d., JHP Papers, 8:31.

60. Elizabeth Taylor to Miss Abigail [Parker], June 26, 1828, JHP Papers, 8:13–14. See also Michael C. Coleman, "American Indian School Pupils as Cultural Brokers: Cherokee Girls at Brainerd Mission, 1828–1829," in *Between Indian and White Worlds: The Cultural Broker,* ed. Margaret Connell Szasz, 122–35. For extensive letters from other young girls in the mission school at Brainerd such as Mary Ann Vail and Elizabeth Taylor among others, see vol. 8 of the JHP Papers.

61. Cyrus Kingsbury to Ladies of Wilmington, Delaware, *Brainerd Journal,* Apr. 20, 1820, ABCFM Papers, ABC 18.3.1, vol. 2:19. For lists of contributors to the ABCFM, see their *Annual Reports, 1817–1859.*

62. Samuel A. Worcester to William S. Coodey, Mar. 15, 1830, quoted in Walker, *Torchlights,* 250–52.

63. Hatley, *Dividing Paths,* 57. See also Mooney, *Myths of the Cherokees,* 360.

64. Wilma Dunaway, "Rethinking Cherokee Acculturation: Agrarian Capitalism and Women's Resistance to the Cult of Domesticity, 1800–1838," *American Indian Culture and Research Journal* 21, no. 1 (1997): 156–57, 164.

65. Ibid., 155–56. See also Wilma A. Dunaway, *The First American Frontier: Transition to Capitalism in Southern Appalachia, 1700–1860* (Chapel Hill: University of North Carolina Press, 1996), 1–86.

66. Ibid., 165, 167–68, 179–82. As late as 1860, women headed a majority of eastern Cherokee households, and the *gadugi* system survived until 1910.

67. McLoughlin, "Who Civilized the Cherokees?" 55–81, esp. 57–58; McLoughlin, *Cherokees and Missionaries,* 16–17. McLoughlin's overall paradigm of Cherokee history traces the themes of anomie and renaissance from the late eighteenth century to removal. His interpretation stresses to a greater extent than mine the pervasiveness of cultural transformation and acculturation.

68. McLoughlin, *Cherokees and Missionaries,* 7.

69. William G. McLoughlin, *The Cherokee Ghost Dance: Essays on the Southeastern Indians, 1789–1861* (Macon, Ga.: Mercer University Press, 1987), 111–26.

70. Ibid., 114–16; for a detailed account of all of the visions, see 111–52.

71. Dunaway, "Rethinking Cherokee Acculturation," 172–75.

72. Adair, *History of the American Indians,* 133–35. See also Raymond D. Fogelson, "On the 'Petticoat Government,'" 165.

73. McLoughlin, *Cherokees and Missionaries,* 146–47.

74. Among those who converted were Charles and Felicites Hicks, Clement and Mary Christine Vann, Richard Daniel, and Salome Elizabeth Sanders. Others included Major Ridge's wife, Susanna, Stand Watie, John Ridge, and Boudinot. However, as many as half of all men and women who converted were either expelled from the church or abandoned Christianity voluntarily (Diary of Mission at Oothcelaga in the Land of Cherokees, History Branch and Archives, Cleveland Public Library, Cleveland, Tennessee); Walker, *Torchlights,* 37); Berkhofer, *Salvation and the Savage,* 62; McLoughlin, *Cherokees and Christianity,* 25.

75. McLoughlin, *Champion of the Cherokees,* 155.

76. Berkhofer, *Salvation and the Savage,* 51.

77. Daniel Butrick to David Greene, Jan. 1840, ABCFM Papers, ABC 18.3.1, vol. 10.

78. Daniel Butrick, Diary, Sept. 8, 1830, ABCFM Papers, ABC 18.3.3, vol. 4.

79. Starkey, *Cherokee Nation,* 69.

80. Butrick Journal, Sept. 8, 1830, ABCFM Papers, ABC 18.3.3, vol. 4; see journal entries, Jan. 11, 1832, July 3, 1833, Sept. 27, 1833, July 1, 1838, May 30, 1839, Jan. 15, 1844, Feb. 26, 1844, Apr., 1844, Jan. 23, 1845, Mar. 22, 1845, May 3, 1845, May 24, 1845.

81. Butrick Journal, July 1, 1838, ABCFM Papers, ABC 18.3.3, vol. 4.

82. Butrick to Greene, Nov. 10, 1842, ABCFM Papers, ABC 18.3.1, vol. 10.

83. Constitution of the Cherokee Nation (Milledgeville, Ga.: Office of the Statesman and Patriot, 1827); *Constitution and Laws of the Cherokee Nation* (St. Louis: R and T. A. Ennis, 1875); Reid, *A Law of Blood,* 68, 233–34.

84. Dunaway, "Rethinking Cherokee Acculturation," 175.

85. Rennard Strickland, *Fire and the Spirits: Cherokee Law from Clan to Court* (Norman: University of Oklahoma, 1975), 48–49, 58, 60, 95, 100, 188.

86. McLoughlin, *Cherokee Renascence,* 332–33.

87. Reid, *A Law of Blood,* 39.

88. McLoughlin, *Cherokee Renascence,* 333.

89. Strickland, *Fire and Spirits,* 170.

90. See Johnston, "Burning Beds, Spinning Wheels, and Calico Dresses."

Chapter 3

1. James Wooten, *The Cherokee Indians in Bradley County History* (1935; reprinted and revised by Burton Jones, Cleveland, Tenn.: Bradley County, Post 81, American Legion with Cooperation of Tennessee Historical Commission, 1949), 51, 56. There were six stockades in North Carolina: Fort Lindsay in Sevian County, Fort Scott in Macon County, Fort Montgomery in Graham County, Fort Hambric in Clay County, and Fort Delaney and Fort Butler in Cherokee County; there were five stockades in Georgia: Fort Scudder in Lumpkin County, Fort Gilmer in Gilmer County, Fort Coosawatie in Murray County, Fort Talking Rock in Pickens County, and Fort Buffington in Cherokee County; there was a stockade in Tennessee at Rattlesnake Springs, near Fort Cass and the agency near the present town of Charleston, Tennessee; there was a stockade at Fort Turkeytown in Alabama, in addition to other stockades that were built. Historians have written about Cherokee removal from a political perspective and have explored the factionalism resulting from the signing of the Treaty of New Echota by a minority group in 1835. See Copy of New Echota Treaty between the Cherokees and the United States, 1835, Galileo-Southeastern Native American Documents, 1730–1842, Box 78, Folder 12, Document 20, TCC221, Telamon Cuyler Collection, Hargrett Rare Book and Manuscript Library, University of Georgia, Athens. Treaty party: Major Ridge, Elias Boudinot, John Ridge, George Adair, and Andrew Ross.

2. Theda Perdue's groundbreaking article, "Cherokee Women and the Trail of Tears," *Journal of Women's History* 1, no. 1 (1989): 14–30, opened the field of inquiry concerning the role gender played in the removal crisis. For accounts of the political history of the Cherokees' removal, see Francis Paul Prucha, *The Great Father: The United States Government and the American Indians,* 2 vols. (Lincoln: University of Nebraska Press, 1984); Ronald N. Satz, *American Indian Policy in the Jacksonian Era* (Lincoln: University of Nebraska, 1975); Morris L. Wardell, *A Political History of the Cherokee Nation, 1838–1907* (1938; reprint, Norman: University of Oklahoma Press, 1977); Grant Foreman, *Indian Removal: The Emigration of the Five Civilized Tribes of Indians* (Norman: University of Oklahoma Press, 1932); McLoughlin, *After the Trail of Tears, Cherokee Renascence,* and *Champion of the Cherokees.*

3. According to reports, at least sixty-nine newborns arrived in the West. See "Emigration Detachments," *Journal of Cherokee Studies* 3 (1978): 186–87, quoted in Perdue, "Cherokee Women and the Trail of Tears," in *Unequal Sisters: A Multi-Cultural Reader in U.S. Women's History,* ed. Vicki L. Ruiz and Ellen Carol DuBois (New York: Routledge, 1994), 40.

4. Perdue, "Cherokee Women and the Trail of Tears," *Journal of Women's History* 1, no. 1 (1989): 15. See also Theda Perdue and Michael D. Green, eds., *The Cherokee Removal: A Brief History with Documents* (Boston: Bedford Books of St. Martin's Press, 1995).

5. Ibid., 16–17.

6. Ibid., 18. See also Green, *Women in American Indian Society,* 46. Green writes that Nanyehi, Nancy Ward, was among the women addressing the National Council in 1817.

7. Council at Oostanahlee, June 30, 1818, *Brainerd Journal,* July 25, 1818, ABCFM Papers, ABC 18.3.1, vol. 2; excerpt in Perdue and Green, *Cherokee Removal,* 125–26.

8. Green, *Women in American Indian Society,* 46.

9. McLoughlin, *Cherokee Renascence,* 398.

10. *Cherokee Phoenix,* Jan. 6, 1829, 2.

11. David Williams, *The Georgia Gold Rush: Twenty-Niners, Cherokees, and Gold Fever* (Columbia: University of South Carolina Press, 1993), 14, 19.

12. Samuel Carter, *Cherokee Sunset: A Nation Betrayed: A Narrative of Travail and Triumph, Persecution and Exile* (New York: Doubleday, 1976), 13.

13. Henry T. Malone, *Cherokees of the Old South* (Athens: University of Georgia Press, 1956), 69, quoted in Carter, *Cherokee Sunset*, 28–29.

14. Rogin, *Fathers and Children*, 165, 173.

15. William G. McLoughlin, "The Reverend Evan Jones and the Cherokee Trail of Tears, 1838–1839," in *Cherokees and Christianity, 1794–1870: Essays on Acculturation and Cultural Persistence*, ed. Walter H. Conser Jr. (Athens: University of Georgia Press, 1994), 92.

16. Rogin, *Fathers and Children*, 226.

17. Evan Jones to James Barbour, secretary of war, Valley Towns, Nov. 15, 1826, Galileo-Southeastern Native American Documents, Box 1, Folder 10, Document CH003, State Library Cherokee Collection, Tennessee State Library and Archives, Nashville.

18. David M. Wishart, "Evidence of Surplus Production in the Cherokee Nation Prior to Removal," *American Indians*, ed. Nancy Shoemaker (Malden, Mass.: Blackwell, 2001), 146–48, 130–48. Wishart contends, "With at least half of Cherokee households producing substantial surpluses, advocates for the Cherokee removal were on shaky ground when they used economic arguments to justify imposing the costs of forced migration on a developing economy as a humanitarian policy."

19. Opinion of the Supreme Court of the United States, Jan. 1831, Galileo-Southeastern Native American Documents, 1730–1842, Box 3, Folder 7, Document CH076. State Library Cherokee Collection, Tennessee State Library and Archives, delivered by Chief Justice John Marshall on a motion of the Cherokee Nation for a writ of injunction and subpoena against the State of Georgia. See also Worcester's explanation for his actions, Samuel A. Worcester to George R. Gilmer, Governor of Georgia, June 10, 1831, Box 1, Folder 29, Document CH045, State Library Cherokee Collection, Tennessee State Library and Archives. Butler wrote a similar letter explaining his motives; see Elizur Butler to George R. Gilmer, Haweis, June 7, 1831, Box 1, Folder 29, Document CH046, State Library Cherokee Collection, Tennessee State Library and Archives. See also William G. McLoughlin, "The Methodists and the Removal Question, 1831–1832," in *The Cherokee Ghost Dance: Essays on the Southeastern Indians, 1789–1861*, ed. Walter H. Conser Jr. and Virginia Duffy McLoughlin (Macon, Ga.: Mercer University Press, 1987), 397–99, for details regarding James Jenkins Trott, who was married to a Cherokee woman. David B. Cumming, another Methodist minister, left with the Cherokees on the Trail of Tears. At that time, 480 Methodists still remained in the Nation. See McLoughlin, *Cherokee Ghost Dance*, 403, 421.

20. Mankiller and Wallis, *Mankiller*, 92.

21. Grace Steele Woodward, *The Cherokees* (Norman: University of Oklahoma Press, 1963), 192. Only 2,000 Cherokees had emigrated west by the end of 1837 (Carter, *Cherokee Sunset*, 101, 219).

22. Foreman, *Indian Removal*, 284, 286. See also James F. Corn, "Conscience or Duty: General John E. Wool's Dilemma with Cherokee Removal," *Journal of Cherokee Studies* 3, no. 1 (1978): 35–39.

23. Butler to Greene, Red Clay, June 15, 1838, ABCFM, ABC 18.3.1, vol. 10.

24. Sallie Butler, Interview no. 7244, 88:171, WPA, Project S-149, IPHC (collection ed. Grant Foreman). The IPHC consists of 7,105 interviews of elderly Indians, white settlers, and African Americans. These oral histories were collected in the late 1930s. Grant Foreman directed this project, which was sponsored by the WPA. The 112 volumes of oral histories of Indians contain invaluable insights into Indian history.

25. Evan Jones, Letter, June 4, 1838, Missionary Correspondence, 1800–1900, microfilm reel no. 98 (used by permission, American Baptist Historical Society, American Baptist Archives Center, Valley Forge, Pennsylvania).

26. Evan Jones, Journal, June 16, 1838, Missionary Correspondence, 1800–1900, microfilm reel no. 98 (used by permission, American Baptist Historical Society, American Baptist Archives Center, Valley Forge, Pennsylvania); also quoted in McLoughlin, "Evan Jones and the Trail of Tears," 91, 96–97; see CN Papers, Reel 44, RG 2, Treaty Fund Claims, 1831–83, for details of typical claims.

27. Butrick Journal, May 6, 1838, ABCFM Papers, ABC 18.3.1, vol. 4; Butrick, Brainerd, to Greene, Boston, Aug. 21, 1838, ABCFM Papers, ABC 18.3.1, vol. 10:1.

28. Thomas Bluford Downing, Interview no. 13645, 83:386, IPHC.

29. Joanna (McGhee) Jones, 49:168, IPHC.

30. Lucinda Fleetwood, Interview no. 2149, 3:517–18.

31. Eliza Whitmire, a Cherokee freedwoman, Interview no. 12963, 75:250, IPHC.

32. Foreman, *Indian Removal,* 251; Gary E. Moulton, ed., *The Papers of Chief John Ross, 1807–39,* vol. 1 (Norman: University of Oklahoma Press, 1985), 432–33.

33. McLoughlin, *Cherokees and Christianity,* 93–94.

34. Butrick Journal, June 28, 1838, JHP Papers, 9:81.

35. Ibid., June 28, 1838, Aug. 20, 1838, JHP Papers, 9:81, 9:90.

36. Butler to Greene, Red Clay, June 15, 1838, ABCFM Papers, ABC 18.3.1, vol. 10.

37. Foreman, *Indian Removal,* 291–96.

38. Records of the Bureau of Indian Affairs, Records of the Cherokee Indian Agency in Tennessee, 1801–35, RG 75, Microcopy 208, History Branch and Archives, Cleveland Public Library, Cleveland, Tennessee.

39. Mary Cobb Agnew, Interview no. 5978, 66:16, 22; 1:290–91, IPHC.

40. Jobe Alexander, Interview no. 13799, 72:32–33, 45, IPHC.

41. McLoughlin, "Evan Jones and the Trail of Tears," 100; Wardell, *A Political History,* 12.

42. Foreman, *Indian Removal,* 299.

43. McLoughlin, "Evan Jones and the Trail of Tears," 98.

44. William Shorey Coodey to John Howard Payne, JHP Papers, quoted in Carter, *Cherokee Sunset,* 250.

45. Foreman, *Indian Removal,* 302–4.

46. General Winfield Scott to John Ross, Elijah Hicks, J. Brown, and other agents, Aug. 1, 1838, James Corn Collection, Box 1, 608, History Branch and Archives, Cleveland Public Library, Cleveland, Tennessee, quoted in Emmett Starr, *History of Cherokee Indians* (Muskogee, Okla.: Hoffman Printing, 1984), 100–101. Estimate of twelve detachments: Elijah Hicks, 858; Daniel Cohan, 710; John Benge, 1,103; Jesse Bushyhead, 926; Situaki, 1,320; Old Fields, 954; Moses Daniel, 1,056; James D. Wofford, 1,269; James Brown, 840; Richard Taylor, 925; George Hicks, 1,034; Peter Hildebrand, 1,613.

47. Foreman, *Indian Removal,* 302–4.

48. Ibid., 306–7; "A Native of Maine traveling in the Western Country," *New York Observer,* Jan. 26, 1839, 4.

49. Duane H. King, Published Map of Routes, Museum of the Cherokee Indian, Cherokee, North Carolina.

50. Butler, Van Buren, Arkansas, to Greene, Jan. 25, 1839, ABCFM Papers, ABC 18.3.1, vol. 10.

51. See also Dr. C. Lillybridge, Journal, James Corn Collection, Box 3.

52. Butler to Greene, January 25, 1839, ABCFM Papers, ABC 18.3.1, vol. 10. The deaths resulting from the removal may well have been more numerous than previously estimated. See Russell Thornton, *The Cherokees: A Population History* (Lincoln: University of Nebraska, 1990), 73–76.

53. McLoughlin, *Cherokees and Christianity,* 95.

54. Lillian Lee Anderson, Interview no. 7326, 66:57–60, 337, IPHC.

55. Ibid., 338.

56. Bettie (Perdue) Woodall, Interview no. 7551, 67:448, IPHC.

57. Nick Comingdeer, Interview no. 7239, 20:310–11, 439, IPHC.

58. Jennie McCoy Chambers, Interview no. 6320, 17:92, 19:342–43, 104:261–62, IPHC. Chambers was born on Apr. 24, 1854.

59. Rachel Dodge, Interview no. 5765, 25:63, 3:61, IPHC.

60. W. W. Harnage, Interview no. 5162, 4:334–45; L. W. Wilson, Fieldworker, Interviewed Mar. 19, 1937, second interview (no number), 73:416, taken from questionnaire, n.d., IPHC.

61. Ella Coody Robinson, Interview no. 13833, 107:453–54, IPHC.

62. Gloria Jahoda, *The Trail of Tears* (1975; reprint, New York: Random House, 1995), 220, 225.

63. Lillybridge Journal, James Corn Collection, Box 3, 232–45; Thurman Wilkins, *Cherokee Tragedy: The Story of the Ridge Family and the Decimation of a People* (London: Macmillan, 1970), 301–15.

64. William Medill to James McKissick, Mar. 29, 1867, CN Papers, Box 167, Folder 6923, Reel 47.

65. There are at least two references to the death of Quatie Ross on Feb. 1, 1839 in Box 1, Folder 8 of MSS 47 of the James F. Corn Papers. They are J. P. Brown, "Chief John Ross Hated Indian Land Cessions," *Chattanooga News Free Press,* July 17, 1956; Alfred Mynders, "Next to the News," *Chattanooga Times,* Mar. 20, 1958; James Corn Collection, Box 1.

66. Comingdeer, Interview no. 7239, 20:439, IPHC.

67. Anthony F. C. Wallace, *The Long, Bitter Trail* (New York: Hill and Wang, 1993), 103.

68. Cephas Washburn to David Greene, Dwight Mission, July 31, 1838, ABCFM Papers, ABC 18.3.1, vol. 10.

69. McLoughlin, *Cherokees and Christianity,* 107. See also McLoughlin, *After the Trail of Tears,* 37–38.

70. William Medill, commissioner of Indian Affairs, to Hon. W. L. Marcy, secretary of war, Nov. 30, 1848 (Washington, D.C.: GPO, 1848), 386–87.

71. See Butrick Journal, Apr. 30, 1839, May 2, 1839, quoted in Perdue, "Cherokee Women and the Trail of Tears," *Unequal Sisters,* 40. Missionaries commented on Cherokee men's incidences of domestic violence after they arrived in the West.

Chapter 4

1. Scholarship on women who lived during the Civil War has concentrated on Southern women, with more emphasis on the antebellum period than on the war years. The works of George Rable, Catherine Clinton, Drew Gilpin Faust, Jacqueline Jones, and Elizabeth Fox-Genovese have shed light on the responses of Southern (mostly white) women to the insti-

tution of slavery and the Civil War. Mary Chesnut's diary offers a rare glimpse into their lives (C. Vann Woodward, ed., *Mary Chesnut's Civil War* [New Haven: Yale University Press, 1981]). See also George C. Rable, *Civil Wars: Women and the Crisis of Southern Nationalism* (Urbana: University of Illinois Press, 1989); Catherine Clinton's *The Other Civil War: American Women in the Nineteenth Century* (New York: Hill and Wang, 1984), *The Plantation Mistress: Woman's World in the Old South* (New York: Pantheon, 1982), and *Tara Revisited: Women, War and the Plantation Legend* (New York: Abbeville Press, 1995); Elizabeth Fox-Genovese, *Within the Plantation Household: Black and White Women in the Old South* (Chapel Hill: University of North Carolina Press, 1988); Jacqueline Jones, *Labor of Love, Labor of Sorrow: Black Women, Work, and the Family from Slavery to the Present* (New York: Basic Books, 1985); Drew Gilpin Faust, *Mothers of Invention* (Chapel Hill: University of North Carolina Press, 1996); Mary Elizabeth Massey, *Women in the Civil War* (1966; reprint, Lincoln: University of Nebraska, 1994); Anne Firor Scott, *Natural Allies: Women's Associations in American History* (Urbana: University of Illinois Press, 1991); and Mary Jane Warde, "Now the Wolf Has Come: The Civilian War in the Indian Territory," *Chronicles of Oklahoma* 71, no. 1 (1993): 69–87.

2. McLoughlin, *After the Trail of Tears*, 74.

3. Theda Perdue, "Southern Indians and the Cult of True Womanhood" in *The Web of Southern Social Relations: Women, Family, and Education*, ed. Walter I. Fraser, R. Frank Saunders Jr., and Jon L. Wakelyn (Athens: University of Georgia Press, 1985), 35–51.

4. McLoughlin, *Cherokees and Missionaries*, 337.

5. McLoughlin, *Cherokees and Christianity*, 19.

6. William G. McLoughlin, "The Missionaries and the Cherokee Bourgeoisie," in *Cherokees and Missionaries, 1789–1839*, 126–27. For an example of the articles in the *Cherokee Phoenix* espousing genteel constructions of gender, see "Female Delicacy," Nov. 19, 1828, 4, reprinted from *Ariel;* also see July 1, 1839. For articles espousing the virtues of piety, purity, domesticity, and submissiveness of the cult of true womanhood in the *Cherokee Advocate*, see "Influence of a Good Daughter," May 8, 1845; "The Young Wife," Aug. 6, 1846; Oct. 26, 1846; Dec. 18, 1848; "Female Education," July 30, 1849; "Husbands and Wives," "Woman's Sphere," Apr. 22, 1850; "Woman," Jan. 6, 1852; "Tyranny of Petticoats," Mar. 16, 1852; and "A Scolding Wife," "Advice to Young Women," "Women's Rights," July 20, 1853.

7. See *Mt. Holyoke Female Seminary: Female Education Tendencies of the Principles Embraced, and the System Adapted to the Mt. Holyoke Female Seminary* (Boston: n.p., 1839), 3, quoted in Barbara Welter, "The Cult of True Womanhood: 1800–1860," *Dimity Convictions: The American Woman in the Nineteenth Century* (Athens: Ohio University Press, 1976), 23. See also Devon A. Mihesuah, *Cultivating the Rosebuds: The Education of Women at the Cherokee Female Seminary, 1851–1909* (Urbana: University of Illinois Press, 1993), 3, 31, 37, 55–56. For an excellent analysis of the civilization program, see Perdue, "Women, Men, and American Indian Policy," 90–114.

8. Former Cherokee slaves told their stories to interviewers for the WPA in the 1930s, which allows us to see how their experiences differed from those of Cherokee and white women of the period. Too few oral histories survive of Cherokee slave women to make meaningful generalizations about the experiences of all Cherokee slaves. However, the former slave men and women give poignant, richly descriptive accounts of their experiences in Indian Territory and help to provide a picture of that period. Certain patterns do emerge in their stories. Their lives were integrally linked to the economic and political developments

within the Cherokee Nation. See oral histories of Nancy Rogers Bean, Chaney Richardson, Betty Robertson, Katie Rowe, Victoria Taylor Thompson, Patsy Perryman, Phyllis Petite, Aunt Chaney McNair, Lucinda Vann, Rochelle Allred Ward, Charlotte Johnson White, and Sarah Wilson. See T. Lindsay Baker and Julie P. Baker, *The WPA Oklahoma Slave Narratives* (Norman: University of Oklahoma Press, 1996).

9. Baker and Baker, *WPA Oklahoma Slave Narratives*, 435–37.

10. Ibid., 370, 368. Rowe was interviewed by Robert Vinson Lackey, c. spring or summer 1937.

11. Charlotte Johnson White was eighty-eight years old when she was interviewed at Fort Gibson. She was born in the hills east of Tahlequah in the Flint District. Her master was Ben Johnson. Her mother was Elasey Johnson, and her father was Banjo Lastley, who belonged to another master. White slipped away later but was caught and whipped. She was then given to her Aunt Easter Johnson, a mean woman who had beat her own six-year-old child to death for crying. When freedom came, Charlotte said, "I hear about de slaves being free when maybe a hundred soldiers come to de house . . . 'All de slaves is free,' one of de men said, and after dat I jest told everybody. 'I is a free Negro now and I ain't goin to work for nobody!'" After the war she joined the colored Baptist church, and in 1891 she married Randolph White. See Baker and Baker, *WPA Oklahoma Slave Narratives*, 464–66.

12. Baker and Baker, *WPA Oklahoma Slave Narratives*, 49. When she was interviewed, Nancy Rogers Bean was eighty-two years old.

13. Thompson was eighty years old when she was interviewed in Muskogee, Oklahoma. The Taylors (Cherokees) bought her father in the Flint District. Eventually, she married William Thompson, who was born a slave. See Baker and Baker, *WPA Oklahoma Slave Narratives*, 423–24. Thompson was interviewed by Ethel Wolfe Garrison in early winter 1937–38.

14. They did not return to the plantation until a year and a half after the war. Their owners were both dead, and the plantation was devastated. See Baker and Baker, *WPA Oklahoma Slave Narratives*, 440. Vann was interviewed by Anne L. Faulton, c. 1937–39.

15. Baker and Baker, *WPA Oklahoma Slave Narratives*, 445, 447. Ward's mother was Lottie Beck from the Flint District. She belonged to Joe Beck, whereas Ward's father belonged to Sarah Eaton, who presumably stole him from his parents in Georgia when he was eight or nine years old and brought him to Indian Territory near Fort Gibson. Ward's father was born around 1827, and he told her that his mother was a Cherokee named Downing who was related to Chief Downing (Baker and Baker, *WPA Oklahoma Slave Narratives*, 445). Rochelle married Amos Allred, later married Nelson Ward, and had thirteen children. See Baker and Baker, *WPA Oklahoma Slave Narratives*, 447–48. Ward was interviewed by Ethel Wolfe Garrison, c. winter 1937–38.

16. Scott, *Natural Allies;* Drew Gilpin Faust, "Altars of Sacrifice: Confederate Women and the Narratives of War," *Journal of American History* 76, no. 4 (1990): 1200–1228; Anne Firor Scott, *The Southern Lady: From Pedestal to Politics* (Chicago: University of Chicago Press, 1970); Scott, "Women's Perspective on the Patriarchy in the 1850s," in *Half Sisters of History,* ed. Catherine Clinton (Durham, N.C.: Duke University Press, 1994), 78; George C. Rable, *Civil Wars: Women and the Crisis of Southern Nationalism* (Urbana: University of Illinois, 1989). In contrast to Scott, who emphasizes the empowerment of Southern women because of the Civil War, Rable contends that "slight alterations in the southern landscape should not obscure the basic continuity of a class, racial, and sexual hierarchy" (268). Most

historians agree that Southern white women's experiences did not lead to the feminist consciousness that developed in the North. Recent scholarship has focused more on the persistence of gender ideology after the war. See also Suzanne D. Lebsock, *The Free Women of Petersburg: Status and Culture in a Southern Town, 1784–1860* (New York: Norton, 1984; Virginia Bernhard, Betty Brandon, Elizabeth Fox-Genovese, and Theda Perdue, eds., *Southern Women: Histories and Identities* (Columbia: University of Missouri Press, 1992); and Catherine Clinton and Nina Silber, eds., *Divided Houses: Gender and the Civil War* (New York: Oxford University Press, 1992).

17. Albert Pike to Colonel John Drew, July 14, 1862, Headquarters, Department of Indian Territory, Fort McCulloch, GFC, Box 6, 83–229, OHS.

18. See Prucha, *The Great Father*, 2:422; Edward Everett Dale and Gaston Litton, *Cherokee Cavaliers: Forty Years of Cherokee History as Told in the Correspondence of the Ridge-Watie-Boudinot Family* (Norman: University of Oklahoma Press, 1995), xx, xxi; Wardell, *A Political History*, 127, 131, 137, 139; Kenny A. Franks, *Stand Watie and the Agony of the Cherokee Nation* (Memphis: Memphis State University, 1979), 118, 119; Alvin M. Josephy Jr., *The Civil War in the American West* (New York: Alfred A. Knopf, 1991), 319, 322; Daniel F. Littlefield Jr., *The Cherokee Freedmen from Emancipation to American Citizenship* (Westport, Conn.: Greenwood Press, 1978), 15. For other accounts of the Civil War in Indian Territory, see Annie Heloise Abel, *The American Indian and the End of the Confederacy, 1863–1866* (Lincoln: University of Nebraska Press, 1993); Abel, *The American Indian as Slaveholder and Secessionist* (Lincoln: University of Nebraska Press, 1992); Abel, *The American Indian as Participant in the Civil War* (Cleveland: Arthur H. Clark, 1919); W. Craig Gaines, *The Confederate Cherokees: John Drew's Regiment of Mounted Rifles* (Baton Rouge: Louisiana State University, 1989); Laurence M. Hauptman, *Between Two Fires: American Indians in the Civil War* (New York: Free Press, 1996).

19. Mrs. John Falling (Delilah), Interview no. 2197, 3:420–25, 29:20–25; Mary Stockton, Fieldworker, no date for interview, but probably early 1937, IPHC. Delilah Falling was born on Feb. 18, 1844. She was a student at the Cherokee Female Seminary. Her parents became refugees in Texas during the Civil War. See also Wiley Britton, *Memoirs of the Rebellion on the Border, 1863* (Lincoln: University of Nebraska Press, 1993), 309, 312.

20. Lemuel Wright, Interview no. 5139, 75:456, IPHC.

21. Mary Free, Interview no. 4047, 3:592–99; John F. Daugherty, Fieldworker, Interviewed May 13, 1937, IPHC.

22. Julius Pinkey Killebrew, Interview no. 6719, 106:249–57, IPHC.

23. George Lloyd Payson, 40:214–15, IPHC.

24. Sallie Manus, Interview no. 12891, 108:71, 74, IPHC.

25. Ella Coody Robinson, Interview no. 13833, 107:468–69, IPHC. Robinson was born Apr. 28, 1847. Her family owned slaves and supported the Confederacy.

26. The Pin Indians belonged to the Keetoowah Society, formed in 1855, whose goal was to define a "true Cherokee patriot" as faithful to traditional values and upholding Cherokee self-determination. They opposed slavery and sought to preserve many of the ancient ceremonies and aspects of their old religion. See McLoughlin, *After the Trail of Tears*, 155–59.

27. Susan Riley Gott, Interview no. 5088, 4:122–29; Ella Robinson, Fieldworker, Interviewed Mar. 31, 1937, IPHC. Gott was born in 1857.

28. Emma Sixkiller, Interview no. 6468, 40:47, 50, IPHC.

29. Dale and Litton, *Cherokee Cavaliers*, xx; Warde, "Now the Wolf Has Come," 69.

30. George W. Collamore to William P. Dole, Annual Report of the Commissioner for Indian Affairs, Apr. 21, 1862 (Washington, D.C.: GPO, 1863), 155–58. Collamore recorded 7,640 people: 240 Cherokees, 5,000 Creeks, 1,096 Seminoles, 140 Chickasaws, 315 Quapaws, 544 Uchees, 83 Keeshies, 197 Delaware, 17 Ironeyes, 3 Caddoes, and 5 Witchitas.

31. Angie Debo, "Southern Refugees of the Cherokee Nation," *Southwestern Historical Quarterly* 35, no. 4 (1932): 255–57.

32. Ibid., 258.

33. After the war, the U.S. government did take up the work of caring for Southern refugees. They were supported during the winter of 1865–66 and well into the following summer. In July 1862, Congress suspended all treaties with any Indian nations that supported the Confederacy effective July 1862. Then the annuities of the five major tribes were placed in a common fund that was available to support loyal Indian refugees. The Cherokees were eligible for funds after 1862. Debo, "Southern Refugees of the Cherokee Nation," 259–61; McLoughlin, *After the Trail of Tears*, 217.

34. Dale and Litton, *Cherokee Cavaliers*, xxi.

35. McLoughlin, *After the Trail of Tears*, 122.

36. Sarah C. Watie to Stand Watie, Oct. 9, 1864, quoted in Dale and Litton, *Cherokee Cavaliers*, 200.

37. Moulton, *Papers of Chief John Ross*, 2:601. See also McLoughlin, *After the Trail of Tears*, 216. In a tribal population of 21,000, the Cherokees owned 3,500 to 4,000 slaves by 1860. Four hundred out of 4,200 or 10 percent of Cherokee families owned slaves (McLoughlin, 125).

38. For a definition of "true womanhood," see Welter, "The Cult of True Womanhood," 21. In the Nave family papers at the John Vaughan Library at Northeastern State University in Tahlequah, Oklahoma, there is a notice of the family's subscription to *Godey's Lady's Book,* a nineteenth-century magazine that espoused the tenets of true womanhood.

39. John Ross to Mary B. Stapler, Washington City, June 27, 30, and July 1, 1844, quoted in Moulton, *Papers of Chief John Ross,* 2:212–14, 229–30; also John Ross to Mary B. Stapler, New York, Howard's Hotel, July 30, 1844, 230–31, 243.

40. Edith Hicks Smith Walker, Interview, Mar. 24, 1933, GFC, Box 16, Thomas Gilcrease Museum, Tulsa, Oklahoma.

41. Mary Elizabeth Good, introduction to "The Diary of Hannah Hicks," by Hannah Worcester Hicks, *American Scene* 13, no. 9 (1972): 21. Manuscript of Diary of Hannah Hicks, Hicks Collection, Gilcrease Museum. See GFC, Box 5, 83–229, OHS, for details regarding Hannah Hicks's biography.

42. Hicks, "Diary of Hannah Hicks," 5.

43. Nancy Hitchcock left with her husband, Mrs. Worcester (Ermina Nash Worcester, Samuel Worcester's second wife), Mary Covell, and her grandchild, Laura. Nancy Hitchcock, Denmark, Iowa, to Brother and Sister Orr, Sept. 1, 1864, GFC, Box 3, Folder 3, OHS.

44. Hicks, "Diary of Hannah Hicks," 9.

45. Hannah [Hicks] to My dear sister [Ann Eliza?], Ft. Gibson, Sept. 6, 1865, GFC, Folder 3 of 4, no. 82–229.

46. Mary Scott Gordon, Interview no. 1162, 4:101–11, Jennie Selfridge, Fieldworker, Interviewed Mar. 31, 1937, IPHC.

47. Hicks, "Diary of Hannah Hicks," 5, 22.

48. Ibid., 9. Hicks's sister, Mary Eleanor Worcester, also faced physical challenges in un-

accustomed tasks. Worcester had accepted a teaching position in Van Buren, Arkansas, after she completed her education in New England. She married a Confederate army surgeon, Dr. Charles Yancy Nason. He was rumored to have been ordered to the East shortly after their marriage, and Worcester did not hear from him. Consequently, she went to stay with Hicks. See Nettie Terry Brown, "The Missionary World of Ann Eliza Worcester Robertson" (Ph.D. diss., North Texas State University, 1978), 5, 118–19. Worcester recalled the time that she spent alone at her sister's place after Hicks married Dwight Hitchcock and went to live at Fort Gibson. She was there nearly a year, usually having some of the children with her, but during this particular time she was alone. She wrote, "I had my own fences to build, and was making quite a large place for the calves." One day a thorn got stuck in her eye, and she had to pull it out with tweezers. She also had a brush with a panther: "I stooped over, filled my arms with wood and raised up in time to feel the hair of an animal brush my cheek. It had leaped for my shoulders. My arising with my wood prevented his landing on my back as he proposed to do. I naturally quickly dropped my wood, with an exclamation. The animal, which I afterward learned—and then suspected—to be a panther cleared the long porch with two bounds." Shortly after this incident, Worcester started to walk the eighteen miles to Fort Gibson (Mary Eleanor Worcester, Interview, Box 16, GFC, 20–21, Gilcrease Museum).

49. George W. Mayes, Interview no. 4900, 34:285–86, IPHC. Mayes's father was a cattleman, and his family became refugees in Texas.

50. Lizzie Wynn, Interview no. 12286, 52:32, IPHC.

51. Dwight D. Hitchcock to "My very dear friends," Feb. 11, 1863, Brigade Hospital, Camp John Ross, Near Scott's Mill, Missouri, GFC, OHS.

52. Ibid.

53. Sarah Watie to Stand Watie, May 27, 1864, quoted in Angie Debo, "Southern Refugees of the Cherokee Nation," *Southwestern Historical Quarterly* 35, no. 4 (1932): 263. In a similarly laconic style she responded to her husband's capture of a Federal supply train of 250 wagons, the most famous incident of the war in the Indian Territory. Sarah wrote, "I thought I would send you some clothes, but I hear that you have done better" (Oct. 9, 1864 letter in Debo, 263).

54. Hicks, "Diary of Hannah Hicks," 8.

55. W. P. Ross to Colonel Drew, Nov. 27, 1861, Headquarters, Indian Department, Camp Spring Hill near Contacharti, Cherokee Nation, GFC Box 6, 83–229, OHS.

56. Jane to Sarah (handwritten is an archivist's speculation on the identity of the author, "Mary Jane? Mother of Hubbard Ross"), Mar. 22, 1863, GFC, Box 6, Folder 3 of 4, 83–229, OHS.

57. Bettie (Perdue) Woodall, Interview no. 7551, 67:452, 10:196, IPHC.

58. Sylvester Thornton, Interview no. 7784, 47:35, IPHC.

59. Worcester, GFC, Box 16, 84, Gilcrease Museum.

60. Hicks, "Diary of Hannah Hicks," 11. For details, see "Diary," note 9, p. 21.

61. Ibid.

62. Mrs. Edith Hicks Smith Walker, GFC, Box 16, 3, Gilcrease Museum. Herbert Worcester Hicks, Hannah Hicks's son, also remembered being robbed five times (Interview no. 2187, IPHC).

63. Stephen Foreman, Journal, Aug. 26, 1863, Stephen Foreman Collection, WHC.

64. James Anderson Slover, *Autobiography*, 80, WHC.

65. Franks, *Stand Watie,* 148.

66. Watie Papers, Box 115, Folder 3890, Roll 38, WHC, also quoted in Dale and Litton, *Cherokee Cavaliers,* 128–29. For the convenience of readers, I have provided the location of the letters in the published collection also. Obviously, I have not corrected the spelling of the letters.

67. Franks, *Stand Watie,* 148; Stand Watie to Sarah C. Watie, Camp Near North Ford, Nov. 12, 1863, Watie Papers, Box 115, Folder 3893, Roll 38, WHC, also quoted in Dale and Litton, *Cherokee Cavaliers,* 144–45. See also T. L. Ballenger, ed., Nave Letters, 1850–72, John Vaughan Library, Special Collections, Northeastern State University, Tahlequah, Oklahoma. Used by permission.

68. Sarah C. Watie to Stand Watie, Wood Co., Sept. 4, 1864, Watie Papers, Box 115, Folder 3901, Roll 38, WHC, quoted in Dale and Litton, *Cherokee Cavaliers,* 188–89.

69. Mrs. William P. Ross, Aug. 31, 1863, quoted in Woodward, *The Cherokees,* 284–85.

70. Ibid., Feb. 23, 1863.

71. Hicks, "The Diary of Hannah Hicks," 11, 17.

72. Mary B. Stapler Ross to John Ross, Dec. 3, 1863, quoted in Moulton, *Papers of Chief John Ross,* 2:545.

73. Mary S. Ross to John Ross, Washington Place [Philadelphia], Dec. 4, 1863, [708] in Moulton, *Papers of Chief John Ross,* 2:546.

74. Mary S. Ross to John Ross, Mar. 19, 1864, ibid., 2:570, 2:631.

75. Linda Finley, "Notes from the Diary of Susan E. Foreman," *Chronicles of Oklahoma* 47, no. 4 (1969–70): 397; Stephen Foreman, Diary, Aug. 29, 1864, WHC.

76. Dale and Litton, *Cherokee Cavaliers,* 121.

77. Watie Papers, Box 115, Folder 3889, Roll 38, WHC, also quoted in Dale and Litton, *Cherokee Cavaliers,* 124, 126.

78. Faust, "Altars of Sacrifice," 1220–28.

79. Sarah C. Watie to Stand Watie, Rusk Co., Texas, June 12, 1864, Watie Papers, Box 115, Folder 3899, Roll 38, WHC, also quoted in Dale and Litton, *Cherokee Cavaliers,* 172.

80. Sarah C. Watie to Stand Watie, July 2, 1864, Watie Papers, Box 115, Folder 3900, Roll 38, WHC, also quoted in Dale and Litton, *Cherokee Cavaliers,* 178–79.

81. Mary Alice (Gibson) Arendell, Interview no. 5508, 1:155; Dovey P. Heady, Field-worker, interviewed probably in early 1937, IPHC.

82. Stand Watie to Sarah C. Watie, June 23, 1865, Watie Papers, Box 115, Folder 3907, Roll 38, WHC, also quoted in Dale and Litton, *Cherokee Cavaliers,* 228.

83. Wardell, *A Political History,* 178; Steve Cottrell, *Civil War in Indian Territory* (Gretna, La.: Pelican Publishing, 1995), 107. Cherokee women in North Carolina did not face the same violence, terror, and wrenching experiences regarding their status and spheres as their relatives did in Indian Territory. However, factionalism resulting from allegiances during the Civil War seriously fractured the Eastern Band. When the Civil War came, William Holland Thomas, who had been aiding the Eastern Cherokees by buying land, persuaded the North Carolina Cherokees to back the Confederacy, and he organized about 200 Indians into a local force called the Junaluska Zouaves. Then he tried, unsuccessfully, to get the state to recognize their citizenship and muster a detachment, but eventually, in 1862, the Confederates mustered Thomas and a detachment of Quallatown Indians into service. They served three years and were divided into two companies, each with 110 Indian privates and non-commissioned officers. This marked the first Cherokee warfare since their involvement in the Creek campaign in 1813–14. Thomas's Legion of Indians and Highlanders, or simply

Thomas's Legion, consisted of 2,800 officers and enlisted men and included another two companies of Indians, with approximately 400 Cherokees who served in the legion at one time or another. The Indians saw little combat and sustained few casualties in battle, but the Cherokees fought with skill and courage. As was the case in the West, the Indians took scalps only during one battle: they scalped some of the Yankee dead and wounded at Baptist Gap in the Cumberland Mountains in 1862 after Lieutenant Astoogatogeh, the grandson of Junaluska, was killed. The horrified Confederate officers apologized to their Union counterparts. Some of the Cherokee soldiers defected to the Union side in 1864 and joined Colonel George W. Kirk in an impressive Union raid from Tennessee into North Carolina. They served in Kirk's outfit, the 3rd North Carolina Mounted Infantry Volunteers, for the remainder of the war. The Union Cherokees were in a distinct minority in their tribe. Many of the members of Thomas's Legion who were sent to Virginia were killed, and the survivors returned to the legion in North Carolina in 1864. When Colonel Kirk, along with his 600 men, burned Waynesville, the legion stopped him at Soco Creek. Near Waynesville, later that spring in May 1865, members of the legion and some Union soldiers fired at each other, exchanging what were probably the last shots of the war in North Carolina. Subsequently, Thomas surrendered to Lt. Colonel William C. Bartlett. The war was devastating for the Eastern Cherokees. Apparently, a warrior who served in the Union Army brought back smallpox to the Cherokee Nation, precipitating an epidemic within the tribe. By 1866 when the epidemic subsided, 125 Cherokees had died, among them many prominent leaders. The Eastern Band of Cherokees also experienced intense factionalism, an erosion of the harmony ethic, malnutrition, alcoholism, and demoralization after the war. The Cherokees' fields were destroyed, and their lands were vulnerable to seizure even though North Carolina recognized the Cherokees as permanent residents. See John Finger, *The Eastern Band of Cherokees, 1819–1900* (Knoxville: University of Tennessee Press, 1984), 59–60, 80–91, 96–102.

84. Hicks, "Diary of Hannah Hicks," 22.

85. Mary E. James (nee Hudson), Interview no. 7029, 31:143, IPHC. Hudson Creek was northeast of what is now Fairland, Oklahoma.

86. Agnew, Interview no. 5978, 66:16, 22, 296–97, IPHC. When they returned to Indian Territory five years later, at the end of the Civil War, Alice Robertson described the scene: "The ravages of war became more and more apparent; ruined chimneys, marking what had once been great plantation houses, prairie fires had swept through miles and miles of country killing orchards, burning fences, etc. all domestic animals had vanished, but the wild animal denizens of forest and plain had increased alarmingly" (7) (A. Robertson, Presbyterian Mission, Alice Robertson Papers, Box 2, File 1, pp. 82–86, OHS).

87. Wardell, *A Political History of the Cherokees*, 175; McLoughlin, *After the Trail of Tears*, 220.

88. See McLoughlin, *After the Trail of Tears*, 244–47.

Chapter 5

1. McLoughlin, *After the Trail of Tears*, 367, 368.

2. Commissioner of Indian Affairs to Secretary of Interior, *Reports of Superintendent of Schools* (Washington, D.C.: GPO, 1900), 112–13.

3. Mihesuah, *Cultivating the Rosebuds*, see especially 2, 3, 5, 30, 69, 81, 83. See also Johnston, "In the White Woman's Image," 206–9.

4. Isabel Cobb, "Partial History of Dr Isabel Cobb: Earlyday Doctor in Indian Territory," mimeographed by Ruth Cobb Bivins, Folder 5, M-916, C-20, 1, WHC.

5. Cobb, "Partial History," 4–5.

6. Ibid., 1. For a splendid work on a midwife in an earlier period, see Ulrich, *A Midwife's Tale.*

7. Ibid., 1, 4. An account regarding Cobb may be found in what appears to be a report of an article by Ruth Muskrat Bronson in 1923 (Janice J. Sisemore, *Cherokee Quarterly* [summer 1998]). Cobb's mother's neighbor (Mrs. Wash Mayes) came and helped her during labor. The post doctor from Fort Gibson had to assist her before she could get up again (Cobb, "Partial History," 8).

8. Ibid., 3.

9. Cobb delivered a large number of babies in her practice. She even treated herself for pneumonia, recording in great detail her medications and symptoms in Feb. 1900. In her medical journal she recorded the following statistics (my tabulations) in her journal regarding deliveries: 1891: 1; 1893: 4; 1894: 9; 1895: 9; 1896: 6; 1897: 6; 1898: 8; 1899: 5; 1900: 6; 1901: 8; 1902: 5; 1903: 3; 1904: 4; 1905: 4; 1906: 2; 1907: 5; 1908: 4; 1909: 4; 1910: 1; 1911: 5; 1912: 4; 1913: 6; 1914: 3; 1915: 8; 1916: 3; 1917: 4; 1919: 1; 1920: 6; 1921: 1; 1922: 1; 1924: 4; 1927: 1 (Isabel Cobb, Medical Journal, M916 C-20, Folder 2, WHC).

10. Cobb, Medical Journal, WHC, Folder 2.

11. McLoughlin, *After the Trail of Tears,* 242–44.

12. Fanny died in 1896 of tuberculosis. Kathleen Leiper Faux, Faux Collection, Folder 29, FF66, WHC.

13. Kristina Southwell, "The Park Hill Mission: Letters from a Missionary Family," *Chronicles of Oklahoma* 78, no. 2 (2000): 218–20, 216–29.

14. Joseph Leiper to "My Dear Aunts," Jan. 6, 1890, Faux Collection, Box 29, Folder 8; WHC. See also Southwell, *Chronicles,* 78:222. Kathleen Leiper Faux, who found and preserved her grandparents' letters, noted that Maggie claimed that children watched with interest as she served afternoon tea. Faux, her grand-niece, wondered, "if gracious manners were needed skills to truly improve the quality of life of families who in many cases were quite poor." She also commented on the differing responses to the religious influences: "Missionaries during that period [removal] found it was half breeds who were most open to change because they had been exposed to the ways of white people" (Kathleen Leiper Faux, Cincinnati, Ohio, June 8, 1895, Folder 29, FF66, 9, WHC).

15. The ABCFM mission closed in 1859. McLoughlin, *Cherokee Ghost Dance,* 450. As late as 1896, when Principal Chief S. H. Mayes delivered his annual address on Nov. 7, he read it in English, but an official interpreter translated it into Cherokee, paragraph by paragraph (Editorial, *South McAlester Capital,* Nov. 2, 1896, vol. 3, no. 51). Still, the shift to English suggests a move toward assimilation. At one time Maggie Leiper wrote a revealing commentary on the question of Cherokees' assimilation in an offhand statement to her sisters in an undated letter: "I have some curiosity to see. There is not much Indian about these people here. They have been civilized too long." Therefore, her perception about those Cherokees whom she knew was that they were highly assimilated (Faux Collection, Folder 29, FF48, WHC).

16. McLoughlin, *Champion of the Cherokees,* 345.

17. McLoughlin, *Cherokees and Christianity,* 220–24; McLoughlin, *After the Trail of Tears,* 242–44. See also Katja May, "The Cherokee Nation's Political and Cultural Struggle for Independence in the 1870s," *Journal of Cherokee Studies* 11, no. 1 (1986): 30–31.

18. The Cherokees struggled to maintain the sovereignty of their judiciary. This part of the chapter is based on the examination of all of the extant Supreme Court records of the Cherokee Nation and extensive sampling of all of the circuit court records of all the districts in the Cherokee Nation.

19. CHN 119, Supreme Court Records, Oct. 4, 1886–Dec. 10, 1889, vol. 227, WHC.

20. CHN 024, Cooweescoowee District Records–Marriage Records 1869-91, CN Papers. Another explanation for the declining number of Cherokee citizens' marriages in the ledgers may have been their failure to record them in the court records. However, I have seen no evidence supporting this possibility. The Dawes Final Roll listed 286 individuals who were Cherokees by intermarriage, with 185 males and 101 females ("Native American Collection," CD-ROM, GenRef, OHS).

21. CHN 029, Cooweescoowee District Records, Vinita, June 19, 1889, May 12, 1891–June 7, 1894, CN Papers, vol. 57.

22. CHN 029, Cooweescoowee District Record, Jan. 3, 1876–Feb. 25, 1895, CN Papers. Incident on Mar. 22, 1893; murder case tried on May 12, 1893.

23. CHN 38, Flint District Records, May 11, 1877–Jan. 7, 1898, Apr. 21, 1888, and May 15, 1888, CN Papers, vol. 103.

24. CHN 119, Aug. 13, 1892, Supreme Court Records, May 30, 1892–Aug. 19, 1893, CN Papers, vol. 230.

25. CHN 29, Cooweescoowee District Records, Sept. 1887–Oct. 22, 1894, CN Papers, vol. 34. The forty-one divorce cases were in the Cooweescoowee district.

26. CHN 50, Tahlequah District Records, Sept. 25, 1876–Sept. 7, 1897, CN Papers, vol. 212.

27. CHN 50, Tahlequah District Records, Sept. 25, 1865–Nov. 10, 1875, CN Papers, vol. 195.

28. "By mutual foregoing favors Defendant and against Plaintiff for cost" (CHN 119, Supreme Court Records, Oct. 4, 1886–Dec. 10, 1889, vol. 227, WHC).

29. CHN 50, Feb. 1, 1897, Tahlequah District Records, Sept. 25, 1876–Sept. 7, 1897, CN Papers, vol. 212.

30. Tahlequah District Records, vol. 202, 1884-91. See also CHN 50, 208, Sept. 26, 1892–May 28, 1894: 3 divorce suits, 1 initiated by females; CHN 50, Oct. 27, 1877-98, Tahlequah District Records, vol. 222: 8 divorces, 3 by females; CHN 22, Canadian District, 1891: 3 divorce suits, 2 by females; 1892: 3 divorce suits; 2 by females; 1893: 9 divorce suits, 4 by females; CHN 023, Canadian District, Aug. 2, 1894–July 4, 1898, 9 divorce suits, 2 initiated by females; Apr. 24, 1876–Sept. 30, 1897, vol. 14: 12 divorce cases, 6 initiated by females; CHN 23, Apr. 25, 1892, vol. 16: 19 divorces, 10 initiated by females; CHN 23, Jan. 25, 1877–July 1897, vol. 17: 1 divorce; CHN 45, Saline District Records, Sept. 18, 1876–Sept. 20, 1897, vol. 171: 7 divorces, 4 initiated by females; CHN 47, Sequoyah District Records, May 21, 1877–Sept. 20, 1897, vol. 191: 19 divorces, 7 by females.

31. CHN 117, Northern Judicial Circuit Court Records, June 10, 1898–July 1898, CN Papers, vol. 247. The violence allegedly occurred on Nov. 25, 1894.

32. CHN 34, Delaware District Records, May 2, 1868–Oct. 17, 1871, CN Papers, vol. 65, 15 divorce suits, 6 by females; CHN 34, Delaware District Records, Sept. 6, 1876–Nov. 1890, CN Papers, vol. 87, 12 divorce suits, 3 by females.

33. CHN 34, Delaware District Records, Sept. 4, 1876–Nov. 1890, CN Papers, vol. 87. For additional cases see CHN 38, Flint District Records, Sept. 15, 1877–Mar. 10, 1895, vol. 105, 3 divorce suits, 1 initiated by a female; CHN 119, Supreme Court Records, Oct. 4,

1888–Dec. 10, 1889, 3 divorces, 3 by females; May 30, 1892–Aug. 19, 1893, vol. 230, 4 divorces, 3 by females; CHN 119, Oct. 2, 1893–May 2, 1894, Marriage Records, 1894–95, vol. 233, WHC, 1891: 30; 1892: 47; 1893: 55; 1894: 17; 1895: 22; 1896: Cherokee man and white woman, 2, Cherokee woman and white man, 26; 1897: 61.

34. CHN 50, Tahlequah District Records, Jan. 10, 1876–June 1898, CN Papers, vol. 217.

35. Eugenia Davison to J. M. Bell, Chetopa, Kansas, June 6, 1884, CN Papers, Folder 5757, Reel 43.

36. The plaintiff was twenty-one years old. The rape allegedly occurred on Nov. 8, 1876 (CHN 50, Tahlequah District Records, Jan. 10, 1876–June 1898, CN Papers, vol. 217).

37. CHN 23, Aug. 30, 1879 (sentencing), Canadian District Records, Mar. 16, 1876–Apr. 1, 1897, CN Papers, vol. 14. Several individuals named Patsy Johnson appear on the final Dawes Roll. Three are listed as Cherokees by blood and one as a freedwoman. The court records do not shed light on which individual was involved in the case.

38. CHN 38, Aug. 7, 1883, Flint District Records, May 11, 1877–Jan. 7, 1898 (CN Papers, vol. 103). In the rape case of the *Cherokee Nation vs. Lou Latimore* a lack of witnesses prompted a not guilty verdict on July 2, 1877 (CHN 47, Sequoyah District Records, May 8, 1876–June 7, 1897, CN Papers, vol. 182).

39. Fred Eggan, "Historical Changes," 34–52. This essay also appears in Fred Eggan, *Essays in Social Anthropology and Ethnology* (Chicago: University of Chicago Department of Anthropology, 1975), 71–90. Fred Eggan identified a change from a matrilineal emphasis to a patrilineal emphasis in the kinship systems of the southeastern Indians, including the Cherokees, Choctaws, Chickasaws, and Creeks. He saw the period of 1830 to 1860 as dramatic for the Choctaws and the period of 1850 to 1860 especially important for change in the Cherokee Nation because of acculturational pressures. He pointed to the role of missionaries, teachers, and government agents in stimulating changes in behaviors and attitudes that weakened the authority of the clans and promoted patrilineal practices. On the other hand, he pointed to William Gilbert's work regarding the Eastern Cherokees, who had still retained to a large degree the old kinship system, even in the 1930s. Therefore, he contended that the Cherokees formerly had a Crow kinship system. Yet, in the face of acculturational pressures, matrilineal traditions were remarkably persistent. See, for example, the "Narrative of a Cherokee Childhood," by Robert K. Thomas, quoted by Robert D. Cooter, "Individuals and Relatives," in *A Good Cherokee, A Good Anthropologist: Papers in Honor of Robert K. Thomas,* ed. Steve Pavlik (Los Angeles: UCLA American Indian Studies Center, McNaughton and Gunn, 1988), 57–79. Thomas was born in 1925 and grew up in eastern Oklahoma. He confirmed that, in his experience, Cherokee women still directed the household and had a large impact on the broader Cherokee society. His family line was traced through the female, and Cherokee women "owned" the land and the home. He said that most men still lived in their wives' community after marriage (78). Thomas said, "Cherokee women are the givers of life and the nourishers of plants and children, while Cherokee men deal with death—the hunting of animals and, in the old days, the killing of enemies. Cherokee men are 'bloody,' as an old lady put it." He said that when he was around eleven or twelve his grandmother would stare at him penetratingly when he entered the garden where she was working. She probably wondered whether he was becoming a man. "Another time," he recalled, "I remember going into a garden to talk to an old lady. She said, 'Boy, is your thing starting to stand up yet?' and held her hoe up menacingly. I tell you, I got out of there fast" (67).

40. Joseph Epes Brown, *The Spiritual Legacy of the American Indian* (New York: Crossroad, 1993), 65.

Chapter 6

1. Angie Debo, *And Still the Waters Run: The Betrayal of the Five Civilized Tribes* (1940; reprint, Princeton: Princeton University Press, 1991), 165, 171.

2. The Five Civilized Tribes were the Cherokee, Choctaw, Seminole, Creek, and Chickasaw tribes. The federal government designated these tribes as the "civilized tribes" because of their presumed acculturation to Euro-American values. Debo, *And Still the Waters Run,* 292, 170. In the 1890 census of the Cherokees, the following were reported: whites 29,166; Negroes 5,127; Indians 22,015, for a total of 56,309. Therefore, Indians comprised 28.11 percent of the total population (13). The population of 101,228 persons in the Five Civilized Tribes in 1907 included intermarried whites, the freedmen, and 15,603 other Indians. See also Prucha, *The Great Father,* 757. When the Five Tribes Act provided that the rolls close Mar. 4, 1907, the Cherokees counted the following: full-bloods 8,703; mixed 27,916 (Total 36,619); whites 286; freedman 4,919, for a total of 41,824 (Debo, *And Still the Waters Run,* 47). By 1880, 1,821 individuals, representing nearly 10 percent of the 22,000 people in the Cherokee Nation, were living there who had no right to be there. See Marcia Larson Odell, *Divide and Conquer: Allotment among the Cherokee* (New York: Arno Press, 1979), 47.

3. D. S. Otis, *The Dawes Act and the Allotment of Indian Lands,* ed. Francis Paul Prucha (Norman: University of Oklahoma Press, 1973), 6–7; see Francis Paul Prucha, *Documents of United States Indian Policy,* 2nd ed. (Lincoln: University of Nebraska Press, 1975), 190–94, for Report of the Dawes Commission, Nov. 20, 1894, and 171–74 for Dawes Act, Feb. 8, 1887. An amendment to the Dawes Act passed on Feb. 23, 1891, and the president signed it on Feb. 28, 1891. Thereafter, married Indian women were entitled to eighty acres each (see Amendment to Dawes Act, Feb. 28, 1891, 184), and Curtis Act, June 28, 1898, 197–98. See also the *Report of the Commissioner of Indian Affairs,* in *Report of the Secretary of the Interior,* vol. 2, Sept. 21, 1887 (Washington, D.C.: GPO, 1888). "The most potent element of opposition to the allotment act is found in the Five Civilized Tribes of the Indian Territory. They are excepted and excluded from the provisions of the act, yet are busy trying to prejudice others against it, and are using their utmost endeavor to prevent whole tribes of Indians from agreeing to accept its provisions" (x). For a fascinating, perceptive article on the impact of allotment on southern Ute women, see Katherine M. B. Osburn, " 'Dear Friend and Ex-Husband': Marriage, Divorce, and Women's Property Rights on the Southern Ute Reservation, 1887-1930," in *Negotiators of Change,* ed. Nancy Shoemaker (New York: Routledge, 1995), 157–75. See also Katherine M. B. Osburn, *Southern Ute Women: Autonomy and Assimilation on the Reservation, 1887–1998* (Albuquerque: University of New Mexico Press, 1998). A revealing study might focus on whether Cherokee women took allotments near their female kin; this could be accomplished by comparing allotment patterns in a traditional area such as Vian and an acculturated locale such as Park Hill.

4. Otis, *Dawes Act,* 148.

5. *Report of the Commissioner of Indian Affairs,* in *Report of the Secretary of the Interior,* Oct. 1, 1889; published in 1900, 4.

6. Otis, *Dawes Act,* 31.

7. Debo, *And Still the Waters Run,* 91.

8. D'Arcy McNickle, "Indian and European: Indian White Relations from Discovery to 1887," in *The Rape of Indian Lands,* ed. Paul Wallace Gates (New York: Arno Press, 1979), 3, 10.

9. Lewis H. Morgan, a famous American ethnologist, opposed the allotment policy. He argued: "The inevitable result for the Indian would unquestionably be, that in a very short time he would divest himself of every foot of land and fall into poverty" (Wilcomb E. Washburn, *The Assault on Indian Tribalism: The General Allotment Law (Dawes Act) of 1887,* ed. Harold M. Hyman [Philadelphia: J. B. Lippincott, 1975], 9). Historian Mary Young pointed out that the contradictory intentions of the allotment treaties reflected ambivalence in American Indian policy: whether to assimilate the Indians or segregate them. Earlier allotment plans had failed due to extensive fraud, administrative troubles, and negative publicity. Indeed, the allotment process had been suspended in Alabama and Mississippi before the Civil War. It was reintroduced, however, in 1883 as Congress sought to deal with the various tribes pushed west who now occupied land desired by whites. See Mary Elizabeth Young, *Redskins, Ruffleshirts and Rednecks: Indian Allotments in Alabama and Mississippi, 1830–1860* (Norman: University of Oklahoma Press, 1961), 193; Prucha, *The Great Father,* 1:179–81.

10. Francis Paul Prucha, *American Indian Policy in Crisis: Christian Reformers and the Indian, 1865–1900* (Norman: University of Oklahoma, 1976), 154.

11. Janey B. Hendrix, "Redbird Smith and the Nighthawk Keetoowahs," *Journal of Cherokee Studies* 8, no. 1 (1983): 31. Helen Hunt Jackson, *A Century of Dishonor: A Sketch of the United States Government and Dealings with Some of the Indian Tribes* (1881; reprint, Norman: University of Oklahoma, 1995), 336–42.

12. Debo, *And Still the Waters Run,* 21–22; Washburn, *Assault on Indian Tribalism,* 12.

13. Prucha, *The Great Father,* 2:616, 669.

14. Washburn, *Assault on Indian Tribalism,* 19. The following Commissioners of Indian Affairs supported allotment: Manypenny in 1855; Dole in 1863; E. P. Smith in 1873 (Paul W. Gates, "Indian Allotments preceding the Dawes Act" in *The Rape of Indian Lands,* ed. Paul Wallace Gates (New York: Arno Press, 1979), 163.

15. Chief D. W. Bushyhead, Jan. 17, 1881, CN Papers, Box 4, Folder 3, Reel 49.

16. R. Douglas Hurt, *Indian Agriculture in America: Prehistory to the Present* (Lawrence: University Press of Kansas, 1987), 74–75, 65–66.

17. *The Report of the Commissioner of Indian Affairs,* in *The Report of the Secretary of Interior,* Oct. 5, 1885, Department of the Interior, Office of Indian Affairs, V, III.

18. Appeal of the Delegates of the Chickasaw, Creek, and Cherokee Nations to the president of the United States, CN Papers, Folder 3846, Reel 38. The Cherokee delegates were C. J. Harris and H. T. Landrum.

19. Josephine Pennington, Interview no. 7785, 39:407, 50:249, IPHC.

20. Mrs. Minnie L. Miller, Interview no. 13626, 108:303, IPHC. Miller attended and graduated from the old Female Seminary at Park Hill.

21. Agnew, Interview no. 5978, 66:16, 22, 297, IPHC.

22. Minnie L. Miller, Mary Cobb Agnew, and Mary J. Baker were of mixed ancestry. Mary J. Baker, Interview no. 13113, 99:384, 248, IPHC. See also J. W. Brewer, Interview no. 6712, 16:283, IPHC. Brewer said that his family was against allotment of land. Likewise John Bright said that his family was never in favor of allotment. According to Bright, most of the mixed bloods and younger Cherokees favored allotment. See 89:186–88, 208, IPHC.

23. Harvey Chaplen, Interview no. 7909, 65:104–16, 212, IPHC.

24. Comingdeer, Interview no. 7239, 20:310–11, IPHC.

25. Black Bird Doublehead, first interview no. 7537, 22:367–81; Gus Hummingbird, Fieldworker, Interviewed Mar. 21, 1938; Black Bird Doublehead, second interview, no. 13443, 85:293–96, IPHC.

26. Mary Gott, Interview no. 13628, 4:91, 122, IPHC.

27. Benjamin Knight, Interview, 32:272–73, 375, 377, IPHC.

28. Katja May, "Cherokee Nation's Political and Cultural Struggle," 30–31; the Keetoowah Society exists to the present day. See also Hendrix, "Redbird Smith," 73–86, and Katja May, "Nativistic Movements among the Cherokees in the Nineteenth and Twentieth Centuries," *Journal of Cherokee Studies* 15 (1990): 27–39.

29. Debo, *And Still the Waters Run,* 54.

30. "Redbird Smith," <www.cherokee.org/Culture/HistoryPage.asp?ID=14> (June 2002). See also Hendrix, "Redbird Smith," 22–39; Katja May, "Nativistic Movements," 27–39; and Perdue, *Cherokee Women,* 1–2.

31. "Redbird Smith," <www.cherokee.org/Culture/HistoryPage.asp?ID=14>. See also Hendrix, "Redbird Smith," 22–39; May, "Nativistic Movements," 27–39.

32. Redbird Smith went with his son, John, and Ocie Hogshooter to Washington, D.C., in 1914 to appeal to President Wilson. Senator Lane advised them to accept their allotments. Disappointed, the Nighthawks returned home and became more of a religious society than a political one. By 1916 membership in the Nighthawks and Keetoowah societies began to diminish ("Redbird Smith," <www.cherokee.org/Culture/HistoryPage.asp?ID=14>).

The United Keetoowah Band became a federally recognized band of Cherokees under the Indian Reorganization Act of 1934 and the Oklahoma Indian Welfare Act of 1936. The membership was approximately 7,700 members in 1995, with a blood quantum requirement of one-quarter Cherokee blood for membership. The band traces its lineage to the Keetoowah people who, in 1817, were the first to migrate from the East to Indian Territory (Stephen M. Fabian, Letter to *National Geographic,* Apr. 25, 1995, <www.uark.edu/depts/comminfo/UKB/three.html> [June 2002]). Since it became federally recognized, the United Keetoowah Band has conflicted with the Cherokee Nation and the United States government as members have attempted to preserve Cherokee traditions and ceremonies.

33. Debo, *And Still the Waters Run,* 153.

34. Ibid., 57–58.

35. Frank B. Long, ed., *Nowata Advertiser,* May 5, 1905, vol. 11, no. 6, CN Papers, Folder 7656, Reel 50.

36. In reporting the story of his defection, the reporter betrayed his biases as he wrote, "He [Red Bird Sixkiller] used to tell his story in quaint and graphic language that stirred the hearers. Those days are gone, and the proud Cherokee, like many another proud race[s,] has yielded to the inevitable, having been crushed in the march of progress, swallowed up in the abyss of time." In the same issue of the paper an editorial on the Keetoowah Society appeared. In the article the author wrote: "Peter Wolfe, a fullblood Cherokee Indian, was shot and killed by parties in ambush in the Saline district, Cherokee Nation Wednesday night of last week. An effort is being made to connect the Keetoowah society with the killing. It has been intimated that the Keetoowahs are opposed to the fullblood Cherokees taking their allotment, and they are killing those who do take allotments. There is probably no ground whatever for any such story as this being told. The Keetoowahs are a society of

Cherokees who are opposed to allotment, or to any change in their country. . . . The Cherokee history is the blackest blot in all that dark page of murder committed in the name of civilization by the American people" (*Weekly Examiner,* Bartlesville, Indian Territory, May 2, 1903, vol. 9, no 8, CN Papers, Folder 7632, Reel 50).

37. Editorial on Keetoowahs, *Wagoner Weekly Saying,* Thursday morning, Feb. 1, 1906, vol. 11, no. 50 (CN Papers, Folder 7671, Reel 50). Gritts died at his home near Tahlequah in 1906.

38. Debo, *And Still the Waters Run,* 295.

39. See editorial on Cherokee Resolution, *Daily Capital,* South McAlester, Indian Territory, Monday evening, Aug. 23, 1897, vol. 20, no.6, CN Papers, Folder 7583, Reel 50; another symbol of change in the Nation was the granting of the privilege to erect telephone lines in the Cherokee Nation to J. S. Davenport and others by the Cherokee National Council (CN Papers, Folder 1899, Reel 7). The following principal chiefs served: John Ross, 1826 to 1866; Lewis Downing, 1867 to 1871; William P. Ross, 1871 to 1875; Charles Thompson, 1875 to 1879; Dennis Bushyhead, 1879 to 1887; Joel B. Mayes, 1887 to 1891; C. J. Harris, 1891 to 1895; S. H. Mayes, 1895 to 1899; T. M. Buffington, 1899 to 1903 (D. M. Marrs, ed., "Chiefs Who Have Ruled," *Vinita Daily Chieftain,* June 14, 1904, vol. 6, no. 215, CN Papers, Folder 7645, Reel 50). See also the primary collections of the principal chiefs in the WHC for details on their roles in the allotment controversy.

40. *Nowata Advertiser,* Nov. 25, 1904, vol. 10, no. 35, CN Papers, Folder 7650, Reel 50.

41. CHN 118, Supreme Court Records, Oct. 5, 1868–Dec. 3, 1875, CN Papers. See chapter 5 for analysis of other cases involving divorce, adultery, domestic violence, and rape.

42. CHN 118, Oct. 5, 1868–Dec. 3, 1875, Supreme Court Records, 1868–99, CN Papers. The following probate cases reveal a representative sampling of those recorded in the CN Papers: CHN 24, Cooweescoowee District Records, Aug. 16, 1897–July 3, 1883, Records of Wills, 1869.

43. CHN 24, Cooweescoowee District Records, Aug. 16, 1897–July 3, 1883, Records of Wills, 1869, CN Papers.

44. Ibid., Estate of Nancy Wildcat, July 2, 1872, p. 159; Estate of Peter Proctor to Nancy Proctor, Apr. 4, 1868, Cherokee Court Records, Box 1, Folder 7, WHC.

45. Francis Paul Prucha, ed., *Documents of United States Indian Policy,* 2nd ed. (Lincoln: University of Nebraska, 1990), 197–98.

46. Debo, *And Still the Waters Run,* 34.

47. Petition for citizenship and documents regarding freedmen, CN Papers, Folder 176, Reel 3, Subgroup 5. See also Petition of Moses Whitmire, Trustee of the Freedmen of the Cherokee Nation, *Complainant vs. The Cherokee Nation and the United States,* Respondents, no. 17,209, May 8, 1895. Instructions from the principal chief on Feb. 10, 1870, pointed out that heads of families might be of either sex. The census result in 1880 revealed a total of 19,733 Cherokees—males: 10,011; females: 9,724. Including other residents, the total was Cherokees: 15,307; whites, 1,032; Colored, 1,976; Delaware, 672; Shawnees, 503; Creeks, 232; and miscellaneous, 13, with a total of 19,935 (CN Papers, Folder 84, Reel 2).

48. W. A. Duncan, May 28, 1897, Cherokee Senate Chamber, Cherokee Commission, CN Papers, Folder 384, Reel 4, 3.

49. H. Craig Miner, *The Corporation and the Indian: Tribal Sovereignty and Industrial Civilization in Indian Territory, 1865–1907* (Norman: University of Oklahoma Press, 1988), 14, 19.

50. May, "Cherokee Nation's Political and Cultural Struggle," 20.

51. Miner, *Corporation and the Indian,* 53, 58, 101, 115, 143.

52. Craig Miner wrote, "When the derrick joined the steam locomotive, the slag pile, and the roll of barbed wire in the vista of the frightened full blood, it seemed to him the equipment of doom was complete" (Miner, *Corporation and the Indian,* 102, 143, 209). See also the front page of the *Cherokee Advocate,* "Investigation of Sundry Indian Problems," Apr. 13, 1878, for a protest against the railroad companies issuing bonds upon land and homes in their territory (Augustus E. Ivey, ed., "Special to the Standard," *Stillwell Standard,* Dec. 20, 1901, vol. 2, no. 11, CN Papers, Folder 7984, Reel 51).

53. Prucha wrote, "The Choctaws and Chickasaws received 320 acres each, the Cherokees 110 acres, Creeks 160 acres, and Seminoles 120 acres. Freedmen among Cherokees, Creeks, and Seminoles shared equally with the Indians; those among the Chickasaws and Choctaws received 40 acre allotments." Congress made every Indian in the territory a citizen of the United States in 1901 (Prucha, *The Great Father,* 2:754). Debo recorded that before allotment the Cherokees owned 4,420,068 acres in Indian Territory in the northeast corner. The Cherokees owned $2,716,979.98 held in trust for the sale of their Eastern lands. The final disposition of the land in the Five Tribes area follows—Cherokee total acreage: 4,420,068; allotted acreage: 4,346,145; segregated and unallotted acreage: 73,923. Debo claimed that conversion of all the tribes to Christianity had been effected rapidly after removal (Debo, *And Still the Waters Run,* 7, 51).

54. Prucha, *The Great Father,* 2:671.

55. D. M. Marrs, ed., "First Deed Issued," *Vinita Weekly Chieftain,* Apr. 2, 1903, vol. 21, no. 32, CN Papers, Folder 8049, Reel 51. The chief added his autograph to the first deed, a town lot in Vinita, which was the first individual title ever given to land belonging to the Cherokee people. The conveyance was made to Mrs. Ludie Parker, wife of Mayor Luman F. Parker Jr.

56. Hurt, *Indian Agriculture,* 151–53, 172–73. See also Prucha, *The Great Father,* 2:754. From the early 1900s, legislation made it easier for Indians to sell their allotments. The decline in paternalism and protectionism of the Indians was in direct proportion to the discovery of oil in Indian Territory. On Apr. 21, 1904, Congress removed the restrictions from the surplus of adult white and African American allottees, and it gave wide latitude to the secretary of the interior to remove the restrictions on the surplus of any adult Indian. According to Marcia Odell, a historian of the allotment process, on May 27, 1908, Congress "removed the restrictions on all lands belonging to intermarried whites, freedmen, and Indians of less than one-half Indian blood, including minors." By 1907 in the Chelsea oil field, all the freedmen had lost their titles to land (Odell, *Divide and Conquer,* 360, 376, 342).

57. Boudinot's uncle, James M. Bell, received a similar note because of his support of allotment, which read, "Sir We the undersigned Committee of Safety have organized for the purpose of driving from our midst traitors and all persons that are laboring to bring about the allotment and sectionization of our Country do hereby order you and your family from our midst" (Sept. 12, 1881, CN Papers, Folder 7429, Reel 49).

58. "Elias C. Boudinot" from O'Beirne, H. F. and E. S., *The Indian Territory* (St. Louis, 1892), vol. 2:115–16, CN Papers, Folder 7558, Reel 50. See also E. C. Boudinot to James M. Bell, Jan. 13, 1881, CN Papers, Folder 7530, Reel 50. See Memorial of Elias C. Boudinot to the U.S. Congress regarding tobacco taxes, 1869–70, CN Papers, Folder 3791, Reel 38. See also CN Papers, Folders 3948, 3951, Reel 39; E. C. Boudinot to Stand Watie, Fayetteville,

Arkansas, Aug. 15, 1867, CN Papers, Folder 3951, Reel 39; Boudinot to Watie, Washington, D.C., Jan. 9, 1868, CN Papers, Folder 8080, Reel 52.

59. McLoughlin, *After the Trail of Tears,* 267. He reported to Stand Watie on May 10, 1871, "The Supreme Court has decided the tobacco case against me; it is the Death Knell of the Nations. I am totally ruined if you do not run for the Council" (Boudinot to Watie, Mrs. Trotts, May 10, 1871, CN Papers, Folder 3954, Reel 3). See Prucha, *Documents,* 136 (on Cherokee Tobacco Case), WHC. Some white men evidently conspired with an Indian named Eiffert and seized his hotel. Boudinot was able to recover it eventually. See CN Papers, Reel 41, Box 133, 4851; Reel 47, Box 165, 6763; Boudinot, ed., "The White Citizens Have Equal Rights So States Col. Boudinot—Mr. Bushyhead Quoted," Oct. 24, 1889, *Indian Chieftain,* vol. 8, no. 7, CN Papers, Folder 7547, Reel 50. He wrote to his aunt, Sarah C. Watie, on Apr. 23, 1879, "We will soon be strong enough to defy the malice of our enemies and make them pay dearly for all our troubles" (CN Papers, Folder 14322, Reel 40). See also the letters to Sarah C. Watie, Apr. 5, 1880, and Apr. 12, 1880, CN Papers, Folders 4331, 4332, Reel 40. He wrote angrily to James M. Bell, "How is it possible that you allowed the God damned scoundrels to take possession of my Hotel?" (E. C. Boudinot to James M. Bell, Washington, May 5, 1878, CN Papers, Folder 4959, Roll 41).

60. Miner, *Corporation and the Indian,* 19, 24.

61. Debo recounts that "approximately sixty thousand minors with land valued at $130,000,000, besides an oil valuation of $25,000,000, were placed under the jurisdiction of forty county judges." Debo eloquently described the allotment policies as complete failures (*And Still the Waters Run,* 127, 183, 197).

62. Debo, *And Still the Waters Run,* 353. See also *Oklahoma's Poor Rich Indians: An Orgy of Graft and Exploitation of the Five Civilized Tribes-Legalized Robbery,* a report by Gertrude Bonnin, research agent, Indian Welfare Committee, General Federation of Women's Clubs; Charles H. Fabens, American Indian Defense Association; Matthew K. Sniffen, Indian Rights Association (Philadelphia: Office of the Indian Rights Association, 1924). Emmeline Terrell confirmed that the major portion of land that she and her family were allotted had been lost to them by unwise sales and foreclosures of mortgages (Terrell, Interview, 46:287, IPHC). See also George W. Mayes, second interview, no. 8165, 79:129, 71:44, IPHC, and Josephine Pennington, Interview no. 7783, 39:407, IPHC.

63. The allotment policies had less dramatic impact on the Eastern Cherokees than on those in Oklahoma. The Eastern Cherokees became incorporated under state law in 1889. An important court case reaffirmed federal authority in relationship to the tribe. David Boyd, who was a lumberman, offered fifteen thousand dollars to the Indians for the timber on the Cathcart tract of land. He then resold the contract to Harry M. Dickson with William T. Mason for twenty-five thousand dollars. A district court in 1895 said that the Supreme Court had not conferred citizenship on the Eastern Cherokees, nor had any legislative body done so. The decision meant that a state could not set aside federal guardianship, which was established under an 1868 act. The court again affirmed their peculiar status. When the United States appealed the decision, a fourth circuit court of appeals in Richmond ruled in 1897 that the Indians were not citizens, and that the U.S. government had a long recognized right to supervise Indian affairs. The North Carolina Cherokees only gained an undisputed right to vote in 1930. The Boyd decision meant that the Indian Office could consider implementing allotment, a key aspect of its civilization program. However, unlike the Western Cherokees, the Eastern Cherokees had already divided up most of the common

lands among them and were farming almost every available acre. Thus not much more could be gained by severalty. Because of the unusual method of their acquiring their land back with the help of William Holland Thomas, the Eastern Cherokees had already had to formally abandon communal ownership of their land to a great extent. However, the tribal corporation technically held the land, but members could occupy and improve it. For all practical purposes the land became their own (Finger, *Eastern Band of Cherokees,* 172–75). For an excellent discussion of the relationship of federal recognition, citizenship issues, and tribal sovereignty, see George Roth, "Federal Tribal Recognition in the South," in *Anthropologists and Indians in the South,* ed. Rachel Bonney and J. Anthony Paredes (Tuscaloosa: University of Alabama Press, 2001), 49–70. Another insightful article is George Roth, "Overview of Southeastern Indian Tribes Today," in *Indians of the Southeastern United States in the Late Twentieth Century,* ed. J. Anthony Paredes (Tuscaloosa: University of Alabama Press, 1992), 183–202.

64. Daniel F. Littlefield Jr., *The Cherokee Freedmen: From Emancipation to American Citizenship* (Westport, Conn.: Greenwood Press, 1978), 8, 40. This section of the chapter draws primarily on the excellent work of Littlefield, to whom the author is grateful.

65. Ibid., 8–9, 11, 41, 43–44.

66. Odell, *Divide and Conquer,* 189. By the terms of the Cherokee Agreement, the individual's share was set at 110 acres of average land. This was equivalent to a credit of $325.60 to invest in land. Jan. 1, 1903, marked the beginning of the allotment for the Cherokees. When the Cherokees ran short of land, Congress directed that citizens who did not receive their share would receive $651.20 from tribal funds (Debo, *And Still the Waters Run,* 50). Controversies over Cherokee citizenship continued into the twentieth century with the Dawes Roll and Guion Miller applications. Undoubtedly, as the U.S. government rather than the Cherokee Nation assumed control over defining citizenship, many acquired citizenship who would not have received approval by the Cherokees.

67. Wilma Mankiller, "Rebuilding the Cherokee Nation," Apr. 2, 1993, Sweet Briar College, <http://gos.sbc.edu/m/mankiller.html> (June 2002), 6–7.

Conclusion

1. Mankiller and Wallis, *Mankiller,* 47–48.

2. For a fascinating article on intermarriage as a survival strategy, see Michael H. Logan and Stephen D. Ousley, "Hypergamy, Quantum, and Reproductive Success—The Lost Indian Ancestor Reconsidered," *Anthropologists and Indians in the New South,* ed. Rachel A. Bonney and J. Anthony Paredes (Tuscaloosa: University of Alabama Press, 2001), 184–202. Out of the 29,610 Cherokees in Oklahoma in 1910, almost 80 percent had a non-Indian ancestor (185). Logan and Ousley address the question of why so many Americans claim to have some Indian ancestry and most frequently claim a great-grandmother who was a Cherokee princess. Vine Deloria spoke of this phenomenon in his book *Custer Died for Your Sins* (1969; reprint, Norman: University of Oklahoma, 1941). Logan and Ousley cite Russell Thornton's findings that in 1980 the U.S. census data recorded 6,754,800 Americans who claimed some degree of Indian ancestry. This was a figure five times greater than the figure of 1,366,676, recorded in the same year for American Indians (198–99). The authors contend, "Admixed women also enjoyed greater fecundity and reduced childhood mortality than their full-blood counterparts" (200–201). Thus, they argue, "During the 19th cen-

tury, native females who intermarried with whites and admixed tribal members enjoyed a decided reproductive advantage" (202). Many people may claim Cherokee ancestry because the tribe has been perceived as highly acculturated, but the fact remains that a large number of Cherokees did intermarry with whites. Former president Bill Clinton acknowledged a Cherokee ancestor. In addition to intermarriage, the other reason so many Americans claim Cherokee heritage is the fact that many white Americans with genuine Cherokee background—Cherokee freedmen, members of other tribes, and whites without any background—were enrolled on the Dawes Roll. Moreover, the Seminoles and other tribes are currently receiving petitions from a number of African Americans who are requesting tribal enrollment based on intermarriage or ancestors who were freedmen and freedwomen.

3. Jack Frederick Kilpatrick, "An Etymological Note on the Tribal Name of the Cherokees and Certain Place and Proper Names Derived from Cherokee," *Journal of the Graduate Research Center*, no. 30 (1962), 37–41. Kilpatrick claims that the term *Anì-Yûñwiyà*, translated usually as "real people" or "principal people," actually denotes more accurately "Indians" and not specifically Cherokees. He questions the translation and believes the "complete" or "unalloyed" would be a more accurate translation of the term. He believes that the tribal name of the Cherokees is and has been within the historic period Anitsàlagí (plural), Atsàlagí (singular), and Tsàlagí (adjectival). The word *tsà^{d}lagí* means "she (or he) turned aside." Thus it refers to someone who turned off a trail and followed an independent way (37–39). Alternate spellings are Ani'-Yûñ'wiyă and Tsa'lăgi'. Mooney, *Myths of the Cherokees*, 15.

4. Mankiller and Wallis, *Mankiller*, 5–6, 181.

5. The Oklahoma Indians were excluded from many of the provisions of the Wheeler-Howard Act. They were not permitted to organize or incorporate (Prucha, *Documents*, 222–29). In the 1960s during the Kennedy and Johnson administrations, federal policy once again emphasized tribal self-determination (Prucha, *The Great Father*, 2:1087–90). The principal chief of the Cherokee Nation of Oklahoma in 2002 was Chad "Corntassel" Smith, who is the great-grandson of Redbird Smith, who was so crucial to the Keetoowah Society. His uncle, the late traditionalist, William Lee Smith, led the Keetoowah Society at Stokes Stomp ground beginning in the 1950s. Chad Smith holds a master's degree in public administration from the University of Wisconsin and a J.D. from the University of Tulsa. He has strong ties with traditional Cherokee beliefs and values ("Chad Corntassel" Smith Chief, "Cherokee Nation Official Website," <www.cherokee.org/TribalGovernment/CouncilPage/> [June 2002]). At the time this book was published, the principal chief of the Eastern Band of Cherokees was Leon Jones, who was elected in 1999. Jones was chief magistrate and a former council representative (Virginia Moore Carney, "A Testament to Tenacity: Cultural Persistence in the Letters and Speeches of the Eastern Band Cherokee Women" [Ph.D. diss., University of Kentucky, 2000], 275).

6. Mankiller and Wallis, *Mankiller*, 226.

7. Ibid., 86.

8. Carney, "A Testament to Tenacity," 244, 238, 247–48, 268–69 (section on Joyce Dugan, inclusive 236–50).

9. Ibid., 245–46.

10. June 5, 2001, *News Sentinel*, Knoxville, Tenn. See also Andrew Curry, "Cherokee Holy of Holies," *Archaeology* (Sept./Oct. 2002), 70–75. Curry wrote that some archaeologists estimate that the site has been occupied for at least ten thousand years, and evidence gath-

ered in some preliminary investigations indicates the Cherokee presence for at least eight hundred years (71). Archaeologists working for the Eastern Band of Cherokees discovered the presence of the sacred hearth, which is centuries old. Cherokee prophecy held that they would lose Kituwha and their way but regain it and recover their "Kituwha Way." However, the prophecy also predicted that if the tribe lost Kituwha a second time, they would not remain Cherokee, and the world would end (72).

11. Elie Wiesel, *The Gates of the Forest* (Geneva: Bibliophile Library, 1986), 14–15.

Bibliography

Manuscript Collections

Allen, Penelope Johnson. "History of the Cherokee Indians." Manuscript, 1935. James D. Hoskins Library, Special Collections. University of Tennessee, Knoxville.

American Baptist Historical Society, Valley Forge, Pennsylvania Missionary Correspondence 1800–1900.

American Board of Commissioners for Foreign Missions. Archive. Houghton Library, Harvard University.

American State Papers. Library of Congress.

Cherokee Nation Papers. Oklahoma Historical Society and Western History Collections. University of Oklahoma Libraries, Norman. Reels 19, 20, 22, 23, 24, 29, 32, 38, 41, 42, 43, 44, 45, 46, 47, 50, 51, 52, 53, 117, 118, 119.

Corn, James, Collection. Records of the Cherokee Indian Agency in Tennessee, 1801–35. History Branch and Archives, Cleveland Public Library, Cleveland, Tennessee.

Galileo Project. Southeastern Native American Documents, 1730–1842. <http://galileo.usg.edu>.

Indian-Pioneer History Collection. Indian Archives, Oklahoma Historical Society, Oklahoma City.

National Archives, Washington, D.C. Records of the Bureau of Indian Affairs, Record Group 75, Microcopy 208.

Nave Letters, 1850–72. Ed. T. L. Ballenger. Northeastern State University, John Vaughn Library, Special Collections, Tahlequah, Oklahoma.

Museum of the Cherokee Indian, Cherokee, North Carolina
    Baptist Missionary Records
    David Brown Letters
    Elias Boudinot Letters
    Evan Jones Journals and Letters

Frans Olbrechts Collection
Hargrett Collection
James Mooney Collection
John Ross Papers
Photographic Archives
Samuel E. Beck Collection
Springplace Diary
Trail of Tears Research Data
Oklahoma Historical Society, Archives and Manuscripts Division, Oklahoma City, Oklahoma
Alice Robertson Papers
Barde Collection
C. C. Torrey Collection
Dwight Mission Church and School Records
Edward Deas Collection
Emmet McDonald Starr Collection
Evaluation of Claims, Alabama, 1838
Grant Foreman Collection
H. L. Buckner Collection
John Ross Collection
Kenneth Phillips Collection
Photographic Archives
Records of the Dawes Commission to the Five Civilized Tribes
Return J. Meigs Collection
Samuel Worcester Collection
Thomas J. Harrison Collection
Oklahoma State Museum of History, Oklahoma City, Oklahoma.
Payne, John Howard, Papers. MSS 10 volumes. Newberry Library, Chicago.
Smithsonian Institution, National Anthropological Archives, Washington, D.C.
Thomas Gilcrease Museum, Tulsa, Oklahoma.
Grant Foreman Collection
Ross Papers
Watie Papers
Western History Collections, University of Oklahoma Libraries, Norman
Ann Ross Piburn Collection
C. Johnson Harris Collection
Dennis Bushyhead Collection
Isabel Cobb Collection
James Anderson Slover Collection
Joel Bryan Mayes Collection
Kathleen Faux Collection
Oochalata Collection
Photographic Archives
Samuel Houston Mayes Collection
Stephen Foreman Collection
T. M. Buffington Collection
Watie-Boudinot Papers
Woolaroc Museum, Bartlesville, Oklahoma.

Books, Articles, and Theses

Abel, Annie Heloise. *The American Indian and the End of the Confederacy, 1863–1866*. Lincoln: University of Nebraska Press, 1993.

———. *The American Indian as Slaveholder and Secessionist*. 1915. Reprint, Lincoln: University of Nebraska Press, 1992.

Adair, James. *Adair's History of the American Indians*. Ed. Samuel Cole Williams. 1775. Reprint, Johnson City, Tenn.: Watauga Press, 1930.

———. *The History of the American Indians Particularly Those Nations Adjoining to the Mississippi East and West Florida, Georgia, South and North Carolina, and Virginia*. With an introduction by Robert F. Berkhofer Jr. New York: Johnson Reprint Corporation, 1968.

Ahenakew, Freda, and H. C. Wolfart, eds. *Our Grandmothers' Lives As Told in Their Own Words*. Saskatoon, Saskatchewan: Fifth House, 1992.

Albers, Patricia, and Beatrice Medicine. *The Hidden Half: Studies of Plains Indian Women*. New York: University Press of America, 1983.

Anderson, Karen. *Chain Her by the Foot: The Subjugation of Women in Seventeenth-Century New France*. New York: Routledge, 1993.

Anderson, Rufus, ed. *Memoir of Catharine Brown: A Christian Indian of the Cherokee Nation*. 3rd ed. Boston: Crocker and Brewster, 1828.

Annual Reports of the Commissioners of Indian Affairs, 1800–1907, Reports of the Secretary of the Interior. Washington, D.C.: GPO.

Axtell, James. *The Indian Peoples of Eastern America: A Documentary History of the Sexes*. New York: Oxford University Press, 1981.

Baker, T. Lindsay, and Julie P. Baker. *The WPA Oklahoma Slave Narratives*. Norman: University of Oklahoma Press, 1996.

Bartram, William. "Observations on the Creek and Cherokee Indians, 1789." *Transactions of the American Ethnological Society* 3, pt. 1. (1853): 39.

———. *Travels and Other Writings*. New York: Literary Classics of the United States, 1996.

Bass, Althea. *Cherokee Messenger*. 1936. Reprint, Norman: University of Oklahoma Press, 1968.

Bataille, Gretchen M., and Kathleen Mullen Sands. *American Indian Women: Telling Their Lives*. Lincoln: University of Nebraska Press, 1984.

Bell, Amelia Rector. "Separate People: Speaking of Creek Men and Women." *American Anthropologist* 92 (1990): 332–45.

Berhard, Virginia, Betty Brandon, Elizabeth Fox-Genovese, and Theda Perdue. *Southern Women: Histories and Identities*. Columbia: University of Missouri Press, 1992.

Berkhofer, Robert F., Jr. *Salvation and the Savage: An Analysis of Protestant Missions and American Indian Response, 1787–1862*. Lexington: University of Kentucky Press, 1965.

Bonney, Rachel A., and J. Anthony Paredes, eds. *Anthropologists and Indians in the New South*. Tuscaloosa: University of Alabama Press, 2001.

Bonnin, Gertrude. *Oklahoma's Poor Indians: An Orgy of Graft and Exploitation*. Philadelphia: Office of the Indian Rights Association, 1924.

Bowden, Henry Warner. *American Indians and Christian Missions*. Chicago: University of Chicago Press, 1981.

Braund, Kathryn E. Holland. "Guardians of Tradition and Handmaidens of Change: Women's Roles in Creek Economic and Social Life during the Eighteenth Century." *American Indian Quarterly* 14 (summer 1990): 239–58.

———. *Deerskins and Duffels: The Creek Indian Trade with Anglo-America, 1685–1815.* Lincoln: University of Nebraska Press, 1993.

Britton, Wiley. *Memoirs of the Rebellion on the Border.* Lincoln: University of Nebraska Press, 1993.

Brown, John P. *Old Frontiers: The Story of the Cherokee Indians from Earliest Times to the Date of Their Removal to the West, 1838.* Kingsport, Tenn.: Southern Publishers, 1938.

Brown, Joseph Epes. *The Spiritual Legacy of the American Indian.* New York: Crossroad, 1993.

Brown, Nettie Terry. "The Missionary World of Ann Eliza Worcester Robertson." Ph.D. diss., North Texas State University, 1978.

Butler, Judith. *Gender Trouble: Feminism and the Subversion of Identity.* New York: Routledge, 1990.

Calloway, Colin G. *New Directions in American Indian History.* Norman: University of Oklahoma Press, 1987.

Carney, Virginia Moore. "A Testament to Tenacity: Cultural Persistence in the Letters and Speeches of Eastern Band Cherokee Women." Ph.D. diss., University of Kentucky, 2000.

Carter, Samuel, III. *Cherokee Sunset: A Nation Betrayed: A Narrative of Travail and Triumph, Persecution and Exile.* New York: Doubleday, 1976.

Chase, Marybelle W. *Cherokee Claims: Skin Bayou District.* Nashville: Tennessee State Library and Archives, 1988.

Clinton, Catherine. *The Other Civil War: American Women in the Nineteenth Century.* New York: Hill and Wang, 1984.

———. *The Plantation Mistress: Woman's World in the Old South.* New York: Pantheon, 1982.

———. *Tara Revisited: Women, War and the Plantation Legend.* New York: Abbeville Press, 1995.

Clinton, Catherine, and Nina Silber. *Divided Houses: Gender and the Civil War.* New York: Oxford University Press, 1992.

Cochran, Thomas C, ed. *New American State Papers.* Wilmington, Del.: Scholarly Resources, 1972.

Colbert, Alice Taylor. "Cherokee Women and Cultural Change." In *Women of the American South: A Multicultural Reader,* ed. Christie Anne Farnham, 43–55. New York: New York University Press, 1997.

Coleman, Michael C. *American Indian Children at School, 1850–1930.* Jackson: University of Mississippi, 1993.

Constitution and Laws of the Cherokee Nation. St. Louis: R and T. A. Ennis, 1875.

Constitution of the Cherokee Nation. Milledgeville, Ga.: Office of the Statesman and Patriot, 1827.

Corkran, David H. *The Cherokee Frontier: Conflict and Survival, 1740–1762.* Norman: University of Oklahoma Press, 1962.

Crouch, William W. "Missionary Activities among the Cherokee." Master's thesis, University of Tennessee, 1932.

Dale, Edward Everett, and Gaston Litton. *Cherokee Cavaliers: Forty Years of Cherokee History as Told in the Correspondence of the Ridge-Watie-Boudinot Family.* Norman: University of Oklahoma Press, 1995.

Davis, Natalie Zemon. "Iroquois Women, European Women." In *Women, "Race," and Writing in the Early Modern Period,* ed. Margo Hendricks and Patricia Parker, 243–58, 350–61. New York: Routledge, 1994.

de Beauvoir, Simone. *The Second Sex*. Translated by H. M. Parshley. New York: Alfred A. Knopf, 1952.

Debo, Angie. *And Still the Waters Run: The Betrayal of the Five Civilized Tribes*. 1940. Reprint, Princeton: Princeton University Press, 1991.

———. *The Road to Disappearance*. Norman: University of Oklahoma Press, 1941.

———. "Southern Refugees of the Cherokee Nation." *Southwestern Historical Quarterly* 35, no. 4 (1932): 255–66.

Deloria, Vine. *Custer Died for Your Sins: An Indian Manifesto*. 1969. Reprint, Norman: University of Oklahoma Press, 1988.

Devens, Carol. *Countering Colonization: Native American Women in the Great Lakes Missions, 1630–1900*. Berkeley: University of California Press, 1992.

Douglas, Mary. *Purity and Danger: An Analysis of the Concepts of Pollution and Taboo*. 1966. Reprint, London: Routledge and Kegan, 1984.

Dunaway, Wilma. "Rethinking Cherokee Acculturation: Agrarian Capitalism and Women's Resistance to the Cult of Domesticity, 1800–1838." *American Indian Culture and Research Journal* 21, no. 1 (1997): 155–92.

Dunaway, Wilma A. *The First American Frontier: Transition to Capitalism in Southern Appalachia, 1700–1860*. Chapel Hill: University of North Carolina Press, 1996.

Eaton, Rachel Caroline. *John Ross and the Cherokee Indians*. Chicago: University of Chicago Libraries, 1921.

Eggan, Fred. *The American Indian: Perspectives for the Study of Social Change*. Chicago: Aldine, 1966.

———. *Essays in Social Anthropology and Ethnology*. Chicago: University of Chicago Department of Anthropology, 1975.

———. "Historical Changes in the Choctaw Kinship System." *American Anthropologist* 39 (1937): 34–52.

———. *Social Anthropology of North American Tribes: Essays in Social Organization, Law, and Religion*. Chicago: University of Chicago Press, 1937.

Ehle, John. *Trail of Tears: The Rise and Fall of the Cherokee Nation*. New York: Doubleday, 1988.

Engels, Friedrich. *The Origin of the Family, Private Property, and the State*. 1884. Reprint, New York: Pathfinder Press, 1972.

Etienne, Mona, and Eleanor Leacock, eds. *Women and Colonization: Anthropological Perspectives*. New York: Praeger, 1980.

Evans, J. P. "Sketches of Cherokee Characteristics." *Journal of Cherokee Studies* 4, no. 1 (1979): 16–20. Prepared in 1835, originally JHP Papers, vol. 6.

Evarts, Jeremiah. *Cherokee Removal: The "William Penn" Essays and Other Writings*. Ed. Francis Paul Prucha. Knoxville: University of Tennessee, 1981.

Everett, Diana. *The Texas Cherokees: A People between Two Fires, 1819–1840*. Norman: University of Oklahoma Press, 1990.

Farnham, Christie. *The Impact of Feminist Research in the Academy*. Bloomington: Indiana University Press, 1987.

———. *Women of the American South: A Multicultural Reader*. New York: New York University Press, 1997.

Faust, Drew Gilpin. "Altars of Sacrifice." *Journal of American History* 76, no. 4 (1990): 1220–28.

Fenton, William N., and John Gulick, eds. *Symposium on Cherokee and Iroquois Culture.*

Smithsonian Institution, Bulletin 180, Bureau of American Ethnology. Washington, D.C.: U.S. GPO, 1961.

Filler, Louis, and Allen Guttmann. *The Removal of the Cherokee Nation: Manifest Destiny or National Dishonor?* Boston: D. C. Heath, 1962.

Finger, John R. *Cherokee Americans: The Eastern Band of Cherokee in the Twentieth Century.* Lincoln: University of Nebraska Press, 1991.

———. *The Eastern Band of Cherokees, 1819–1900.* Knoxville: University of Tennessee Press, 1984.

Fogelson, Raymond D. "The Cherokee Ball Game: A Study in Southeastern Ethnology." Ph.D. Diss. Ann Arbor, Mich.: University Microfilms, 1962.

———. *The Cherokees: A Critical Bibliography.* Published for the Newberry Library. Bloomington: Indiana University Press, 1978.

———. "On the 'Petticoat Government' of the Eighteenth-Century Cherokee." In *Personality and the Cultural Construction of Society: Papers in Honor of Melford E. Spiro,* ed. David Jordan and Marc Swartz, 161–81. Tuscaloosa: University of Alabama Press, 1990.

Fogelson, Raymond D., and Amelia B. Walker. "Self and Other in Cherokee Booger Masks." *Journal of Cherokee Studies* 5, no. 2 (1980): 88–102.

Foreman, Carolyn. *Indian Women Chiefs.* Muskogee, Okla.: Hoffman Print Co., 1954.

———. *Park Hill.* Muskogee, Okla.: n.p., 1948.

Foreman, Grant. *The Five Civilized Tribes.* Norman: University of Oklahoma Press, 1934.

———. *Indian Removal: The Emigration of the Five Civilized Tribes of Indians.* Norman: University of Oklahoma Press, 1932.

———, ed. *A Traveler in Indian Territory: The Journal of Ethan Allen Hitchcock-Late Major-General in the United States Army.* Cedar Rapids, Iowa: Torch, 1930.

Fox-Genovese, Elizabeth. *Within the Plantation Household: Black and White Women in the Old South.* Chapel Hill: University of North Carolina Press, 1988.

Franks, Kenny A. *Stand Watie and the Agony of the Cherokee Nation.* Memphis: Memphis State University, 1979.

Fraser, Walter J., Jr., Frank Saunders Jr., and Jon L. Wakelyn. *The Web of Southern Social Relations: Women, Family, and Education.* Athens: University of Georgia Press, 1985.

Gaines, W. Craig. *The Confederate Cherokees: John Drew's Regiment of Mounted Rifles.* Baton Rouge: Louisiana State University Press, 1989.

Gates, Paul Wallace, ed. *The Rape of Indian Lands.* New York: Arno Press, 1979.

Gearing, Fred O. *Priests and Warriors: Social Structures for Cherokee Politics in the Eighteenth Century.* Vol. 64, no. 5, pt. 2, Memoir 93. Menasha, Wis.: American Anthropological Association, 1962.

Gero, Joan M., and Margaret W. Conkey. *Engendering Archaeology: Women and Prehistory.* Oxford: Basil and Blackwell, 1991.

Gilbert, William Harlen, Jr. *The Eastern Cherokees.* Bulletin 133. Anthropological Papers, 19–26. Bureau of American Ethnology. Washington, D.C.: U.S. GPO, 1943.

Green, Michael D. *The Politics of Indian Removal: Creek Government and Society in Crisis.* Lincoln: University of Nebraska Press, 1982.

Green, Rayna. *Native American Women: A Contextual Bibliography.* Bloomington: Indiana University Press, 1983.

———. *Women in American Indian Society.* New York: Chelsea House, 1992.

Gregory, Jack, and Rennard Strickland, eds. *Starr's History of the Cherokee Indians*. Fayetteville, Ark.: Indian Heritage Association, 1967.

Gridley, Marion E. *American Indian Women*. New York: Hawthorn Books, 1974.

Gulick, John. *Cherokees at the Crossroads*. Rev. ed. Chapel Hill: University of North Carolina Press, 1973.

Gutierrez, Ramon A. *When Jesus Came the Corn Mothers Went Away: Marriage, Sexuality, and Power in New Mexico, 1500–1846*. Stanford: Stanford University Press, 1991.

Hale, Janet Campbell. *Bloodlines: Odyssey of a Native Daughter*. New York: Harper Perennial, 1993.

Haskins, Shirley Coats. *Cherokee Property Valuations in Tennessee, 1836*. Cleveland: n.p., 1984.

Hatley, M. Thomas, "The Three Lives of Keowee: Loss and Recovery in Eighteenth-Century Villages." In *Powhatan's Mantle*, ed. Peter H. Wood, Gregory A. Waselkov, and M. Thomas Hatley, 223–48. Lincoln: University of Nebraska Press, 1989.

———. *The Dividing Paths: Cherokees and South Carolinians through the Era of Revolution*. New York: Oxford University Press, 1993.

Hauptman, Laurence M. *Between Two Fires: American Indians in the Civil War*. New York: Free Press, 1995.

Hawkins, Benjamin. *A Sketch of Creek Country in the Years 1798 and 1799 and Letters of Benjamin Hawkins, 1796–1806*. Spartanburg, S.C.: Reprint, 1974.

Haywood, John. *The Natural and Aboriginal History of Tennessee up to the First Settlements Therein by the White People in the Year 1768*. Ed. Mary U. Rothrock. 1823. Reprint, Jackson, Tenn.: McCowat-Mercer Press, 1959.

Hendricks, Margo, and Patricia Parker, eds. *Women, "Race," and Writing in the Early Modern Period*. New York: Routledge, 1994.

Hendrix, Janey B. "Redbird Smith and the Nighthawk Keetoowahs." *Journal of Cherokee Studies* 8, no. 1 (1983): 22–39.

Henry, Jeannette. *The American Indian Reader*. San Francisco: Indian Historian Press, 1972.

Hicks, Hannah Worcester. "The Diary of Hannah Hicks." *American Scene* 13 (1972), 2–24.

Hill, Sarah H. *Weaving New Worlds: Southeastern Cherokee Women and Their Basketry*. Chapel Hill: University of North Carolina Press, 1997.

Horton, Wade Alston. "Protestant Missionary Women as Agents of Cultural Transition among Cherokee Women, 1801–1839." Ph.D. diss., Southern Baptist Theological Seminary, 1992.

Hoxie, Frederick. *A Final Promise: The Campaign to Assimilate the Indians, 1880–1920*. New York: Cambridge University Press, 1989.

Hudson, Charles M. "Red, White, and Black: Symposium on Indians in the Old South." In *Southern Anthropological Society Proceedings*, no. 5. Athens: University of Georgia Press, 1971.

———. *The Southeastern Indians*. Knoxville: University of Tennessee Press, 1976.

———, ed. *Ethnology of the Southeastern Indians: A Source Book*. New York: Garland, 1985.

Hungry Wolf, Beverly. *The Ways of My Grandmothers*. New York: William Morrow, 1980.

Hurt, Douglas R. *Indian Agriculture in America: Prehistory to the Present*. Lawrence: University Press of Kansas, 1987.

Jackson, Helen Hunt. *A Century of Dishonor: A Sketch of the United States Government and*

Dealings with Some of the Indian Tribes. 1881. Reprint, Norman: University of Oklahoma Press, 1995.

Johnston, Carolyn. "Burning Beds, Spinning Wheels, and Calico Dresses: Controlling Cherokee Female Sexuality," *Journal of Cherokee Studies* 19 (1998): 3–17.

———. "In the White Woman's Image? Resistance, Transformation, and Identity in Recent Native American Women's History," *Journal of Women's History* 8, no. 3 (1996): 205–18.

———. *Sexual Power: Feminism and the Family in America.* Tuscaloosa: University of Alabama Press, 1992.

———. "The 'Panther's Scream Is Often Heard': Cherokee Women in Indian Territory during the Civil War," *Chronicles of Oklahoma* 78, no. 1 (2000): 84–107.

Jones, Jacqueline. *Labor of Love, Labor of Sorrow: Black Women, Work, and the Family from Slavery to the Present.* New York: Basic, 1985.

Jordan, David K., and Marc J. Swartz. *Personality and the Construction of Society.* Tuscaloosa: University of Alabama Press, 1990.

Kappler, Charles J., ed. *Indian Affairs, Laws, and Treaties.* Washington, D.C.: GPO, 1904–75.

Keller, Robert H., Jr. *American Protestantism and United States Indian Policy, 1869–1982.* Lincoln: University of Nebraska Press, 1983.

Kersey, Harry, and Helen Bannan. "Patchwork and Politics: The Evolving Roles of Florida Seminole Women in the Twentieth Century." In *Negotiators of Change: Historical Perspectives on Native American Women,* ed. Nancy Shoemaker, 193–212. New York: Routledge, 1995.

Kersey, Harry A., Jr. *An Assumption of Sovereignty: Social and Political Transformation among the Florida Seminoles, 1953–1979.* Lincoln: University of Nebraska Press, 1996.

———. *The Florida Seminoles in the Depression and New Deal, 1933–1942: An Indian Perspective.* Boca Raton: Florida Atlantic University Press, 1989.

Kidwell, Clara Sue. "Choctaw Women and Cultural Persistence in Mississippi." In *Negotiators of Change: Historical Perspectives on Native American Women,* ed. Nancy Shoemaker, 115–34. New York: Routledge, 1995.

———. *Choctaws and Missionaries in Mississippi, 1818–1918.* Norman: University of Oklahoma Press, 1995.

———. "Indian Women as Cultural Mediators." *Ethnohistory* 39 (spring 1992): 97–107.

Kilpatrick, Jack Frederick. "An Etymological Note on the Tribal Name of the Cherokees and Certain Place and Proper Names Derived from Cherokee." *Journal of the Graduate Research Center* 30 (1962): 37–41.

Kilpatrick, Jack Frederick, and Anna Gritts Kilpatrick. *New Echota Letters: Contributions of Samuel A. Worcester to the Cherokee Phoenix.* Dallas: Southern Methodist University Press, 1968.

———. *Notebook of a Cherokee Shaman.* Washington, D.C.: Smithsonian Institution Press, 1970.

———. *The Shadow of Sequoyah: Social Documents of the Cherokees, 1862–1964.* Norman: University of Oklahoma Press, 1965.

———. *Walk in Your Soul: Love Incantations of the Oklahoma Cherokees.* Dallas: Southern Methodist University Press, 1965.

Kilpatrick, Jacquelyn. *Celluloid Indians: Native Americans and Film.* Lincoln: University of Nebraska Press, 1999.

King, Duane H., ed. *The Cherokee Indian Nation: A Troubled History.* Knoxville: University of Tennessee Press, 1979.

Klein, Laura F., and Lillian A. Ackerman, eds. *Women and Power in Native North America.* Norman: University of Oklahoma Press, 1995.

Klinck, Carl, and James J. Talman, eds. *The Journal of Major John Norton, 1816.* Toronto: Champlain Society, 1970.

Kupferer Harriet J. *Ancient Drums, Other Moccasins: Native North American Cultural Adaptation.* Englewood Cliffs, N.J.: Prentice Hall, 1988.

——. *The "Principal People," 1960: A Study of Cultural and Social Groups of the Eastern Cherokee.* Washington, D.C.: GPO, 1966. Also Smithsonian Institution, Bureau of American Ethnology Bulletin, 196. Anthropological Papers No. 78, 215–325.

Lamphere, Louise. "Historical and Regional Variability in Navajo Women's Roles." *Journal of Anthropological Research* 45 (winter 1989): 431–56.

Landes, Ruth. *The Ojibwa Woman.* New York: Columbia University Press, 1938. Reprint, Lincoln: University of Nebraska, 1997.

Lawson, John. *A New Voyage to Carolina, 1709.* Ed. Hugh Talmage Lefler. Chapel Hill: University of North Carolina Press, 1967.

Leacock, Eleanor, and Mona Etienne, eds. *Essays on Women and Colonization: Anthropological Perspectives.* New York: Praeger, 1980.

Lebsock, Suzanne D. *The Free Women of Petersburg: Status and Culture in a Southern Town, 1784–1860.* New York: Norton, 1984.

Leeds, Georgia Rae. *The United Keetoowah Band of Cherokee Indians in Oklahoma.* New York: Peter Lang, 1996.

Lewis, David Rich. *Neither Wolf nor Dog: American Indians, Environment and Agrarian Change.* New York: Oxford University Press, 1994.

Lewis, Thomas M. N., and Madeline Kneberg. *Tribes That Slumber: Indians of the Tennessee Region.* Knoxville: University of Tennessee Press, 1958.

Littlefield, Daniel F., Jr. "Utopian Dreams of the Cherokee Fullbloods: 1890–1934." *Journal of the West* 10 (n.d.): 404–27.

——. *The Cherokee Freedmen: From Emancipation to American Citizenship.* Westport, Conn.: Greenwood Press, 1978.

Lomawaima, K. Tsianina. *They Called It Prairie Light: The Story of Chilocco Indian School.* Lincoln: University of Nebraska Press, 1994.

Lumpkin, Wilson. *The Removal of the Cherokee Indians from Georgia.* 2 vols. in 1. 1907. Reprint, New York: Arno Press and *New York Times,* 1969.

Lurie, Nancy Oestreich, ed. *Mountain Wolf Woman, Sister of Crashing Thunder: The Autobiography of a Winnebago Indian.* Ann Arbor: University of Michigan Press, 1961.

——. *Women and the Invention of American Anthropology.* Prospect Heights, Ill.: Waveland Press, 1999.

Malone, Henry T. *Cherokees of the Old South: A People in Transition.* Athens: University of Georgia Press, 1956.

Mankiller, Wilma, and Michael Wallis. *Mankiller: A Chief and Her People.* New York: St. Martin's Press, 1993.

Martin, Joel. *Sacred Revolt: The Muskogees' Struggle for a New World.* Boston: Beacon Press, 1991.

Massey, Mary Elizabeth. *Women in the Civil War.* 1966. Reprint, Lincoln: University of Nebraska Press, 1994.

May, Katja. "Nativistic Movements among the Cherokees in the Nineteenth and Twentieth Centuries." *Journal of Cherokee Studies* 15 (1990): 27–39.

McLoughlin, William G. *After the Trail of Tears: The Cherokees' Struggle for Sovereignty, 1839–1880.* Chapel Hill: University of North Carolina Press, 1993.

———. *Champion of the Cherokees: Evan and John B. Jones.* Princeton: Princeton University Press, 1986.

———. *The Cherokee Ghost Dance: Essays on the Southeastern Indians, 1789–1861.* Ed. Walter H. Conser Jr. and Virginia Duffy McLoughlin. Macon, Ga.: Mercer University Press, 1984.

———. *Cherokee Renascence in the New Republic.* Princeton: Princeton University Press, 1986.

———. *The Cherokees and Christianity, 1794–1870: Essays on Acculturation and Cultural Persistence.* Ed. Walter H. Conser Jr. Athens: University of Georgia Press, 1994.

———. *Cherokees and Missionaries, 1789–1839.* New Haven: Yale University Press, 1984.

Medicine, Bea. *The Native American Woman: A Perspective.* Austin: National Educational Laboratory, 1978.

Meisch, Deborah. "An Ethnographic Study of Keetoowah Women." Master's thesis, University of Arkansas, 1993.

Merrell, James H. *The Indians' New World: Catawbas and Their Neighbors from European Contact through the Era of Removal.* Chapel Hill: University of North Carolina Press for the Institute of Early History and Culture, 1989.

Merriam, Lewis. *The Problem of Indian Administration.* N.p., 1928.

Mihesuah, Devon A. *Cultivating the Rosebuds: The Education of Women at the Cherokee Female Seminary, 1851–1909.* Urbana: University of Illinois Press, 1993.

Miller, Christopher, and George R. Hamell. "A New Perspective on Indian-White Contact: Cultural Symbols and Colonial Trade." *Journal of American History* 73 (Sept. 1986): 311–28.

Miner, H. Craig. *The Corporation and the Indian: Tribal Sovereignty and Industrial Civilization in Indian Territory, 1865–1907.* Norman: University of Oklahoma Press, 1988.

Minges, Patrick Neal. "The Keetoowah Society and the Avocation of Religious Nationalism within the Cherokee Nation, 1855–1867." Ph.D. diss., Union Theological Seminary, 1999.

Mintz, Steven, ed. *Native American Voices: A History and Anthology.* St. James, N.Y.: Brandywine Press, 1995.

Mitchell, Robert D. *Appalachian Frontiers: Settlement, Society and Development in the Preindustrial Era.* Lexington: University of Kentucky Press, 1991.

Mooney, James. *Myths of the Cherokees and Sacred Formulas of the Cherokees.* Nashville: Cherokee Heritage, 1982.

———. *The Swimmer Manuscript: Cherokee Sacred Formulas and Medicinal Prescriptions.* Rev., comp., and ed. Frans M. Olbrechts. Washington, D.C.: Smithsonian Institution, U.S. Bureau of American Ethnology Bulletin 99, 1932.

Moore, Henrietta L. *Feminism and Anthropology.* Minneapolis: University of Minnesota Press, 1988.

Moraga, Cherrie, and Gloria Anzaldua, eds. *This Bridge Called My Back: Writings by Radical Women of Color.* New York: Kitchen Table, Women of Color Press, 1981.

Morgan, Lewis Henry. *Ancient Society.* New York: Henry Holt, 1877.

——. *Laws of Descent of the Iroquois.* N.p., 1858[?].

——. *League of the Iroquois.* 1851. New York: Corinth, 1962.

——. *Systems of Consanguinity and Affinity of the Human Family.* Washington, D.C.: Smithsonian Institution, 1870.

Moulton, Gary E. *John Ross: Cherokee Chief.* Athens: University of Georgia Press, 1978.

——. *The Papers of Chief John Ross.* 2 vols. Norman: University of Oklahoma, 1985.

Nabokov, Peter, ed. *Native American Testimony: A Chronicle of Indian-White Relations from Prophecy to the Present, 1492–1992.* New York: Viking, 1991.

Neely, Sharlotte. *Snowbird Cherokees: People of Persistence.* Athens: University of Georgia Press, 1991.

Odell, Marcia Larson. *Divide and Conquer: Allotment among the Cherokee.* New York: Arno Press, 1979.

Olbrechts, Frans M. "Cherokee Belief and Practice with Regard to Childbirth." *Anthropos* 26 (1931): 18–31.

Opler, Marvin K. *Acculturation in Seven American Indian Tribes,* Ed. Ralph Linton. Gloucester, Mass.: Peter Smith, 1963.

Ortner, Sherry B., and Harriet Whitehead. *Sexual Meanings: The Cultural Construction of Gender and Sexuality.* New York: Cambridge University Press, 1981.

Osburn, Katherine, M. B. "'Dear Friend and Ex-Husband': Marriage, Divorce, and Women's Property Rights on the Southern Ute Reservation, 1887–1930." In *Negotiators of Change: Historical Perspectives on Native American Women,* ed. Nancy Shoemaker, 176–92. New York: Routledge, 1995.

——. *Southern Ute Women: Autonomy and Assimilation on the Reservation, 1887–1998.* Albuquerque: University of New Mexico Press, 1998.

Otis, D. S. *The Dawes Act and the Allotment of Indian Lands.* Ed. and intro. Francis Paul Prucha. Norman: University of Oklahoma Press, 1973.

Owen, Narcissa. *Memoirs of Narcissa Owen, 1831–1907.* Washington, D.C.[?]: n.p., 1907[?].

Paredes, J. Anthony. *Indians of the Southeastern United States in the Late Twentieth Century.* Tuscaloosa: University of Alabama Press, 1992.

——. "Paradoxes of Modernism and Indianness in the Southeast." *American Indian Quarterly* 19, no. 3 (1995): 341–60.

Pavlik, Steve, ed. *A Good Cherokee, A Good Anthropologist.* Papers in honor of Robert K. Thomas. Los Angeles: University of California American Indian Center, McNaughton and Gunn, 1998.

Payne, John Howard. *John Howard Payne to His Countrymen.* Ed. Clemens de Baillou. Athens: University of Georgia Press, 1961.

Pearce, Roy Harvey. *The Savages of America: A Study of the Indian and the Idea of Civilization.* Baltimore: Johns Hopkins University Press, 1953.

Perdue, Theda. "Cherokee Women and the Trail of Tears." *Journal of Women's History* 1, no. 1 (1989): 14–30.

——. *Cherokee Women: Gender and Culture Change, 1700–1835.* Lincoln: University of Nebraska Press, 1998.

——. *Nations Remembered: An Oral History of the Five Civilized Tribes, 1865–1907.* Westport, Conn.: Greenwood Press, 1980.

——. *Native Carolinians: The Indians of North Carolina.* Raleigh: Division of Archives and History, North Carolina Department of Cultural Resources, 1985.

——. *Sifters: Native American Women.* New York: Oxford University Press, 2001.

——. *Slavery and the Evolution of Cherokee Society, 1540–1866.* Knoxville: University of Tennessee Press, 1979.

——. "Southern Indians and the Cult of True Womanhood." In *Half Sisters of History: Southern Women and the American Past,* ed. Catherine Clinton, 36–55. Durham, N.C.: Duke University Press, 1994.

——. "The Traditional Status of Cherokee Women." *Furman Studies* 26 (Dec. 1980): 19–25.

——. "Women, Men and American Indian Policy: The Cherokee Response to 'Civilization.'" In *Negotiators of Change: Historical Perspectives on Native American Women,* ed. Nancy Shoemaker, 90–114. New York: Routledge, 1995.

——, ed. *Cherokee Editor: The Writings of Elias Boudinot.* Knoxville: University of Tennessee Press, 1983.

Perdue, Theda, and Michael D. Green, eds. *The Cherokee Removal: A Brief History with Documents.* Boston: Bedford Books of St. Martin's Press, 1995.

Perrone, Bobette, H. Henrietta Stockel, and Victoria Krieger. *Medicine Women, Curanderas, and Women Doctors.* Norman: University of Oklahoma Press, 1989.

Prucha, Francis Paul. *Documents of United States Indian Policy.* 2nd ed. Lincoln: University of Nebraska Press, 1990.

——. *The Great Father: The United States Government and the American Indians.* 2 vols. Lincoln: University of Nebraska Press, 1984.

——. *United States Indian Policy: A Critical Bibliography.* Bloomington: Indiana University Press for the Newberry Library, 1977.

Rable, George C. *Civil Wars: Women and the Crisis of Southern Nationalism.* Urbana: University of Illinois Press, 1989.

Reid, John Philip. *A Better Kind of Hatchet.* University Park: Pennsylvania State University Press, 1976.

——. *A Law of Blood: The Primitive Law of the Cherokee Nation.* New York: New York University Press, 1970.

Ridge, John. "John Ridge on Cherokee Civilization in 1826." Ed. William C. Sturtevant. *Journal of Cherokee Studies* 6, no. 2 (1981): 79–91.

Riley, Glenda. *Women and Indians on the Frontier, 1825–1915.* Albuquerque: University of New Mexico Press, 1984.

Rogin, Michael Paul. *Fathers and Children: Andrew Jackson and the Subjugation of the American Indian.* New York: Alfred A. Knopf, 1975.

Rosaldo, Michelle Zimbalist, and Louise Lamphere, eds. *Woman, Culture, and Society.* Stanford: Stanford University Press, 1974.

Ross, Mrs. William P. *The Life and Times of Hon. William P. Ross.* Entered according to the Act of Congress in Office of Librarian of Congress at Washington, 1892.

Royce, Charles C. *The Cherokee Nation of Indians.* Chicago: Aldine, 1975.

Rozema, Vicki. *Footsteps of the Cherokees.* Winston-Salem, N.C.: John F. Blair, 1995.

Ruff, Rowena McClinton. "To Ascertain the Mind and Circumstance of the Cherokee Nation, Springplace, Georgia, 1805–1821." Master's thesis, Western Carolina University, 1992.

Ruiz, Vicki L., and Ellen Carol DuBois. *Unequal Sisters: A Multi-Cultural Reader in U.S. Women's History.* 2nd ed. New York: Routledge, 1994.

Satz, Ronald N. *American Indian Policy in the Jacksonian Era*. Lincoln: University of Nebraska Press, 1975.

Saunt, Claudio. *A New Order of Things: Property, Power, and the Transformation of the Creek Indians, 1733–1816*. Cambridge: Cambridge University Press, 1999.

Scott, Anne Firor. *Natural Allies: Women's Associations in American History*. Urbana: University of Illinois Press, 1991.

Sheehan, Bernard W. *Seeds of Extinction: Jeffersonian Philanthropy and the American Indian*. Chapel Hill: University of North Carolina Press, 1973.

Shoemaker, Nancy. "How Indians Got to Be Red." *American Historical Review* 102 (June 1997): 625–44.

———. "The Rise or Fall of Iroquois Women." *Journal of Women's History* 2 (winter 1991): 39–57.

———, ed. *American Indians*. Malden, Mass.: Blackwell, 2001.

———, ed. *Clearing a Path: Theorizing the Past in Native American Studies*. New York: Routledge, 2002.

———, ed. *Negotiators of Change: Historical Perspectives on Native American Women*. New York: Routledge, 1995.

Sider, Gerald M. *Lumbee Indian Histories: Race, Ethnicity, and Indian Identity in the Southern United States*. Cambridge: Cambridge University Press, 1993.

Singer, Beverly R. *Wiping the War Paint off the Lens: Native American Film and Video*. Minneapolis: University of Minnesota Press, 2001.

Southwell, Kristina L. "The Park Hill Mission: Letters from a Missionary Family." *Chronicles of Oklahoma* 78, no. 2 (2000): 216–29.

Speck, Frank G., and Leonard Broom, in collaboration with Will West Long. *Cherokee Dance and Drama*. Berkeley: University of California Press, 1951.

Spicer, Edward, ed. *Perspectives in American Indian Culture Change*. Chicago: University of Chicago Press, 1961.

Starkey, Marion L. *The Cherokee Nation*. 1946. Reprint, New York: Russell and Russell, 1972.

Starr, Emmet. *History of the Cherokee Indians*. Muskogee, Okla.: Hoffman Printing, 1984.

Strickland, Rennard. *Fire and the Spirits: Cherokee Law from Clan to Court*. Norman: University of Oklahoma Press, 1975.

Sturm, Circe. *Blood Politics: Race, Culture, and Identity in the Cherokee Nation of Oklahoma*. Berkeley: University of California Press, 2002.

Swanton, John. R. *Indians of the Southeastern United States*. 1946. Reprint, Washington, D.C.: Smithsonian Institution Press, 1979.

Szasz, Margaret Connell. *Between Indian and White Worlds: The Cultural Broker*. Norman: University of Oklahoma Press, 1994.

Thoburn, Joseph B., and Isaac M. Holcomb. *A History of Oklahoma*. San Francisco: Doub, 1908.

Thomas, Robert K. "The Origin and Development of the Redbird Smith Movement." Ph.D. diss., University of Arizona, 1953.

Thornton, Russell. *The Cherokees: A Population History*. Lincoln: University of Nebraska Press, 1990.

Timberlake, Henry. *The Memoirs of Lieutenant Henry Timberlake*. Ed. Samuel Cole Williams. 1756. Reprint, Marietta, Ga.: Continental Book, 1948.

Underhill, Ruth M. *Papago Woman*. New York: Holt, Rinehart and Winston, 1979.

Van Kirk, Sylvia. *Many Tender Ties: Women in the Fur Trade Society, 1670–1870.* Winnipeg, Manitoba: Watson and Dwyer, 1982.

Wahrhaftig, Albert L. "Making Do with the Dark Meat: A Report on the Cherokee Indians in Oklahoma." In *World Anthropology: American Economic Development,* ed. Sol Tax, 409–510. Chicago: Aldine, 1978.

———. "We Who Act Right: The Persistent Identity of Cherokee Indians." *Currents in Anthropology* (1979): 40–53.

Walker, Robert Sparks. *Torchlights to the Cherokees: The Brainerd Mission.* 1931. Reprint, Johnson City, Tenn.: Overmountain Press, 1994.

Warde, Mary Jane, "Now the Wolf Has Come: The Civilian War in the Indian Territory." *Chronicles of Oklahoma* 71, no. 1 (1993): 69–87.

Wardell, Morris L. *A Political History of the Cherokee Nation, 1838–1907.* 1938. Reprint, Norman: University of Oklahoma Press, 1977.

Warren, Mary B., and Eve B. Weeks. *Whites among the Cherokees in Georgia, 1828–1838.* Danielsville, Ga.: Heritage Papers, 1987.

Waselkov, Gregory A., and Kathryn E. Holland Braund, eds. *William Bartram on the Southeastern Indians.* Lincoln: University of Nebraska Press, 1995.

Washburn, Cephas. *Reminiscences of the Indians.* Richmond: Presbyterian Committee of Publication, 1869.

Washburn, Wilcomb E. *The Assault on Indian Tribalism: The General Allotment Act.* Philadelphia: J. B. Lippincott, 1975.

Welter, Barbara. *Dimity Convictions.* Athens: Ohio University Press, 1976.

White, Richard. *The Middle Ground: Indians, Empires, and Republics in the Great Lakes Region, 1650–1815.* New York: Cambridge University Press, 1999.

———. *The Roots of Dependency: Subsistence, Environment, and Social Change among the Choctaws, Pawnees, and Navajos.* Lincoln: University of Nebraska Press, 1983.

Whitmire, Mildred E., ed. *Noland's Cherokee Diary: A U.S. Soldier's Story from inside the Cherokee Nation.* Spartanburg, S.C.: Reprint, 1990.

Wiesel, Elie. *The Gates of the Forest.* Geneva: Bibliophile Library, 1986.

Wilkins, Thurman. *Cherokee Tragedy: The Story of the Ridge Family and the Decimation of a People.* London: Macmillan, 1970.

Williams, David. *The Georgia Gold Rush: Twenty-Niners, Cherokees, and Gold Fever.* Columbia: University of South Carolina Press, 1993.

Williams, Walter L., ed. *Southeastern Indians since the Removal.* Athens: University of Georgia Press, 1979.

———. *The Spirit and the Flesh: Sexual Diversity in American Indian Culture.* Boston: Beacon, 1986.

Witthoft, John. "An Early Cherokee Ethnobotanical Note." *Journal of Washington Academy of Sciences* 37, no. 3 (1947): 73–75.

———. *Green Corn Ceremonialism in the Eastern Woodlands.* Ann Arbor: University of Michigan Press, 1949.

———. "Will West Long, Cherokee Informant." *American Anthropologist* 59 (1948): 355–59.

Wood, Peter H., Gregory A. Waselkov, and M. Thomas Hatley, eds. *Powhatan's Mantle.* Lincoln: University of Nebraska Press, 1989.

Wooten, John Morgan. *The Cherokee Indians in Bradley County History.* Published by Bradley Co., Post 81, American Legion with cooperation of Tennessee Historical Commission, 1949.

Woodward, C. Vann, ed. *Mary Chesnut's Civil War.* New Haven: Yale University Press, 1981.

Woodward, Grace Steele. *The Cherokees.* Norman: University of Oklahoma Press, 1963.

Wright, Mary C. "Economic Development and Native American Women in the Early Nineteenth Century." *American Quarterly* 33, no. 5 (1981): 525–36.

Wright, Muriel H. *Springplace Moravian Mission and the Ward Family of the Cherokee Nation.* Guthrie, Okla.: Cooperative Publishing, 1940.

Young, Mary Elizabeth. *Redskins, Ruffleshirts, and Rednecks: Indian Allotments in Alabama and Mississippi.* Norman: University of Oklahoma Press, 1961.

Index